John Ewart

Architect for a New World: Upper Canada's First Architect in York and London

Janet Ewart FitzGerald

with

Harry van Bommel

A Canada 150 Book

Resources Supporting Family
and Community Legacies Inc.

Toronto, Ontario 2005

National Library of Canada Cataloguing in Publication

FitzGerald, Janet Ewart, 1918-

John Ewart : Architect for a New World : Upper Canada's First Architect in York and London/Janet Ewart FitzGerald; with Harry van Bommel.

(A Canada 150 book)

Includes bibliographical references and index.

ISBN 1-55307-015-1

1. Ewart, John, 1788-1856. 2. Historic buildings--Ontario--Toronto.

3. Historic buildings--Ontario--London Region.

4. Architects--Canada--Biography.

I. van Bommel, Harry II. Resources Supporting Family and Community Legacies Inc.

III. Title. IV. Series: Canada 150 book.

NA749.E93F58 2005 720'.92 C2005-900936-5

To contact the author, write or call:

Janet Ewart FitzGerald, c/o the Publisher
Resources Supporting Family and Community Legacies Inc.
11 Miniot Circle, Toronto, ON Canada M1K 2K1
(416) 264 4665, harry@legacies.ca, www.legacies.ca

Canada 150 is a 20-year project ending in 2017 to celebrate Canada's 150th birthday. We hope to encourage 150,000 Canadians to record their life stories and/or family histories and deposit these stories with ***Library and Archives Canada*** where their descendants will be able to find these stories in perpetuity.

Dedication

To my mother, Mabel Ewart Steele Grubbe,

whose tales of her ancestors prompted

me to begin this project.

Table of Contents

Table of Illustrations **7**

Acknowledgements **11**

Introduction **15**

CHAPTER 1 The Early Years (1788-1818) **23**

Ewart's Early History 25

Origins and Early History of the Town of York 30

Physical Layout of the Town 32

Ewart's New Neighbours 34

The Town in 1818 and 1819 39

CHAPTER 2 Foundations of a New Life in Upper Canada (1819-1824) **48**

York General Hospital (1820) 52

Hazelburn (1822) 55

St. Paul's Roman Catholic Church (1822-23) 58

Second Courthouse and Jail in York (1823-24) 62

CHAPTER 3 Building Upon a Respected Reputation (1825-1829) **70**

Founding Trustee of Strangers' Burial Ground (1825) 72

Bank of Upper Canada (1825-27) 75

Workers' Residence in London, Upper Canada (1826)
London Court House and Jail (1827-31) 81

Moss Park (1827-29) 91

Coffin Block (circa 1828-1830) 94

CHAPTER 4 Constructing a New City (1829-1833) 103

Upper Canada College (1829-31) 107

Third Parliament Buildings (1829-32) 110

Osgoode Hall (1829-32) 113

Ewart Wharf (1829-31) 125

Emigrants' Asylum 1830 130

Mechanics' Institute 1830 131

St. Andrew's Presbyterian Church (1830-31) 136

Wholesale Grocer's Store (1833) 140

CHAPTER 5 A New Era for the Growing City (1834-1856).... 147

Ewart's Politics 150

Life in the New Toronto 152

St. Andrew's Society of Toronto (1836) 155

City of Toronto and Lake Huron Railroad Company (1836) 155

St. James' Church/Cathedral 158

Great West Railway Company (1845) 160

Ewart's Positions on Boards of Directors and Commissions 163

Provincial Lunatic Asylum (1846-1850) 167

Ewart's Diverse Interests 169

Family Life 171

John Ewart's Death (1856) 177

APPENDIX 1 John Ewart (1788-1856) Family Tree 190

APPENDIX 2 Historical Timeline 191

APPENDIX 3 John Ewart's Buildings 203

APPENDIX 4 Toronto/York Street Names 211

APPENDIX 5 Members of the Family Compact 212

Glossary 214

Bibliography 215

Index 231

About the Authors 240

Table of Illustrations

The following abbreviations are used in the text:
CTA = City of Toronto Archives
DH = Devin Hunt Illustration
JEF = Janet Ewart FitzGerald Collection
LAC = Library and Archives of Canada
LSUC = Law Society of Upper Canada
OA = Ontario Archives
ROM = Royal Ontario Museum
TPL = Toronto Public Library
UWO = University of Western Ontario

Cover

John Ewart [LSUC, P252]
Osgoode Hall, East Wing [JEF]
London Courthouse and Jail [JEF]
John G. Howard's drawing of the Jail and Courthouse in 1835 [TPL T-12633]
Author's photo by Irina Buzenkova of the Michael Wong Studio in Toronto [JEF]

Introduction

1. John Ewart (1788-1856) [LSUC, P252]
2. Jane Wilson Ewart (1787-1867) [JEF]
3. Early road from Kingston to York [LAC C-012632]

Chapter 1

1 Thomas Young lithograph of Second Court House and Jail [TPL T-35162]
2 Lieutenant R.E. Phillpotts 1818 Map [TPL BB 37]
3 Portion of the Plan of the Town of York 1834 [TPL City of Toronto Map (east) 1834]
4 Dr. W.W. Baldwin (1775-1844) [TPL T-31037]
5. Robert Baldwin (1804-1858) [TPL T-13649]
6. William Allan [TPL T-16678]
7. *The Grange* [TPL T-11141]
8. *Campbell House* [TPL T-11161]
9. Rev. Strachan's Home, The Palace [TPL T-11530]
10. The York Water Front circa 1815 [TPL T-12567]
11. Portion of the Plan of the Town of York, March 1839 [TPL City of Toronto March 30 1839]

12. Land Petition to Sir Peregrine Maitland [LAC, C-001888 Upper Canada Land Petitions, RG 1, L3, Vol. 177A, petition E12/26]

Chapter 2

1. Two General Maps of Toronto showing all of Ewart's Building Projects [DH]
2. York General Hospital [TPL T-10937]]
3. *Hazelburn* [TPL J Robertson Vol. 2 p 1024]
4. St. Paul's Roman Catholic Church [TPL T-10805]
5. St. George's Parish Church in Glasgow (by permission of the congregation)
6. John G. Howard's drawing of the Jail and Courthouse in 1835 [TPL T-12633]

Chapter 3

1. Thomas Carfrae [TPL T-16701]
2. William Lyon Mackenzie [TPL T-31909]
3. Sketch of The Bank of Upper Canada [TPL T- 10484]
4. The Bank of Upper Canada circa1872 [TPL T-10485]
5. The Bank of Upper Canada (2004) [JEF]
6. London Courthouse and Jail (2004) [JEF]
7. Colonel Thomas Talbot [TPL T-16586]
8. "The Old Log Court House" in London, Ontario [UWO, Regional Collection]
9. Early Photo of the Courthouse [OA ACC 3619 S 12569]
10. First Floor Plan of the Courthouse [DH]
11. Second Floor Plan [DH]
12. London Courthouse Jail Cell (2004 photo) [JEF]
13. Sketch of *Moss Park* [TPL T-30698]
14. *Moss Park* in late 19th century [TPL T-33502]
15. The Coffin Block circa 1860s [TPL T-12553]
16. The Coffin Block Map 1830s [DH]
17. The Old Fish Market [TPL T-32138]
18. The Coffin Block front view [CTA Fonds 1478 Item 15]

Chapter 4

1. Upper Canada College Lithograph by Thomas Young in 1835 [TPL T-30087]
2. Upper Canada College photo [TPL T-31168]
3. Thomas Young's 1835 lithograph of the Third Parliament Buildings [TPL T-10249]

4. The Third Parliament Buildings in late nineteenth century [CTA Fonds 1498 Item 10]
5. Osgoode Hall circa 1850s [CTA Fonds 1498 Item 9]
6. Toronto panorama 1857 View including Osgoode Hall [CTA Fonds 1498 Item 16]
7. Basement Floor Plan of Osgoode Hall [DH]
8. First Floor Plan of Osgoode Hall [DH]
9. Second-Floor Plan of Osgoode Hall [DH]
10. "Muddy York" in 1909 photo [CTA Fonds 1244 Item 31]
11. Wood engraving by F.E. Wyman [TPL T-33830]
12. Osgoode Hall in 1868-69 [TPL T-12016]
13. City of Toronto Map (east) 1834 cropped to highlight area shown [TPL map room]
14. Maitland's Wharf circa 1845 as engraved by W.H. Bartlett [TPL T-32137]
15. York Harbour in 1828 [TPL T-10339]
16. The Mechanics Institute [TPL T-11997]
17. St. Andrew's Presbyterian Church in 1840 [TPL T-10706]

Chapter 5

1. Political boundaries after 1834 to 1880 [DH]
2. A streetscape of 1847 looking east [TPL Illustrated London News, January 30, 1847, Vol. 10, page 68]
3. A streetscape of 1847 looking west [TPL Illustrated London News, January 30, 1847, Vol. 10, page 68]]
4. The Toronto locomotive [TPL T-13602]
5. St. James Cathedral [TPL Illustrated London News, January 30, 1847, Vol. 10, page 68, close-up view]
6. Sir Allan MacNab [TPL T-13738]
7. The Great Western Railway [TPL T-12182]
8. Toronto General Hospital [TPL 10971]
9. The Provincial Lunatic Asylum [TPL T-10262]
10. John G. Howard [TPL T-13710]
11. Photo of the asylum [TPL T-10966]
12. Jane Ewart [ROM 991.181.2]
13. Oliver Mowat [JEF]
14. Modern view of "*Northfield*" [JEF]
15. Thomas Ewart [JEF]
16. Catherine Skirving Ewart [JEF]
17. John Ewart Jr. [TPL T-35169]
18. Ewart Monument in the Necropolis Cemetery, Toronto [JEF]
19. Map of Ewart's Estate in the Beach [TPL Goad's 1884 Map]

20. Cropped view of harbour in W. Whitfield 1854 lithograph of Toronto [TPL T-32081]
21. Cropped view of city in W. Whitfield 1854 lithograph of Toronto [TPL T-32081]

Appendix 1

1. Ewart Family Tree [DH]

Acknowledgements

The concept for this book began years ago when my mother, **Mabel Ewart Steele Grubbe**, started collecting letters and photographs of the Ewart and Skirving families. Her notes show her preliminary studies into the early history of her families, John Ewart's work and the stories of his descendants. My father, **Talbot 'Tab' Page Grubbe**, contributed research from his family history because his family and that of my great grandmother (Catharine Seaton Skirving Ewart) were connected.

In the late 1990s I retained **Jocelyn Honeyman**, an architectural student entering her fifth and final year at the University of Toronto to do preliminary research on the buildings that Ewart designed and/or built. Although this research has been greatly expanded by many hours of further research, I am grateful to her for giving me a good start.

Harry van Bommel took my initial research and that of Ms. Honeyman and added his own. He then drafted the body of this book. His experiences as a researcher and writer have helped me put together a history of John Ewart and his family that I hope will help historians, architectural students and genealogists alike understand early York life and architecture. I have tried to add sufficient background history to put Ewart's work into the context of the time (the early to mid-1800s in York and London, Ontario) so that we can all better appreciate what the early pioneers of these towns accomplished under very difficult circumstances.

I am indebted to the published works of those with specialties that affect various aspects of this book. Works by authors such as **Frederick H. Armstrong**, **Edith Firth**, **Robert Gourlay**, **Edwin Guillet**, **J. Ross Robertson** and **Henry Scadding** continue to help all researchers understand the history and peoples of early York. More recently, **Mike Filey's** collections of early photos and sketches, **William**

Kilbourn's perceptive analysis of the times, and the architectural histories so thoroughly researched and presented by **Eric Arthur**, **Marion MacRae** and **Anthony Adamson**, **Patricia McHugh** and **Stephen Otto** have helped immensely.

I am further indebted for the assistance of **Pleasance K. Crawford**, a writer in the fields of Canadian landscape and garden history and **Stephen Otto**, an eminent author who updated Eric Arthur's *Toronto: No Mean City*, and who has been heavily involved in the Ontario heritage conservation movement. The Horwood Collection of architectural drawings was presented to the Ontario Archives in 1979 based on his efforts. Mr. Otto provided me with leads to little known archival sources including several newspaper articles about Ewart's works.

Librarians are the unsung heroes of all researchers and I sincerely appreciate all of those who were always ready to take on the challenge of finding a new source. Particularly, I am thankful for the efforts of the librarians at the ***Toronto Public Library*** who work at ***Answerline*** (their Internet-based research centre), those who work throughout the ***Reference Library***, including the outstanding librarians in the ***Baldwin Room***, and the librarians at the ***Albert Campbell Library***. For those interested in photographs or illustrations of early York and Toronto, I would start at the Toronto Reference Library as they charge less for reproduction rights than other archives and have many of the items you might also find at other archives. As well, I am grateful to the staffs at the ***Law Society of Upper Canada***, ***Library and Archives Canada***, ***City of Toronto Archives***, ***Royal Ontario Museum***, ***Ontario Archives***, ***University of Toronto's Thomas Fisher Rare Books Library***, and the ***University of Western Ontario*** who assisted in finding sources and photos that we could reproduce in this book.

Toronto and London are richly endowed with local historians, some of whom work at historical sites providing the public and researchers with memorable insights into the early years of Upper Canada. I am grateful to: **Joel Barker**, Assistant Curator at the ***1st Hussars Museum, Middlesex County Building*** in London, Ontario; **Elise Brunet** and **Paul Leatherdale**, archivists at ***Osgoode Hall***; **Shirley E. Hartt**, Curator of the ***Enoch Turner Schoolhouse*** for referring me to ***York's First Post Office*** book and three-dimensional model of York in 1834; **Judi Prigion** of ***The Guelph Historical Society*** for information on Guelph; **Jenny Rieger** of ***The Grange*** and **Melissa Wright** of ***Campbell House*** for help in understanding the construction of such early buildings in York; **Kathleen Wall** of the ***Guelph Museums*** for information on Ewart's possible work there; **Janet Walters** of ***Toronto's First Post Office*** for information regarding the model of York in 1834; **Louise Winton**, public relations and communications co-ordinator at ***Mount Pleasant Group of Cemeteries*** for help with questions about the Ewart family, and Potters' Field and the Necropolis Cemeteries.

Modern research is greatly helped by the Internet. People in Scotland were easily reached through e-mails that uncovered invaluable information. **Derek Barber** is a family historian who led us to further contacts in tracing John Ewart's Scottish roots; **David Ewart** is the founder of the web site dedicated to the Ewart extended family around the world; **Alison Hair** of ***St. George's-Tron Church*** in Glasgow sent a sketch of the church to compare with Ewart's St. Andrew's Presbyterian Church; **Veronica Wallace** and **Ray Halliday** work at the ***Local History Centre*** in East Lothian, Scotland (the area where John Ewart was born). They helped us with research and sent us a copy of the Ewart's genealogy from that region done by **John Richard Layton**.

I am grateful to the following people: **Stephen Langmead**, Professor (retired 2004) in the Department of Architectural Science, Faculty of Engineering and Applied Science, ***Ryerson University*** and a registered architect in Ontario (retired 2002). He read the first draft and provided insightful recommendations to improve the text. **Richard Stromberg** suggested changes to the early draft of the text and his comments, based on his extensive experience with ***Heritage Toronto*** and the ***Ontario Ministry of Housing***, were incorporated into the text. **Howard Joy**, a descendant of George Ewart (1828-1870) provided family history never before recorded. **Janet Klees** did a preliminary edit of the text to ensure that the content could be easily read by those not familiar with Toronto's early history.

Beverley Powell-Vinden did a superb job in designing the book and cover to highlight Ewart's accomplishments. To **Devin Hunt** I am grateful for his timely and expert help in recreating floor plans and Toronto street maps. Many thanks to **Albert Pinhas** for his advice on photographic reproductions and donation of suitable software for the project.

I am very grateful to my daughter, **Shelagh FitzGerald**, for her help with the launch and promotion of this book, and her many good ideas. Also, my son, **Michael Ewart FitzGerald**, has helped immeasurably in the research and editing. His interest in our ancestors increased through researching some of the primary documents of Ewart's period. He has come to appreciate the richness of our family history and I am sincerely grateful for his help in bringing alive my dream of publishing this book.

Introduction

We shape our buildings and they shape our lives.

Attributed to Winston Churchill[1]

In 2001, I published my father's papers about his Scottish ancestors, the Grubb family of Edinburgh and Weston, Ontario. During the process, I continued to add information to my mother's collection of documents and photos of her ancestors, the Ewart family of Edinburgh and early York. [To help you visually understand my family's history, please see the abbreviated family tree in Appendix 1.]

My father, Talbot Page Grubbe, wrote about his family:

> *There is nothing spectacular about it [our family history], but for years the families appear to have been highly respectable citizens who took leading parts in the life of their communities and in which their descendants can take considerable pride.*[2]

I have always thought of John Ewart in a similar vein—a largely unknown, hardworking Scottish immigrant trying to make a living in the small town of York in the 1820s and 1830s. Instead I found that his work on many of the key civic, religious, legal and educational buildings in York between 1819-1834 was fundamental to the growth of the town into the City of Toronto in 1834. Furthermore, his work in London, Upper Canada, helped turn an uninhabited forest into a new centre of legal activity for the region.

John Ewart was, in fact, Upper Canada's first professional architect in York and London.

1. John Ewart (1788-1856) [LSUC, P252]

2. Jane Wilson Ewart (1787-1867) [JEF]

In Ewart's prime he was involved as an architect and/or builder on all three principal churches in York: ***St. Paul's Roman Catholic Church***, ***St. Andrew's Presbyterian Church***, and ***St. James Church of England***. He was the architect and/or builder of many of the most important civic buildings of his era: the ***District Courthouse and Jail***, ***Osgoode Hall*** and the ***Third Parliament Buildings***. He was the architect and/or builder of the main preparatory school and the only public hospital in town: ***Upper Canada College*** and the ***York General Hospital***. His involvement on the ***Bank of Upper Canada*** had him at the forefront of the commercial and property community of his time. The two homes in which he was involved, ***Hazelburn*** and ***Moss Park*** were key estates for the Jarvis and Allan families. Later he would be a commissioner to build the largest building in town, the ***Provincial Lunatic Asylum***, overseeing John G. Howard's mental health hospital design. No one matched his versatility of designs (civic, legal, public, and religious) nor the number of projects on the go at the same time.

3. This main road leading to York illustrates the kind of wilderness in which Ewart worked and travelled. These roads were not passable for much of the later spring and early fall due to muddy conditions. [LAC C-012632]

John was already 30 years old when he arrived in York with his wife, Jane, (31) and their children, William and Margaret, ages 6 and 5. They arrived in a town that only 25 years before was nothing but virgin forest. York had grown by 1818 to include nearly a thousand people living and working within the ten-block boundaries of the original town. In these short years the town had moved from single-storey wooden buildings to multi-storey brick and stone edifices similar to those in New York and London.

During these early years, York required men who could do the work. John Ewart was such a man as he designed and built according to possibilities of the materials on hand (wood and brick) and the labour available. Yet, he used his commissions to construct buildings that went beyond the typical ones already in the town.

Unlike my father's side of the family, Ewart's legacy is not recorded in drawings, journals or letters. But it can be seen in the finished buildings, in the land he accumulated, and his contributions to the communities of York and London.

For the first few decades of the Town of York's history, people had to design and build their own homes, offices, and civic buildings. The town was not significant enough (only 720 people in 1815[3]) to attract professional architects. There was neither the money, materials nor demand for larger civic projects that would attract professionals to "Muddy York".

Whether by design, accident, or by a personal invitation from someone in York, Ewart arrived from New York City in about 1818, having emigrated to America from Britain two years earlier. He was already an accomplished architect and builder[4], having trained and worked for about 15 years. Ewart's first commission was the York General Hospital, which also served as the temporary Parliament Buildings for Upper Canada. Such a first commission likely would not have been given to an untrained architect or builder.

Ewart stood alone as York and London's first architect for the next 13 years of his professional life. When other professionals were attracted to Toronto starting in the 1830s, it was partly due to Ewart's buildings, which testified to the desire for large and imposing civic, religious, educational and legal edifices. It was obvious to others that Toronto was no longer just another swampy backwater town but a place where buildings of worth were being commissioned and built. As Marion MacRae wrote in *Hallowed Halls*, Ewart was "the first architectural designer of demonstrable merit to appear in York."[5] Nancy Zwart Tausky and Lynne Delehanty DiStefano confirm this in their 1986 book, *Victorian Architecture in London and Southwestern Ontario, Symbols of Aspiration* when they write that Ewart was "one of the most talented architects then in Upper Canada."[6]

Later professionals of the 1830s and 1840s competed with each other to win commissions. Ewart, however, competed and collaborated only with the wealthy amateur architects of York including government officials, legal, clerical, commercial professionals and landowners. These amateur architects, like so many of their generation in Europe and America, were passionate about their buildings and as skilled in basic architecture as they were in the arts, law, politics and commerce.[7] They knew that buildings reflected their owners' view of the world and reflected the town's place within a region or nation. They had come mostly from cities in Great Britain where the latest trends in architecture were evident everywhere. When the need arose, they could be called upon to help design a church or courthouse.[8]

These so-called amateurs used "pattern books", filled with drawings and specific instructions on how to construct and decorate homes and civic or religious buildings, to create their own designs. Skilled tradesmen would translate these drawings, using the same pattern books, to help them construct the buildings.[9] One need look only at ***The Palace*** (John Strachan's house, 1818), ***The Grange*** (1817-18) and ***Campbell House*** (1822)[10] to realize that these very early examples of Toronto mansions, constructed in the forested wilderness, were probably designed by their owners and/or with the help of talented tradesmen familiar with the Georgian architectural style popular back in Britain.

Ewart shared the passion of the town's amateur architects and worked closely with them to build such long-lasting institutions as the original ***Osgoode Hall***, ***York General Hospital***, ***St. Paul's Roman Catholic Church***, the second ***Courthouse and Jail***, the ***London Court House and Jail***, ***Upper Canada College***, the ***Bank of Upper Canada***, and ***St. Andrew's Presbyterian Church***. Besides being an architect, Ewart was also a builder and contractor. For example, he worked on the ***Third Parliament Buildings*** and was responsible for the restoration of ***St. James' Church*** after a fire in 1839, even though he was not its architect.

Ewart's many talents enabled him to obtain the help of many of the skilled tradesmen (the largest industry in the town at the time). There is also evidence that he was able to work within a budget and get the job done on time.

While some of the wealthy men in town designed and built beautiful homes as a legacy of their own professional abilities and lives, Ewart's own home was torn down later in the century and replaced by the city's largest wholesale manufacturing firm of John Macdonald.[11] Ewart's legacy is in his commissioned buildings and the family he and his wife Jane raised. They experienced the uncertainty of pioneer life in early "Muddy York" after the cosmopolitan lifestyle of London and New York City. They lived through the cholera epidemics of the 1830s and the 1837 Rebellion. Jane experienced the worst of all life's sorrows—outliving her husband and nine of her eleven children before her death in the year of Confederation, 1867.

In writing this book I wanted to help family historians, architectural students and historians learn something new about the early buildings and history of York and London. Family historians will find the footnotes and bibliography helpful in searching out information about their own ancestors from that era. Architectural students and historians will find information collected about some of the earliest Georgian, Regency and Gothic buildings of note in York and London. Although there may be little new for academic historians, the book pulls together sources to make a case for a neglected part of Toronto history—who designed and built the earliest buildings that showcased the influence and dreams of the first settlers?

Architecture is a visual medium. I have included many photographs and illustrations to help you see the impact of some of these magnificent buildings on daily life. I also include some illustrations to remind us all that these buildings were often constructed in the forest or on the cleared farmlands of York and London.

I will provide details of daily life in York where Ewart lived and worked and also in London (Upper Canada) where he constructed the first buildings in the town's history. To help us comprehend such details, I have used the words of people from that time. Ewart left no diaries, journals or architectural drawings. Therefore, I have relied on his colleagues and contemporaries to give us a sense of the language and flavour of those times as well as insights into the man himself. Without these quotes I believe it would be difficult to grasp the tone, energy, politics, entrepreneurship, foresight and town life of early York and London.

Present day street names will be used rather than the cumbersome style of giving both original and current names. For example, Osgoode Hall's location will be given on Queen Street rather than Lot Street even though the street name was not changed until 1844.[12]

I have placed endnotes at the end of each chapter rather than at the bottom of each page so they will not get in the way of a 'good read'.

One of Toronto's leading architectural historians, Eric Arthur, described John Ewart as a "shadowy figure who appears sporadically between 1824 and 1844" in his 1964 book *Toronto: No Mean City*.[13] Subsequent research by some of Toronto's current architectural historians has evolved to the point where Ewart's accomplishments are acknowledged, but still largely unknown. This book aims to cast a brighter light on Ewart's work, achievements and character. He is a substantial figure in

Upper Canada from 1818 until his death in 1856, at the age of 68. He can be legitimately recognized now as the first professional architect of York and London.

Janet Ewart FitzGerald
Toronto, May 2005

---

1 William Dendy and William Kilbourn. (1886). *Toronto Observed,* p. viii.

2 Talbot Page Grubbe in Janet Grubbe FitzGerald. (2001). *The Grubb Pioneers of Etobicoke,* p. 40. The 'e' on Grubbe was added in the late 19th century by a vowel-loving descendant.

3 F.H. Armstrong. (1983). *Toronto: The Place of Meeting*, p. 63.

4 *Dictionary of Canadian Biography*. Vol. VIII, pp. 280-282 "John Ewart", by Marion MacRae, p. 280.

5 Marion MacRae. (1975). *Hallowed Walls: Church Architecture of Upper Canada,* p. 83.

6 Nancy Zwart Tausky and Lynne Delehanty DiStefano. (1986). *Victorian Architecture in London and Southwestern Ontario, Symbols of Aspiration*, p. 12.

7 William Dendy and William Kilbourn. (1986). *Toronto Observed,* pp. 26-27.

8 *Ibid,* p. 25.

9 *Ibid,* pp. 26-27.

10 Harold Kalman. (2000). *A Concise History of Canadian Architecture,* pp. 125, 127.

11 J. Ross Robertson. (1974). *Landmarks of Toronto*, Vol. 3 of 1898 original, p. 110.

12 Leonard Wise and Allan Gould. (2000). *Toronto Street Names*, p. 170.

13 *Ibid*, p. 246.

CHAPTER 1
The Early Years (1788-1818)

Ewart's Early History
Origins and Early History of the Town of York
Physical Layout of the Town
Ewart's New Neighbours
The Town in 1818-1819

Almost every book about early York prominently features the Thomas Young lithograph of the town's Second Courthouse and Jail. The drawing shows the importance these authors give to the civic buildings in the evolution of a great city. What is often missing is acknowledgement that this York landmark was designed by John Ewart, York's first professional architect.

1. Thomas Yong's lithograph in 1835 looking east along King Street from Toronto Street is one of the most famous illustrations of early York. On the left is Ewart's jail (1827-1840), then his courthouse (1827-1853), followed by St. James Church (1833-1849), which he rebuilt in 1839 after a fire. The steeple was not built when the drawing was made. [TPL T-35162]

Stephen Otto has made a career of studying the architecture of Toronto and Upper Canada. He is an eminent author who updated Eric Arthur's seminal *Toronto: No Mean City* in 1983 and has been heavily involved in the Ontario heritage conservation movement. He says, "John Ewart is well worth studying. He would have had a good grounding in design but professional architects were just coming into their own at that time in England. They wouldn't have arrived in Toronto until after Ewart's time."[14]

In fact, it was not until 1837 that royal charters established the Institute of British Architects to separate architects from builders.[15] An equivalent body would not exist in Ontario until the late nineteenth century. Within two years of Ewart's arrival in Upper Canada, there were only three architect-builders of note: "John Ewart was at work in York, and Archibald Fraser and Thomas Rogers were busy in Kingston."[16]

Ewart has been credited with many projects, "among them, the Court House, Jail, Parliament Buildings, Osgoode Hall, St. Andrew's Church of Scotland, and St. Paul's Roman Catholic Church. He was the first president of the York Mechanics' Institute in 1830-31. His youngest daughter Jane married Sir Oliver Mowat"[17] the longest serving provincial Premier in Canadian history. He also designed and/or built the London Courthouse and Jail (Middlesex County), Upper Canada College, the Bank of Upper Canada, York General Hospital, and rebuilt St. James' Church after a 1839 fire.

What kind of background, education and personal history leads a Scottish immigrant from a small town in County East Lothian to achieve so much in such a short time? What sort of town was York when he arrived in 1818?

Ewart's Early History

John Ewart was born on January 31, 1788 to William and Margaret Ewart in Tranent, county East Lothian, Scotland,[18] fourteen kilometres from Edinburgh and within three kilometres of the narrow sea inlet, the Firth of Forth. He was baptized in the Scottish Presbyterian Church of which he would later become a leading member in his new parish in York. Other notable men from East Lothian of the previous generation were Scottish designers John Rennie and Peter Nicholson. Ewart's own professional ambitions would follow these leaders in architecture to Edinburgh and eventually to London.[19]

Tranent was by far the largest village in the parish with a 1790's population of 1,300. It was substantially larger than the town of York would be 30 years later when Ewart and his family immigrated to Upper Canada. While Tranent was primarily an agricultural parish, it was also a substantial mining community, and had been so since the 13th century. In total, more people were working in 'trade' jobs of one sort or another than on the land. Three coal mines employed some 350 men, women and children at the time of Ewart's youth.[20]

Ewart was born into a family with a long history of working and farming the land. His Uncle John Ewart (b.1763) was "a contemporary of Robert Burns and Sir Walter Scott". During the uncle's lifetime the transition from subsistence farming to commercial production gathered momentum in the Lothians. However, Uncle John became a brewer's assistant in Haddington (age 11 years) rather than work the land. He would know the town from "trips to the market as a small boy with his father, who had probably made several friends and contacts there." That town had 3,000 people with traditional wool, linen and cloth factories, plus many long established, rather primitive taverns.[21]

Literacy was widespread in the county of East Lothian where Ewart grew up. Reading centred on the Bible and a few religious tracts. It was the aim of John Knox and the reformers to see one parochial school in each parish funded by the heritors (landowners) but under the control of the church. This had been achieved in the Lothians by the end of the 17th century. So the children of William and Margaret Ewart may well have attended the parochial school. Reading, writing and arithmetic were taught for fees of 1s. 6d., 2s., and 2s. 6d. per quarter, respectively. The fees and books for poor children were met from a bequest left for that purpose. There were about 60 pupils for each schoolmaster. Attendance was voluntary, with absenteeism common whenever there was work to be done on the farm.[22]

Nine-year old John Ewart may have been present at the Massacre of Tranent on August 29, 1797. The 1797 Militia Act required local military recruiting quotas in anticipation of a war with the French revolutionary army. A "huge crowd of protesters, led by the miners, gathered outside the inn where the conscription balloting station was held and attacked the building. Troops were called in and the mob was eventually quelled; eleven people were killed and twelve wounded."[23] Ewart's Uncle John (the brewer now in Tranent) and Aunt Margaret probably kept safely indoors with their three children while the troops were clearing the streets. It was a day they would long remember and "they probably had a hard time in restraining the curiosity of the children."[24] Whether our nine-year old John saw the riot or not, it would have made a significant impression on his young mind, at least until the 1837 Rebellion in Toronto.

In the surrounding areas of Tranent, Ewart would have seen everything from the hilltop castles and manor houses to the elegance and sophistication of the city of Edinburgh. Marion MacRae writes that Ewart would have completed his apprenticeship in the building trade and qualified as a free craftsman by the time of his marriage to Jane Wilson on October 3, 1810. "Presumably he was employed on construction projects in Edinburgh's New Town [designed by Robert Adams] but after 1811, like many other ambitious Scottish builders, he moved to London, possibly in the hope of securing lucrative commissions or recognition as an architect."[25] "Ewart stemmed from the Scots background which had sent Watt, Nicolson, Telford and the Rennies to London to join that milling reserve of building practice, His Majesty's Department of Works. As a group they were inquisitive, inventive and prepared to experiment, generally basing their imaginative flights on a good sound training in practical building. John Ewart was a typical example of the export model of the species."[26]

Architects had no formal training in Ewart's time other than informal apprenticeships. One architect in 1909 said, "Then, if students read Paley and Ryckman [sic], that was about all that was expected of them, aside from looking out the window when the boss was out."[27] It was not until 1889 that the Toronto School of Practical Science appointed the first lecturer in architecture.[28]

Along with an apprenticeship, many architects and builders learned through books and working with more experienced colleagues. There was a surprising wealth of reading material to help these men. Although we know little of what Ewart might have read himself, we do know that he owned a copy of Loudon's 1833 book Encyclopaedia of Cottage, Farm and Villa Architecture and Furniture. This book bears Ewart's signature and was later owned by Toronto architect William Storm. It is now in the Rare Book Collection at the University of Toronto.

Loudon's book is a sample of what are called 'pattern books'[29]. These volumes provided detailed information and drawings on every aspect of architecture and building. Whatever the books Ewart would have owned in his library, it is clear that he had resources available to him to help him in designing works of Georgian, Regency and Gothic styles for churches, civic, health, education and residential buildings.

While in London, John and Jane Ewart settled into St. Marylebone parish, the home to many builders. London was becoming the world's largest city. John Nash was building St. Marylebone Estate at Regent's Park and Regent Street. James Wyatt's Gothic style in Woolwich produced the castellated Royal Military Academy. John Rennie's Waterloo Bridge and Nicholson's publications of pattern books were all happening at the same time.[30]

The young couple were now parents of six children, including sets of twins and triplets. Four of the six children were to die young, of unknown causes. Perhaps this sorrow combined with the economic difficulties from the building slump after the Napoleonic war led the Ewarts to emigrate to New York City. They would live there for well over a year and would have seen some of the most ambitious architecture in North America.[31]

Nothing is known of their time in New York. We can presume that Ewart found work there and that he visited and studied the various styles of architecture in and around America's greatest commercial city. His understanding of colonial architecture in the New York area would have influenced his own work in a much smaller frontier town where the amount and quality of labour and materials would constrain any designs he had conceived when he was still in Britain.

We don't know why the Ewarts chose to move to the British Colony of Upper Canada rather than remain in republican America.[32] Whether their move to York in 1818 was based on a desire to be with other Scottish and English immigrants in a British colony or whether he was invited by one of the town's leading families is not known. It is a fact, however, that Ewart took very little time to acquire property and commissions to begin his work.

T.W. Magrath describes the passage from New York City to York in the 1820s. The "inland navigation from New York…by the delightful Hudson, and the canal to Oswego, occupies but four or five days, with the advantage of seeing the most interesting parts of the States. In short, the election, when practicable, is decidedly in favour of the passage to New York from Liverpool [rather than via Quebec and the St. Lawrence River], where merchant ships, (or packets of the first class) with every accommodation that the most luxurious person could desire, are always to be met with. The passage in the best merchantmen can be engaged for twenty guineas[33], with every delicacy of the table, and spirits of all kinds, ad libitum. In the noble packets, called Liners, the total charge, including wines of the best description, is thirty-five guineas. If the emigrant has money to spare, he can pass a few days agreeably at New York; if not, he has the power of immediately removing his kit to the first steamer that starts for Albany, a distance of 150 miles, to which place he will be conveyed for nine shillings. His passage thence to Oswego, on the lake Ontario, by Canal boat, all expenses included, will be 3£ 10s.; and from Oswego to York 1£ 15s.; making a total cost, from New York to York, the grand point of his destination, in either case, of 5£ 4s."[34]

The rest of this book will look at Ewart's legacies of design and construction as well as his contributions to the civic development of York and Toronto. There are conflicting sources of information on his time in the city because the records kept during this period are sketchy at best, with none of Ewart's personal papers to provide guidance. We have several eminent authors crediting Ewart with work that he could not possibly have done.[35] A respected architectural researcher and writer, Eric Arthur, claims that Ewart was "a shadowy figure who appears sporadically between 1824 and 1844."[36]

Yet in his own time, Ewart was already recognized as a leading figure. Henry Scadding writes in 1873 that Ewart was a "Scottish emigrant who became a leading contractor in York. Among his buildings were the Court House, Parliament Buildings and Osgoode Hall. He was the first president of the Mechanics' Institute in 1831 and became the father-in-law of Sir Oliver Mowat."[37] Stephen Otto agrees that "Ewart was part of the early wave of carpenter builders. He quickly moved on to building designs. He was intelligent and the kind of man that would pull up his bootstraps to get the job done. Later in his career he probably became a shareholder in various building supply companies and along with his wharf spent more time supplying the industry rather than doing the actual building. He probably made more money at it too."[38]

So what was York like for the young Ewart family upon their arrival? What kind of government and military town was it? Who were the leading people who would become his neighbours and colleagues? Was it just a "Muddy York", or was there more to the little town than what he might have expected?

Origins and Early History of the Town of York

When Ewart arrived in York in 1818, Toronto's history as a town was only 25 years old. This remarkable fact is often forgotten when we think of modern Toronto. Before 1793, the land we know as Toronto was a virgin forest.[39]

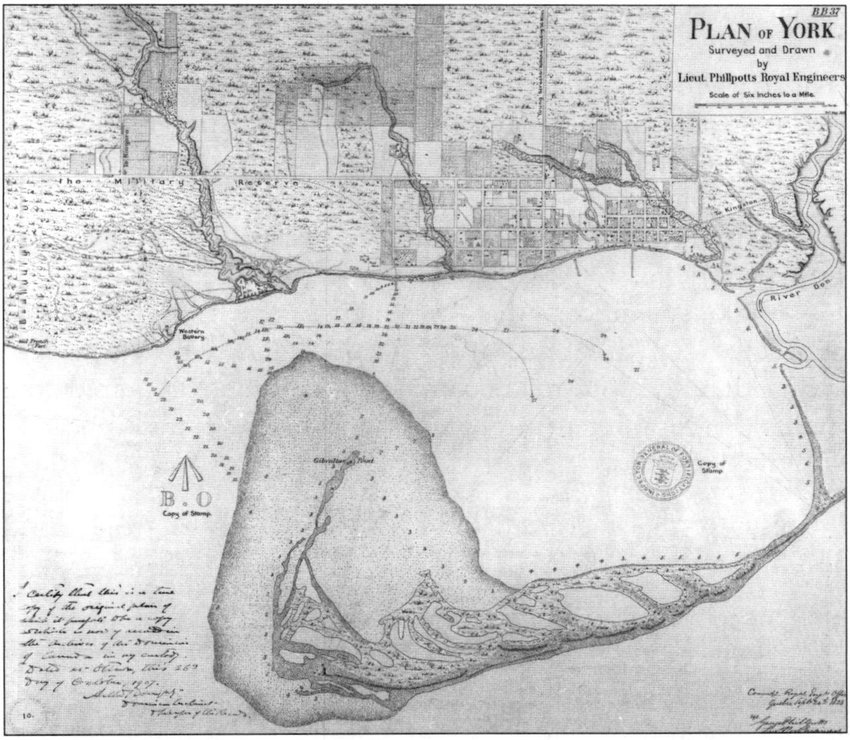

2 Lieutenant R.E. Phillpotts' (Royal Engineers) 1818 Map of the York area shows the western harbour entrance with the main town on the eastern edge of the shoreline. The peninsula that would become the Toronto Islands is on the bottom. A storm separated the eastern end of the harbour from the mainland in 1858 at Ashbridges Bay which completely severed the Toronto Islands from the city.[40] [TPL BB 37]

In 1810 the town's 600 inhabitants lived amongst only two brick buildings (the legislature and Laurent Quetton St. George's house on King Street). The rest of the buildings were all constructed of wood. Nineteen years after York was founded as a military and administrative settlement, the War of 1812 put the town to the test and it survived invasion by American troops and the burning down of its legislative buildings. The town enjoyed an economic boom after the war. There were food and other shortages in town partly because of increased military buying and war shortages. This was quickly followed by inflated prices on all goods. Shopkeepers were in a position to make small fortunes, and many of them did. A growing middle class of tradesmen began to infuse new energy into the unmotivated civil-servant society, and the frontier settlement expanded quickly. New and finer homes were needed so that the leading citizens could publicly display their wealth. Construction was required for civic, hospital, educational, legal and religious edifices that reflected a growing sense of importance for this small provincial capital. The town was moving rapidly toward becoming a city and required the expertise of immigrant architects, builders and tradesmen to fulfill the demand.

This was the energized town that John Ewart would find upon his arrival in 1818.

Physical Layout of the Town

York was divided into town lots and farm lots for houses and shops south of Queen Street to the lake. North of Queen up to Bloor Street were 100-acre park lots numbered westward from the Don River. North of Bloor Street were 200-acre farm lots. "Land was virtually the only thing the colonial government had to give its settlers; and though its real worth was untested, it attracted many people from Britain who had an almost mystical respect for land and the status it conferred."[41]

3. The Plan of the Town of York 1834 on the next page shows a close up of land lots, with Yonge Street on the west, Parliament on the east and Queen (Lot) Street East on the north. You can see the different sizes of land parcels that were available at the time. You can also notice Ewart's Wharf at the southeastern end of Church Street, Ewart's courthouse and jail on the north side of King Street between Toronto and Church Streets, and the Bank of Upper Canada building at the northeast corner of Adelaide and George Streets. [TPL City of Toronto Map (east) 1834 cropped to highlight area shown]

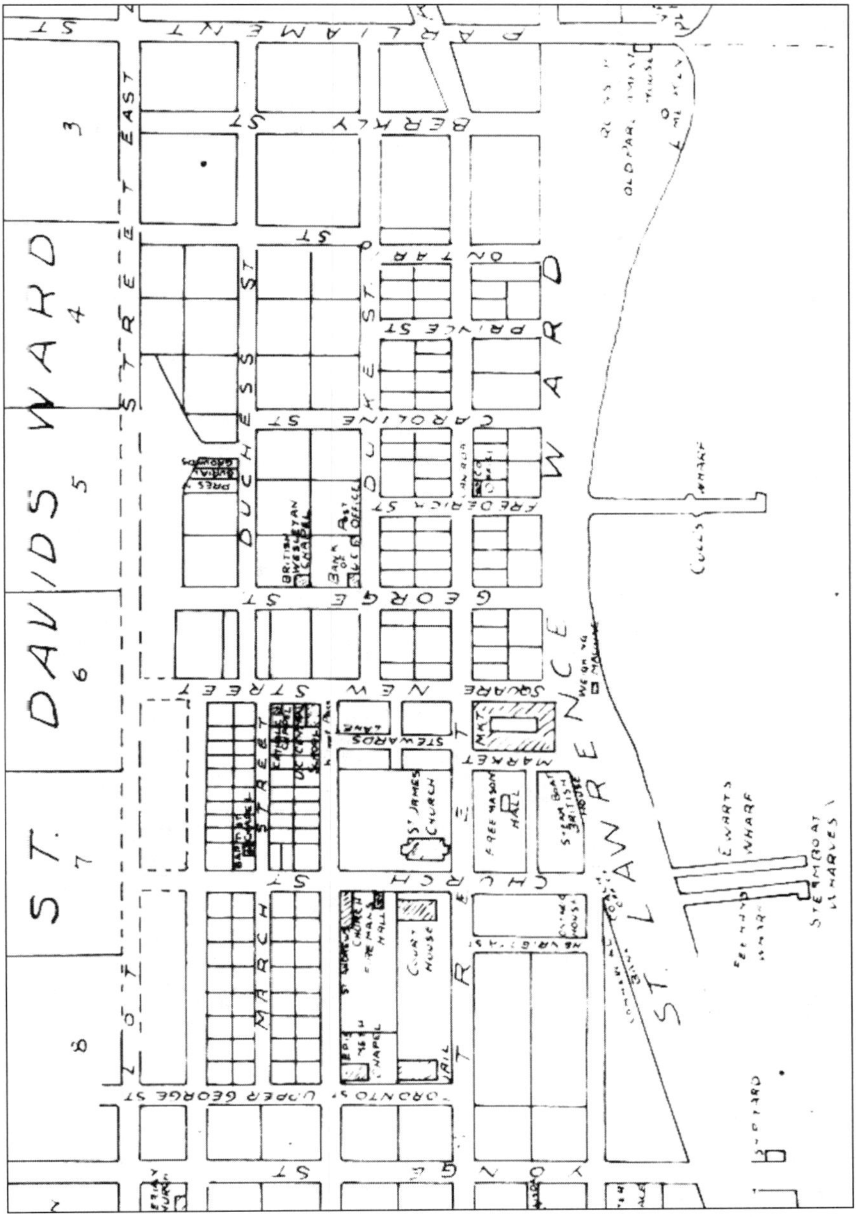

The early officials from Niagara-on-the-Lake were rewarded for their move to the wilderness of York with grants of park lots[42]. The most popular and valuable ones were just north of the town limits and provided the kind of land people wanted on which to build their large estates. "Virtually any of the early settlers were eligible for town lots or farm lots. But the most important men in the colonial establishment were granted park lots, which were intended to be suburban estates—an appropriate setting for the colonial gentry. From the 1820s on, the park lots were subdivided by their owners and profitably sold in building lots to create a series of new districts for the town."[43]

The waterfront was under provincial control until 1850[44], at which time lots were awarded for the construction of wharves and waterfront warehouses. Ewart would secure one of these lots after many of the "founding aristocracy" (as Dendy and Kilbourn call them)[45] had their first chances.

Ewart's New Neighbours

The early years of the nineteenth century saw the evolution of a new class in York: the Family Compact.[46] It "derived from the absence of British leadership in the colony. Provincial Administrators were largely absent, and subsequent Lieutenant-Governor Francis Gore was also absent from 1811-15, essentially the period of the War of 1812."[47] York's citizens were effectively left to govern themselves. Under the leadership of Rev. John Strachan, a member of the Family Compact, the York colonists successfully negotiated the end of hostilities with the Americans.[48]

When Ewart's family arrived in York in 1818, there were already over 1,000 people in town, up considerably from 720 a few years earlier. His trade brought him into contact with many of the most powerful men in the town who had been here for most of the town's early history. Although York was relatively small, the Family Compact and wealthy merchants had a reach far beyond the town's borders. Five of the most visible leaders were: Dr. W.W. Baldwin (1775-1844), who would have the most contact with Ewart during his career; William Allan (1772-1853), D'Arcy Boulton, Jr. (1785-1846), Sir William Campbell (1758-1834), and John Strachan (1778-1867).

4. Lithograph of Dr. William Warren Baldwin portrait by Théophile Hamel ca 1850s. [TPL T-31037]

Dr. William Warren Baldwin[49] immigrated to Upper Canada from Ireland in 1799 with his father, brother and four sisters upon the request of Peter Russell (Simcoe's subsequent administrator in the earliest days of York). Baldwin practiced medicine first and then asked permission of the Lieutenant Governor to practice law as well, which was granted. He conducted a school for boys and was a leader in the later reform movement that his son, Robert, would eventually lead. His marriage to Phoebe Willcocks led to their inheriting thousands of acres belonging to Peter Russell and his cousin William Willcocks. Baldwin was an 'amateur' architect and built his own home, *Spadina House*, as well as laying out the Spadina Avenue as a wide, tree-lined street beyond the town's northern border.

Ewart would meet with him on several projects including the York Courthouse and Jail, Osgoode Hall and the Third Parliament buildings. Baldwin was 13 years older and may well have been Ewart's introduction to the other townsmen likely to commission his work.

5. Robert Baldwin portrait by Théophile Hamel circa 1840s. [TPL T 13649]

Robert Baldwin would have been 14 or 15 years old when Ewart first met him. Like his father, Robert became an advocate for the politics of 'the vital centre.' Robert would lead the triumph of moderate Reform, west of the Ottawa River, in the later 1840s. In the eyes of their Tory (conservative) opponents, the Baldwins were among the few real 'gentlemen' who supported the Reform, or more liberal, cause.[50]

6. Lieutenant Colonel William Allan established the first Customs House in York and became the financial force of the Family Compact. [TPL T-16678]

William Allan was the economic strategist and financial wizard behind the Family Compact. He immigrated to Montreal from Huntley, Aberdeenshire in 1789 and worked his way to York in 1795. He opened a store that was looted twice. These events actually helped him, as he used the government compensation for his losses as investment capital. Ewart would work on his home, *Moss Park*, as well as the Bank of Upper Canada, of which Allan was the President. During his career he was also a postmaster, collector of customs, militia officer, commissioner of the Canada Company, president of the British America Assurance Company, legislative and executive counsellor and Canadian manager of the financial affairs of Edward Ellice, the prominent British financier and politician.[51]

D'Arcy Boulton, Jr. built the first brick manor house, *The Grange*, which survives to the present day. Built in 1817-18 during the reconstruction period after the War of 1812, it was certainly one of the first homes that Ewart would have seen upon his arrival. *The Grange* was a symbol of the aristocratic society the town leaders hoped to perpetuate by promoting a supremely romantic image of colonial Toronto.[52] Even though the roads to and from the house were just as muddy as the rest of town, and it stood amongst farmland, *The Grange's* majesty nevertheless rose above all around it as a true beacon of what was possible in this small town. *The Grange* was built before Ewart's arrival but his awareness of its grandeur and prominence could not be lost on the entrepreneurial builder from Scotland.

7. *The Grange* looking south toward the lake. [TPL T- 11141]

Sir William Campbell was a leading jurist who had moved to York in 1811. He was a judge of King's Bench before becoming the Chief Justice in 1825. Although his home was relocated to University Avenue on the west side opposite Osgoode Hall on

Queen Street in 1972, it was originally at Frederick[53] and Adelaide Streets. Ewart would have seen the original construction of this mansion, as it was not completed until 1822. Campbell would comment very favourably on a number of Ewart's designs, including Osgoode Hall and the York Courthouse and Jail.

8. Sketch of *Campbell House* from J. Ross Robertson's Landmarks of Toronto. [TPL T 11161]

The Reverend John Strachan (pronounced Strawn) was the first Anglican Archbishop of Toronto and founder of Trinity College. He was the spiritual and *de facto* leader of the Family Compact through his church and political connections with the other families. His home, *The Palace*, was completed in 1818. It would have been a second elegant home that Ewart might have first noted upon his arrival in the small town of otherwise wooden dwellings. Strachan was from Aberdeen, Scotland and ordained in 1793 in Kingston, Upper Canada.

9. *The Palace* was Rev. Strachan's home on the present northwest corner of University and Front Street. [TPL 11530]

Strachan married Ann McGill in 1807, the rich widow of fur trader Andrew McGill. They built their 'palace' and entertained the province's wealthy and influential families. Strachan worked to maintain the Anglican dominance over education and politics.[54] One of the reasons that Osgoode Hall was built by the Law Society of Upper Canada, with Ewart as the architect, was to prevent Strachan from taking over the legal education of lawyers through the university he was developing.

Ewart's arrival in York came at a turning point for the young town. The war was over, the town was repairing the damage from the Yankee invasion and the demand for housing and grander buildings to reflect the town's view of itself was increasing exponentially.

The Town in 1818 and 1819

Sailing into York harbour after the lake voyage from the U.S., Ewart would have rounded the sheltering peninsula near the ten-year old hexagonal limestone Gibraltar Lighthouse.[55] Lt. George Phillpotts' map (see early part of this chapter),[56] drawn in that same year, shows Queen Street as the dividing line of the city going west from Yonge Street with large areas of cleared land to its north. The most important street remained King, which goes on a diagonal to Kingston Road, the rough road heading toward the Don River. The rectangular block of houses and shops near the mouth of the Don River was the old centre of the town, bounded by Berkeley, Jarvis, Front, and Richmond Streets. Other less sparsely settled streets had been laid out west of Yonge. The area between the present Jarvis and Yonge was largely swamp, though it contained a dozen or more houses and St. James' Church. Queen Street was laid out as the northerly boundary and ran as far east as Parliament Street. "In 1818, York was only a city in miniature…."[57]

William Kilbourn describes the town as "a jauntier forest [that] meets the eye: masts, rigging, sails, warehouses, and the bell-towers on the docks. The waterfront was noisy. The fishwives in the fish-market at the foot of Church Street cried their wares. The hammers and saws of the shipwrights were busy on the hulls of new ships. Captains of small ships, the truckers and taxi-men of their day, loudly offered to carry freight or cattle or passengers to any of the hundred tiny ports and creeks on the lake."[58]

10. We do not know where Ewart landed in York, but upon docking in the harbour he would have passed by the newer Western frontage of the town featured in this circa 1815 drawing. Looking north from the lake to Peter Street on the left and John Street on the right he would have seen, from left to right: the Crookshank and John Beikie homes, the military storehouse in the foreground, and the Halfway Tavern on the right that served mostly the Garrison soldiers.[59] [TPL T-12567]

The "presence of government officials, officers of the army and navy, and other 'gentlemen', gave a higher tone to social life than was usually to be found elsewhere during the early period of settlement. …Both women and men were fond of visiting their friends and associates, and such calls, especially on New Year's Day, were of a much more formal nature than visits in the rural districts, where the elements of spontaneity and surprise predominated in the interchange of civilities. Class distinctions were very rigid in the early days, and the fashionable society of these first towns was restricted to a comparatively small section of the population. The military and civilians alike were fond of horse-racing and field sports, fishing and sailing, football and cricket in the summer, and of skating and caroling in winter; while at all seasons dancing, chess, whist, wine and conversation served to while away the time."[60]

The postwar years saw the legislators of York and Upper Canada trying to limit the number of immigrants from the United States. Ewart and his family were part of an influx of

British immigrants who increased the population of York from 720 in 1816 to 1,270 in 1821. The first significant wave of British immigrants, however, would not arrive until the late 1820s and early 1830s, reaching a peak in 1832, when 66,000 new immigrants arrived in Upper Canada.[61] The ongoing immigration was aided by books encouraging Britons to leave the homeland for a colony with real promise of economic success combined with adventure. One such book was Robert Gourlay's 1822 publication, *Statistical Account of Upper Canada.* He uses 630 pages to covers all aspects of living in Upper Canada based on his years in York at the turn of the century.

By June of 1818, Ewart had purchased the Custom House Reserve on the waterfront just west of Yonge Street. He also acquired his own wharf lot at the base of east side of Church Street just beside that of D'Arcy Boulton, Jr., owner of *The Grange.*[62] He clearly arrived in York with funds saved up from his time in London and New York City and invested wisely in the most precious commodity of the time: land and water access.

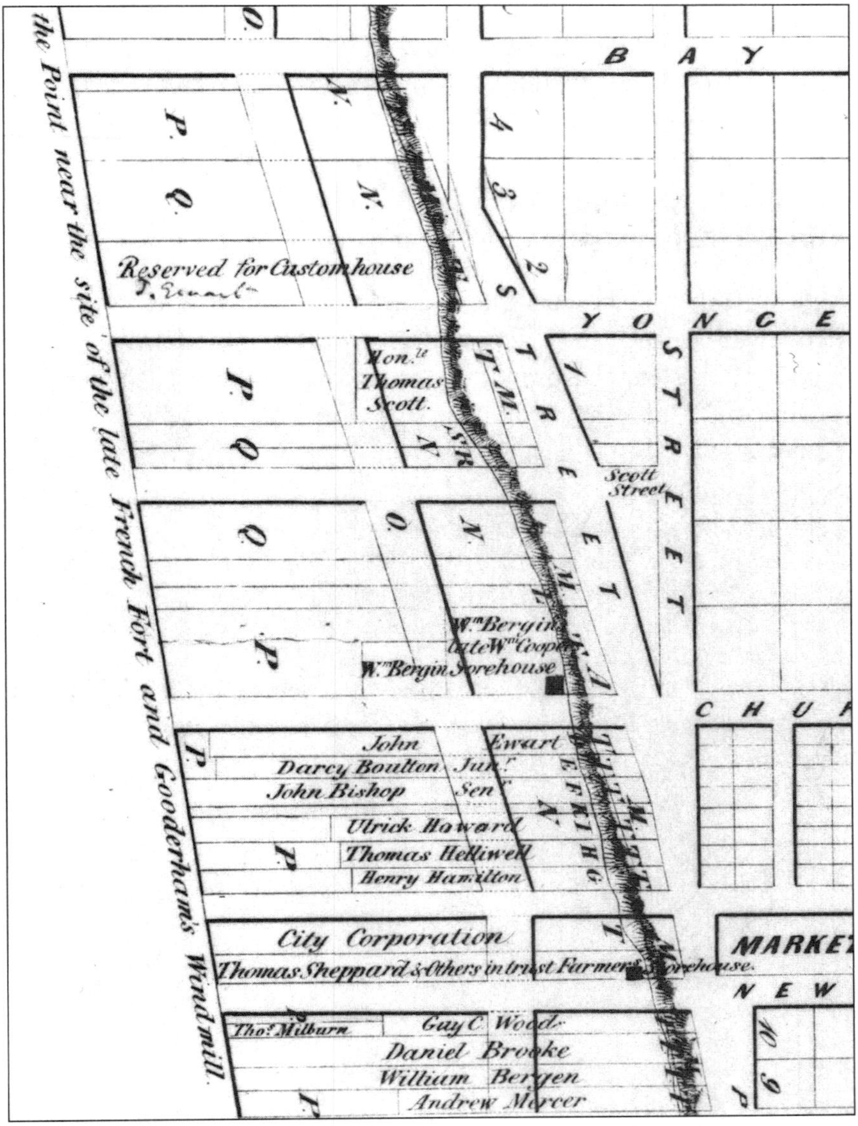

11. Ewart's water lots as shown on the Plan of the Town of York 1839. The first is a reserve for the Custom House in Ewart's name and the second is the wharf lot just east of the bottom of Church Street. The street labelled "O" just above the water lots was a 100-foot wide esplanade. [TPL City of Toronto March 30 1839]

Both of Ewart's purchases are still evident twenty years later on the Toronto Map of 1839.[63] What happened to Ewart during those twenty years? What buildings was he involved with and how did his family grow in the early years of Toronto's history? How did the Family Compact help or hinder his work and who were the people he worked with to secure his own family's future and also that of our growing town of York?

To begin to answer these questions, we end this chapter with Ewart's first land acquisition through his petition, on 1 June 1819, to the Lieutenant Governor of Upper Canada (JF Collection). This is also the first signature of John Ewart known to exist:

To His Excellency, Sir Peregrine Maitland, Lieutenant-Governor of the province of Upper Canada, and Major General commanding His Majesty's forces therein. In Council, The Petition of John Ewart, of the Town of York – Carpenter – Humbly Herewith – That Your Excellency's Petitioner is a native of East Lothian Scotland, and has just arrived in this Province, has a wife and two children, and has the means of cultivating 200 acres of lands, has taken and subscribed the oath of allegiance, and has never received any Land or order for Land from the Crown. Wherefore humbly prays that Your Excellency may be pleased to Grant him such portion of the waste Lands of the Crown as to Your Excellency may seem meet and as in duty bound will ever pray. (Signed John Ewart)[64].

12. The original Land Petition (on the next page) to Sir Peregrine Maitland, Lieutenant Governor of Upper Canada on June 1, 1819. [LAC, C-001888 Upper Canada Land Petitions, RG 1, L3, Vol. 177A, petition E12/26]

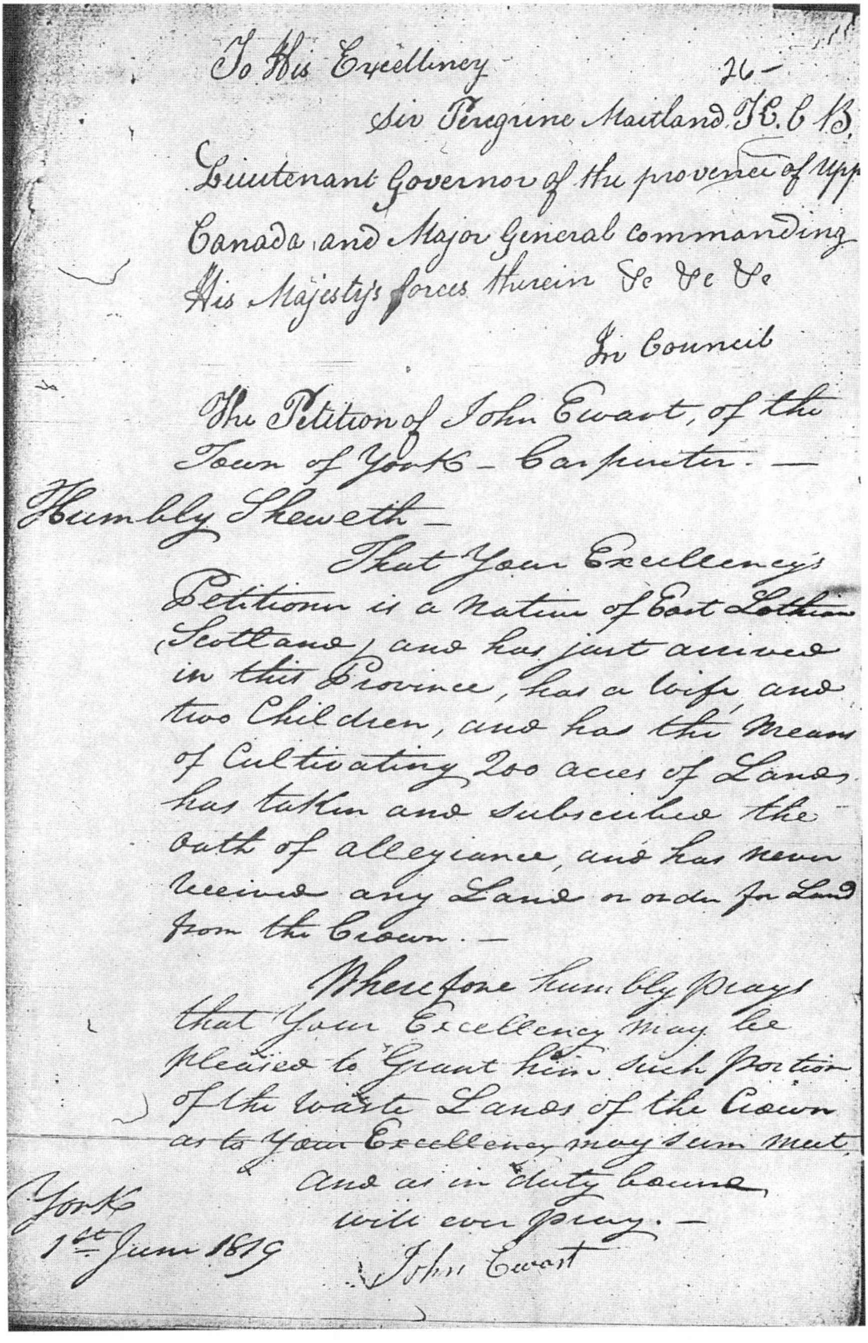
To His Excellency 26 –

Sir Peregrine Maitland K.C.B.

Lieutenant Governor of the province of Upp

Canada and Major General commanding

His Majesty's forces therein do Vc Vc

In Council

The Petition of John Ewart, of the

Town of York – Carpenter. –

Humbly Sheweth –

That Your Excellency's

Petitioner is a Native of East Lothian

(Scotland) and has just arrived

in this Province, has a wife, and

two Children, and has the Means

of Cultivating 200 acres of Land.

has taken and subscribed the

oath of allegiance, and has never

received any Land or order for Land

from the Crown. –

Wherefore humbly prays

that Your Excellency may be

pleased to Grant him such portion

of the waste Lands of the Crown

as to Your Excellency may seem meet,

and as in duty bound

will ever pray. –

York

1st June 1819

John Ewart

14 Interview with Stephen Otto, April 16, 2004.

15 Marion MacRae and Anthony Adamson. (1983). *Cornerstones of Order,* p. 37.

16 *Ibid*, p. 39.

17 Edith Firth. (1962). *The Town of York 1815-1834*, pp. 41-42, footnote 17.

18 *Dictionary of Canadian Biography*. Vol. VIII, "John Ewart", by Marion MacRae, p. 280.

19 Marion MacRae and Anthony Adamson. (1983). *Cornerstones of Order,* p. 41.

20 John Richard Layton. (1993). *The Ewarts of Tranent, East Lothian,* p. 11.

21 *Ibid*, p. 9.

22 *Ibid*, p. 8.

23 *Ibid*, p. 11.

24 *Ibid*, p. 11.

25 *Dictionary of Canadian Biography*. Vol. VIII, "John Ewart", by Marion MacRae, p. 280.

26 Marion MacRae and Anthony Adamson. (1975). *Hallowed Walls*, p. 83.

27 Angela Carr. (1995). *Toronto Architect Edmond Burke*, p. 6.

28 *Ibid*, p. 5.

29 See bibliography for a sample of these.

30 Marion MacRae and Anthony Adamson. (1983) *Cornerstones of Order*, p. 41. A sample of Peter Nicholson's work, undated but between 1785-1844, (when he died) is: *Architectural Directory: The Student's Instructor in Drawing and Working with the Five Orders of Architecture.* London: M. Taylor. Two large volumes. See also, the appendix on architecture for other pattern books that Ewart may have used in his career.

31 *Dictionary of Canadian Biography*. Vol. VIII, "John Ewart", by Marion MacRae, p. 280.

32 1818, June 3. *Plan of the Town of York* in the Toronto Reference Library clearly shows two Ewart properties: The Custom House Reserve and the wharf property at the eastern base of Church Street.

33 F.H. Armstrong. (1988). *A City in the Making*, p. 11. Until 1857, before we adopted the decimal system, Upper Canada used the imperial system of pounds, shilling and pence: the pound consisting of 20 shillings and the shilling divided into 12 pennies (240 pennies equalled one pound). Figures were written in £/s./d.—pounds/shillings/pence. To complicate matters further, there were two types of pounds used in Upper Canada, the British pound or pound Sterling (abbreviated St.), and the local pound or pound Currency (Cy.). The latter, which was originally only a bookkeeping currency since there were no local coins or paper notes, was less valuable with five shillings Currency equalling four shillings Sterling. There are no monetary equivalents to 2004 dollars due to the complex variables in financial equivalents from 1820s to 2004. However, the assessment rolls and daily incomes in the mid 1830s, described later in the book, can provide a useful comparison.

34 Thomas Radcliff. (Ed.). (1953). *Authentic Letters from Upper Canada*, pp. 10 and 11. This book provides a collection of letters up. to 1833, originally published in Dublin.

35 For example, Lucy Booth Martyn (1982) *The Face of Early Toronto*, p. 25, credits him with the First Government Buildings in 1797 when Ewart was only 9 years old; Harold Kalman (1994) *A History of Canadian Architecture*, p. 174, credits Ewart with Elmsley House [later Government House for Lieutenant-Governor of Upper Canada] and built in 1798 when Ewart was 10.

36 Eric Arthur. (1964) *Toronto: No Mean City*, p. 246.

37 *Toronto of Old.* (1873), p. 364.

38 Interview April 16, 2004.

39 Glazenbrook, G.P. DeT. (1971). *The Story of Toronto*, p. 3.

40 Edith Firth. (1962). *The Town of York 1793-1815*, p. 239.

41 William Dendy and William Kilbourn. (1986). *Toronto Observed*, p. 4.

42 Edith Firth. (1962). *The Town of York 1793-1815*, p. xxxvi.

43 William Dendy and William Kilbourn. (1986). *Toronto Observed.* p. 16.

44 Eric Rosen. (1998). *The Don: The History of the Don Valley*, p. 59.

45 William Dendy and William Kilbourn. (1986). *Toronto Observed*, p. 5.

46 The Family Compact was the group of early families who established the financial and political power of the early town of York. For a complete listing of these families, see Appendix 5.

47 William Dendy and William Kilbourn. (1986). *Toronto Observed*, p. 12.

48 Jennifer Parsons and Kevin Lillian. (1995). *Toronto 1837: A Model City*, p. ii.

49 Austin Seton Thompson. (1975). *Spadina: A Story of Old Toronto*, p. 44.

50 Randall White. (1985). *Ontario 1610-1985: A Political and Economic History*, p. 92.

51 F.H. Armstrong. (1983). *Toronto: The Place of Meeting*, p. 40.

52 William Dendy and William Kilbourn. (1986). *Toronto Observed*, p. 22.

53 Sketch from J. Ross Robertson. (1896). *Landmarks of Toronto*, Vol. 1, p. 80.

54 Leonard Wise and Allan Gould. (2000). *Toronto Street Names*, p. 203.

55 Harold Kalman. (1994). *A History of Canadian Architecture*, Vol. 1, p. 203.

56 Eric Arthur. (1964). *Toronto: No Mean City*, p. 36.

57 *Ibid*, pp. 34-36.

58 William Kilbourn. (1956). *The Firebrand*, p. 4.

59 William Dendy and William Kilbourn. (1986). *Toronto Observed*, p. 12.

60 Edwin Guillet. (1933). *Pioneer Days in Upper Canada*, p. 169.

61 F.H. Armstrong. (1983). *Toronto: The Place of Meeting*, p. 53.

62 June 3, 1818 *Plan of the Town of York* map, Toronto Reference Library.

63 *Toronto Map*, 30 March 1839 by Rordans, Carter, and Lan. Toronto Reference Library.

64 Library and Archives Canada C-1888.

CHAPTER 2
Foundations of a New Life in Upper Canada (1819-1824)

York General Hospital (1820)
Hazelburn (1822)
St. Paul's Roman Catholic Church (1823)
The Second Courthouse and Jail (1823-24)

The early 1820s were increasingly active for John Ewart. His reputation was growing along with his family: a son, Thomas, was born in 1819, followed by John Jr. in 1822 and daughter Jane in 1824. At the time of their births, Ewart was busy with the building of the York General Hospital, *Hazelburn* home, St. Paul's Roman Catholic Church and the Second Courthouse and Jail in York. The town reached just over 1,500 residents by 1823[65] and had "209 houses, 27 shops, and 5 store houses."[66] York had doubled its size in less than ten years.

We do not know the nature of Ewart's first architectural or building commission but it's presumed that he had a few smaller ones of which no records remain. Mike Filey writes that Ewart was engaged in the construction of the early Parliament Buildings near the foot of today's Parliament Street[67] but gives no source for his assertion. Throughout this book, we will only credit Ewart with design or construction of buildings for which we have several reliable sources. His first recorded commission was to design and build a civilian hospital. Architecture was not yet a 'pure science,' so architects were often builders as well. Ewart was following in the tradition of fellow Scotsmen Robert and James Adam, both important architects and builders.

Ewart had no professional competition in York when he began his work. The town was too small and insignificant to attract professional architects from England and America until after the 1820s. Architectural design was left to 'amateur' homeowners, military men, administrators and the educated elite. People like Dr. W.W. Baldwin were excellent examples of how well read and prepared these men were to design homes and buildings to meet their needs in the new settlement.[68]

To help locate Ewart's York buildings over his lifetime, we have commissioned the following maps to serve as our reference point for the rest of the book.

The following two original maps show all of Ewart's York buildings except for the Provincial Asylum located at Queen and Ossington. Most of Ewart's early work was in the original eastern area of York with the exception of the York General Hospital.

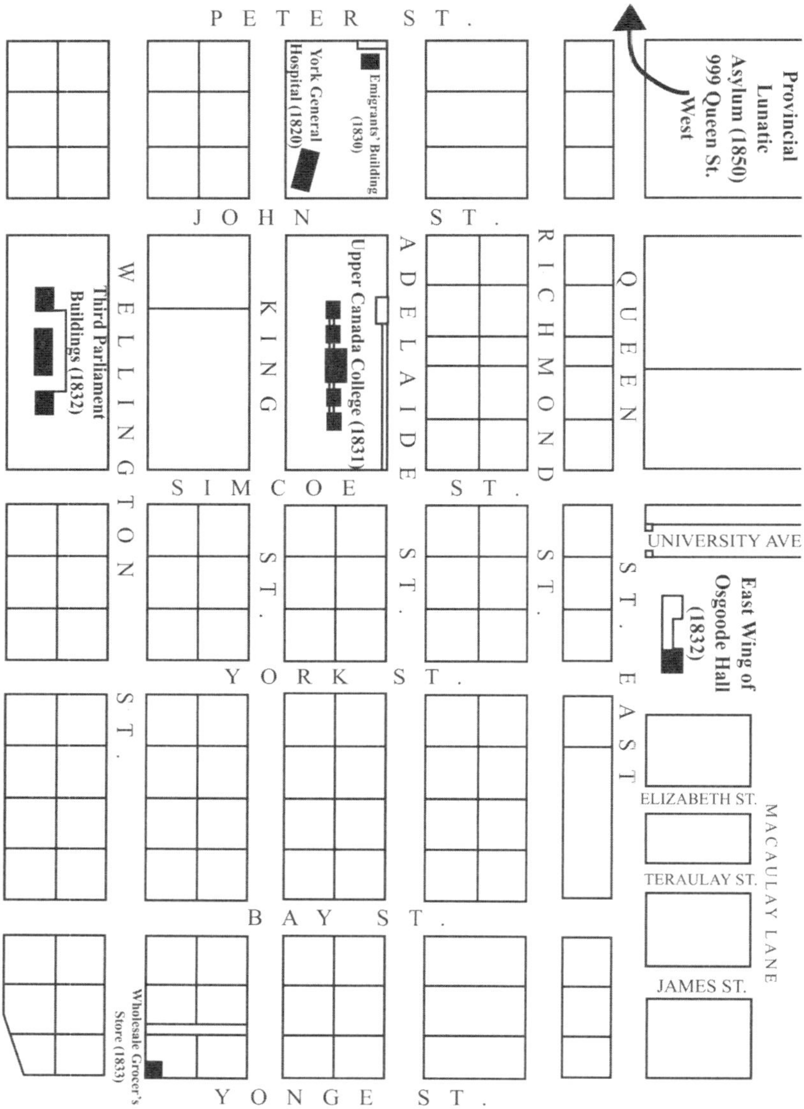
PETER ST.
Provincial Lunatic Asylum (1850) 999 Queen St. West
Emigrants' Building (1830)
York General Hospital (1820)
JOHN ST.
FRONT ST.
Third Parliament Buildings (1832)
WELLINGTON ST.
KING ST.
Upper Canada College (1831)
ADELAIDE ST.
RICHMOND ST.
QUEEN ST. EAST
SIMCOE ST.
UNIVERSITY AVE
East Wing of Osgoode Hall (1832)
YORK ST.
ELIZABETH ST.
TERAULAY ST.
MACAULAY LANE
BAY ST.
JAMES ST.
Wholesale Grocer's Store (1833)
YONGE ST.

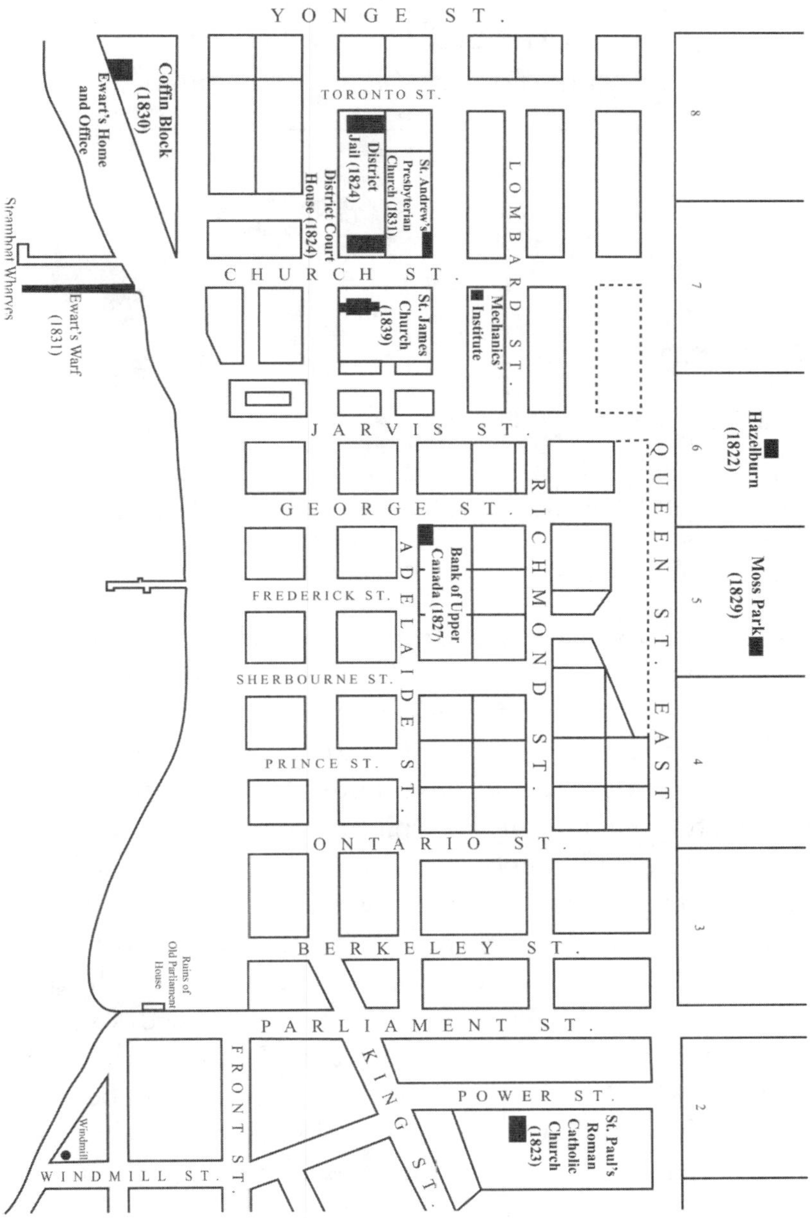

1. Ewart's buildings. Eastern map shows Ewart's wharf at south end of Church St. with his Coffin Block just to the west of where Wellington (north side) meets Front Street (south side). [DH]

York General Hospital (1820)
(Became Toronto General Hospital)

2. York General Hospital built on the northwest corner of King and John Streets in 1820 and used as temporary Parliament Buildings from 1825 to 1829 and as government offices from 1856-1859. [TPL T 10937]

The need for a hospital arose from York's involvement in the short but violent War of 1812-1814 with the United States and the town's siege by President Madison's troops in 1813. During the war, the Loyal and Patriotic Society in York was created. Its purpose was to raise funds to help the war's victims and with the building of a hospital. The society quickly raised funds in York, with some inhabitants pledging an amazing ten-percent of their annual income towards the hospital. People in Quebec City, Montreal, Nova Scotia and even far off Jamaica also contributed along with the Duke of Kent (Princess Victoria's father). These efforts raised £13,000 with over £253 going toward the construction of a small hospital just north of Fort York, where recovering wounded soldiers could be treated. The rest of the money was used to help the victims directly. By 1817 another £4,000 had been raised and put aside for a civilian hospital.[69]

Lieutenant-Governor Maitland endowed the first infirmary with part of the 380-acre reserve that had been intended for

Government House (his official residence). Proceeds from the sale of lots were used to build the hospital but these funds were inadequate.[70] "The tender submitted by Ewart was lowest of those who bid for this work and the contract was awarded to him"[71] to design and build a 107 by 50 feet, 2 storey, 50-bed brick hospital on the six-acre lot bounded by King, John, Adelaide and Peter streets.

The hospital was built in the Georgian style and included recessed galleries on the north and south sides of the interior. It was the only building of the era to face true north so that it was angled southeast to the street. It was likely constructed according to true north under the belief that this would allow it to take advantage of wind direction for proper ventilation and to help insulate against the cold.[72]

A letter from John Sudd (bricklayer) to William Allan[73], chair of the building committee, gives some of the background for tradesmen and labourers in York at the time. Edith Firth has punctuated the letter, but the spelling has not been corrected:

> *I shall be very thankful if you would use your influence for us when the Committee Meets for the Decision of those Estimates That are given in. I hope you think upon the British Subjects. Mr. Young and I have agreed to do the Brickwork if Mr. Ewart should be so fortunate as to get the Job. Mr. Ewart is a very good Carpenter well Qualified for any Building whatever. here is Many good tradesmen in York that will be very glad to work for us Equal to any of the americans if not better. We have com along way from our Nativeland in hops of getting our Bread in this country. we look to you gentlemen for protection and we hop That you will imploy us. we ask not high prices for our work we can work as well as the americans and we will work lower. You Sir have Been very kind to me in given Me the Building of the Brickwork and I hop we hall have The Good will of the Gentlemen. The americans have had Many good Jobs in York. they stick together and are trying to get all the trade in this place and Many of them have*

> *cleared out with a considerable sum of Money with them. I am in no ways stingy against the americans but I Think it is our Duty and Right to be assiduous after the trade as well as they—if the gentlemen of York will incorage us we will Do everything that lay in our power to oblige them.*[74]

Ewart began in 1820 and construction was painfully slow.[75] At a cost of £3,501, there was no money left over to pay for furnishings or staff and the hospital stood empty until the end of 1824.[76] On Christmas Eve of 1824, the Provincial Legislature building fell victim to fire. The hospital was used for a temporary legislature for the next 5 years until 3 June 1829, when it became a hospital as originally intended.[77] Frank Yeigh writes that the "hospital had the honour of being the most important building in the province at that time."[78]

Hazelburn (1822)

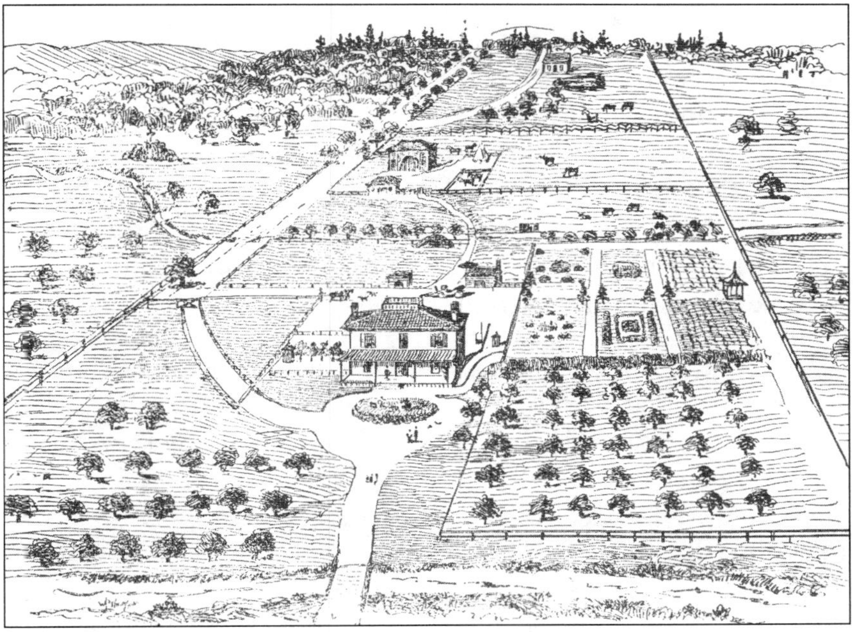

3. *Hazelburn* as reproduced in John Ross Robertson's *Landmarks of Toronto*[79]. The house stood in the centre of today's Jarvis, just south of Shuter Street. [TPL Hazelburn TPL Robertson Vol. 2, p. 1024]

Hazelburn was a home built for Samuel Peters Jarvis (1792-1857) by "John Ewart, who later constructed Osgoode Hall and Upper Canada College. *Hazelburn* was an attractive two-storey brick dwelling with a large verandah that looked out over ten acres of well-kept lawns and gardens. The interior was paneled with black walnut."[80] Its name derived from "the profusion of hazelnut bushes and a small stream (known as a 'burn' in Scotland)."[81]

Robertson writes that *Hazelburn* "was built by the late Mr. John Ewart, as contractor for the masonry work…"[82] The front carriage way was entered from Queen Street over a bridge spanning a small burn and past a hazelnut grove ending in a circle at the front door, hence the home's name. This small stretch of road eventually became Jarvis Street.

Jarvis had acquired the land from his father William, who had been the Provincial Secretary and Registrar of Records from 1792 until his death in 1817. Samuel took over his father's job as Secretary and assumed his father's debts as well. Samuel, 25 years old at the time of his father's death, had been in prison for a deadly duel he fought against 18-year-old John Ridout as a "result of bad feeling between their families and a number of angry exchanges between the two young men."[83]

In 1822 Samuel appealed to Lieutenant-Governor Sir Peregrine Maitland for "part compensation for the Injury suffered by his father" under Lieutenant-Governor Peter Hunter when Jarvis' father was deprived of the full fees to which he was entitled for the issuance of Crown patents of land as provincial secretary. It is likely that Dr. Strachan (his former headmaster) and Chief Justice Powell, (his father-in-law) reviewed his claim and, as they were members of the Executive Council, Sam received £1,000. "It is reasonable to assume that his happy windfall was used by Sam to help build a new house for himself in York on the 100-acre park lot his father had transferred to him just before he died. Construction of the dwelling, which Sam was to name *Hazelburn*, was begun in mid-summer of 1824. It was placed well back from Lot (Queen) Street, at the centre of today's Jarvis Street, a little south of its intersection with Shuter Street. The two-storey house was of brick construction and included a spacious verandah that extended across the front or south elevation. It also provided a covering for Sam's main entrance. John Ewart is said to have been the builder of the house, which was mainly distinguished for its interior woodwork of solid black walnut."[84] John George Howard, a second generation Toronto architect (arrived in 1833) worked under Ewart's direction on the Provincial Lunatic Asylum in the late 1840s, used this same walnut after the demolition of *Hazelburn* in Colonel Arthur Carthew's Deer Park estate home in 1847.[85]

Samuel Jarvis was Chief Superintendent of the Department of Indian Affairs from 1837 to 1845 but was fired for poor management of the department and its finances. His debts forced him to sell off part of his land.[86] Between 1846 and 1851, John Howard supervised the subdivision, creating Jarvis, Mutual and George (north of Shuter) streets. *Hazelburn* was partially demolished as it was in the centre of Jarvis St. and Mutual. Howard laid out Jarvis as a wide, tree-lined boulevard and in the 1870s it became the most fashionable address in Toronto, with rows of mansions.[87] John Ewart bought part of this sub-division in 1843: park lot 6, bounded by Jarvis, Carlton, Mutual and Maitland streets. He gave a large 250-foot by 250-foot square section to his daughter Jane and her husband Oliver Mowat as a wedding present in 1846. In 1856, the Mowats built their home *Northfield* on this property.[88]

St. Paul's Roman Catholic Church (1822-23)

4. Owen Staples sketch of St. Paul's Roman Catholic Church east side of Power Street south of Queen Street East. [TPL T-10805]

There were all of six Catholic citizens in the Town of York area in 1805. The parishioners grew in number to 46 in 1817 and 260 in 1822. The Catholics were mostly Irish with some English, Scottish and French. With the construction of St. Paul's Catholic Church in Cabbagetown in 1822, the Catholic population grew to 1,275 in 1830 and 3,500 by 1834.[89]

As Margaret and Merilyn McKelvey record: "In May of 1822, land on what is now Power Street was purchased for the first Roman Catholic Church between Kingston and Detroit. By December, the Honourable James Baby (Executive Council member and parishioner) wrote to the Roman Catholic Bishop of Kingston: 'Our church is under cover and the walls are secure from frost.'...In 1842 the Diocese of Kingston was divided, and Bishop Michael Power chose Toronto as the seat of the newly created Diocese of Toronto. Thus St. Paul's Church, then the only Catholic church in the community, was for a time a cathedral until St. Michael's was consecrated in 1848."[90]

As the designer[91] and contractor[92] for this church, Ewart built his reputation for fine ecclesiastic structures that would see him involved in all three of the major churches in York: St. Paul's Roman Catholic, St. Andrew's Presbyterian and the rebuilding of St. James' Church of England.

MacRae and Adamson conclude that: "[s]ufficient archival evidence remains on which to base a reconstruction drawing of the principal façade of St. Paul's, and in it one can sense the quality of Ewart's feeling for proportional relationships. He had a designer's eye for the degrees of drama, solemnity, economy and light relief required in a building of urban importance in a semi-pioneer community. All three of his churches would seem to have been based on a close personal knowledge of the design produced by William Stark, in 1808, for St. George's Parish Church in Glasgow, a fanciful Regency simplification of the Baroque idiom, borrowed freely from Nicholas Hawksmoor's London churches. Ewart very sensibly cut his designs to suit his cloth—the townscape of York—telescoping the stages of his bell towers to relate to the mass of his buildings. St. Paul's was dignified but never pompous, and did not mock its humble secular neighbours."[93]

5. St. George's Parish Church in Glasgow inspired Ewart's work on churches in York. [Reprinted with permission from the congregation of St. George's Parish]

Many Protestants readily donated to the building fund for this church including members of the Church of England. Prominent church members included Alexander Macdonell, Sheriff and Mrs. Henry Boulton, wife of the Attorney General. The church was erected with red bricks brought in from Kingston. "At a time when Toronto was almost entirely a town of plain wooden buildings, the new St. Paul's was often described by travellers as its most beautiful. It stood for close to 70 years until a new St. Paul's was built in 1889."[94]

James Baby, a member of the Executive Council of Upper Canada, wrote in 1824 that St. Paul's was the "neatest building of its kind in Upper Canada—to this may be added also the cheapest—the roof, steeple, a neat gallery, a beautiful arched ceiling with cornices all in plaster of Paris complete and painted—the whole ready for public worship."[95] It was Ewart's frugality on this project that helped him secure more than one commission during his career.[96]

Dr. Scadding, York's leading historian of the 19th century, recalled that St. Paul's had been "a substantial brick building, the north and south walls of which had been worked into a 'kind of tessellated pattern, which was considered very extraordinary'...[Ewart] had then instructed his masons, including the aptly named Thomas Bond, to lay up the brick in the Flemish manner—the tessellated pattern [i.e., made from small flat pieces of stone in various colours arranged in a pattern] which had so intrigued the citizens of the wooden town."[97]

Second Courthouse and Jail in York (1823-24) (More accurately the "Home District Courthouse and Jail")

6. When historians write about this period, they invariably display the Thomas Young lithograph produced in 1835 that opens Chapter 1 of this book. John George Howard's print in the same year is more accurate because it does not include the steeple on St. James' Church (far right of photo—northeast corner of King and Church Streets). That steeple was not added until 1839 after a fire burned down the church and Ewart replaced the main building after which Howard added the steeple. The scene above is shown looking north from King Street between Toronto Street on the west and Church Street on the east. Ewart's jail is on the left, on a separate street is the Fireman's Hall designed by Howard and Ewart's Courthouse is on the right. [TPL T-12633]

Stephen Otto writes that the Jail (on the left above) and the Courthouse (on its right) were the most representative architectural structures of their day. When people thought of early York, they imagined these two buildings, connected by a tunnel and set back about sixty-five feet from King Street between Yonge and Church to provide a large public space.[98]

York's first courthouse was in a wing of the 1796 Legislative Buildings at the foot of Parliament Street.[99] After these buildings were burnt by the Americans in the War of 1812, the Home District (centred in York) rented a house for its courts and the legislative work was carried out in Ewart's York

General Hospital building. The justices and leading citizens of York were discouraged that Kingston, under Thomas Rogers' inspiring architecture, had begun to have an urban look compared to York's mostly primitive wooden buildings.[100]

Recognizing that the Home District needed a new courthouse and jail, Lieutenant-Governor Maitland wrote to Lord Bathurst in 1819. He wanted to ensure that the new buildings were both functional for their purposes but also that they set a tone for the provincial capital. He preferred York to have similar stately buildings as towns like Kingston and Newark. He wrote: "As the towns which spring up with great rapidity on the opposite side of the St. Lawrence, generally exhibit a certain sort of exterior decoration in their Churches and other public edifices, it not frequently gives rise among us to a feeling of unsatisfactory comparison; and I am confident that the value of a few such public works as those to which I have alluded, would not be confined to their actual utility, but that they would induce a sense of national pride, and prove a source of attachment to the Government of the Parent State."[101]

The Home District judges "plunged bravely into inevitable debt, determined to save the provincial capital from derisory comment. In 1822, they advertised their wish to receive plans and specifications for a new jail and courthouse to be built in York, and by 3 May 1823, they were seeking expert advice from 'the gentlemen of the Law Society' in arriving at a decision. As a result of these deliberations, they recorded in the Quarter Sessions minutes that: "the plans furnished by Mr. Ewart and Dr. Baldwin were each in part adopted."[102] The judges understood that architecture, as Owen Jones wrote in 1856, was "the material expression of the wants, the faculties, and the sentiments of the age in which it is created."[103]

Baldwin was aware, as a recently arrived architect could not be, that a courtroom in Upper Canada had to serve as a community centre. It was expected to function as an assembly room, as a clearing-house for all manner of municipal concerns, and, every now and then, as a judicial theatre. John Ewart, accustomed to more specialized buildings, had to revise his conception of a courtroom and offer alternative flexible plans for the principal functional space. Fortunately, he was a designer of considerable ingenuity with a nice sense of drama restrained by his firm grip on reality. Ewart had designed the courthouse and jail as pedimented brick buildings with wall pilasters in Roman cement.[104]

As the Minutes of the Magistrates of the Home District Quarter Sessions, 17 May 1823 record: "Mr. Ewart was subsequently required to complete one plan, embracing the parts adopted by the Courts from those now furnished, and Saturday next named to have that plan completed to be laid before the Sessions."[105]

With less than a week at his disposal, John Ewart assimilated the suggestions and worked out a new set of plans. Ewart's energy and initiative is illustrated by the following: "Somewhere along in the discussion it had occurred to Ewart that his clients were not really able to visualize the proposed buildings from plans and elevations, and that the builders selected by them might be even more blinkered; so he made a model to accompany the final plans and specifications, all presented by June 1823. It seems probable from the disposition of the buildings that Ewart made a site plan as well. The Justices had asked for a 'jail and courthouse.' Ewart took them at their word, designing two buildings, set well back from bustling King Street in line with the recently enlarged St. James' Church....Ewart designed the two buildings as wings to be bridged by a truly impressive edifice when the public purse should match public ambition."[106]

The justices liked these so well that they accepted them, after a little soul searching over their earlier decision. Ewart was asked, however, to place round-headed windows in the south front. The tunnel connecting the courthouse and jail was never built due to lack of funds and political will. However, the two buildings costing £6,000[107] stood as testament to how the justices and leaders of York wanted their provincial capital's reputation to be seen by others.

Other changes were made during the construction. Ewart had "specified tin roofing, but the building contractors frustrated that laudable fire precaution by persuading the clients that they had a better scheme. By roofing the building with cedar shingles and reducing the specified internal and external wall thicknesses by depths of from one to two bricks, enough money would be saved, they said, to apply cut stone pilasters to the façade. The flank wall pilasters in Ewart's design were to be omitted as were the roof-lanterns and the jail chapel. The helpful contracting team of Ford and Hayden further recommended that the 'four little rooms' and the courtroom gallery might be omitted."[108] These changes led to easier jail breaks (i.e., thinner brick walls made chiselling out easier), less public access to the courts, and greater fire dangers.

The jail on the left of Thomas Young and John George Howard's 1835 drawings was surrounded on three sides by a fence fifteen feet high. "The jail housed not only debtors, criminals, vagrants, and the Keeper and his family, but also the insane. No one knew what to do with lunatics, so they were shackled in underground dungeons and made to lie on straw that was seldom changed. They were given only bread and water; there was no soap and sanitary arrangements were minimal. Even hardened criminals in basement cells that measured four feet four inches by five feet six inches [shorter than many men of the time] and had brick partitions four feet four inches thick were housed in better conditions than the lunatics. Debtors, and often their families, were confined on the upper floors and lived on charity. The gallows stood in the jail yard."[109]

Writing about Ewart's ingenuity combined with Baldwin's[110] understanding of community needs, J. Ross Robertson's newspaper column said in 1896: "Sufficient credit has not been given to the planners who so arranged the two buildings between Toronto and Church Streets that they formed a public space which, for many years, was called Court House Square. It is one of the earliest attempts in Toronto at civic design."[111] One aspect of their collaboration was probably the prisoner's box inside the courtroom. The box was placed on wheels so that it could be moved easily out of the way for other functions.[112]

William Kilbourn describes the Courthouse square in front of the Courthouse as affording "space for the assembling of the Orangemen's parades, for the country throngs coming in to watch a public hanging, for the promenade of people of fashion on a spring day, or for the small, informal gatherings for gossip and talk and argument which are necessary if a collection of individuals is to become a true community."[113]

In fact public executions could bring out thousands of people to view the end of someone's life. "When two murderers were hanged in 1828, school children were given a holiday. Ten thousand people, four times the entire population of the town, crowded around the jail for the free entertainment."[114] It was also here on 12 April 1838 that Messrs Lount and Matthews, the only two participants of the Rebellion in York sentenced to death, were hanged. By a "curious coincidence, two architectural families were involved—Storm, the builder of the scaffold, was the father of W.G. Storm, the architect, and Joseph Sheard, his foreman, refused on principle to assist in its construction. He, later, was the architect who designed the Cawthra house, and, in 1871-72, was Mayor of Toronto."[115]

Ewart's first five years of known architectural and building work were just the beginning of another decade of unprecedented work in York and in London, Upper Canada. His work during the first five years showed potential clients that he could build a hospital, a courthouse and jail complex, a church, and residential work as well. All of this knowledge and skill would be tested in the next ten years by his taking on some of the most challenging building projects in southwestern Upper Canada.

---

65 J.M.S. Careless. (1984). *Toronto to 1918*, p. 201.

66 Eric Arthur. (1964). *Toronto: No Mean City*, p. 42.

67 Michael Filey, *The Toronto Sun*, March 1976, p. 21.

68 Two authors have compiled excellent lists of these early architects and builders. Stephen Otto who updated Arthur's book, *Toronto: No Mean City* in 1983 with an extensive list of builders and Patricia McHugh's (1989). *Toronto Architecture: A City Guide.* (2nd ed.).

69 W.G. Crosbie. (1975). *The Toronto General Hospital 1819-1965*, p. 6.

70 Lucy Booth Martyn. (1982). *The Face of Early Toronto: An Archival Record 1797-1936*, p. 88.

71 W.G. Crosbie. (1975). *The Toronto General Hospital 1819-1965*, p. 10.

72 C.K. Clarke. (1913). *A History of the Toronto General Hospital*, pp. 13, 39.

73 William Allan would also be responsible for the building of the Bank of Upper Canada and his home *Moss Park*, both of which Ewart worked on.

74 Edith Firth. (1962). *The Town of York 1815-1834*, p. 41.

75 Mike Filey. (1996). *Toronto Sketches 5*, pp. 30-31.

76 Lucy Booth Martyn. (1982). *The Face of Early Toronto: An Archival Record 1797-1936*, p. 88.

77 W.G. Crosbie. (1975). *The Toronto General Hospital 1819-1965*, p. 10.

78 Frank Yeigh. (1893). *Ontario's Parliament Buildings*, p. 21.

79 J. Ross Robertson. (1896). *Landmarks of Toronto*, Vol. 2, p. 1024.

80 Liz Lundell. (1997). *The Estates of Old Toronto*, p. 54.

81 Austin Seton Thompson. (1980). *Jarvis Street: A Story of Triumph and Tragedy*, p. 44.

82 J. Ross Robertson. (1896) *Landmarks of Old Toronto*, Vol. 2, p. 1023.

83 Leonard Wise and Allan Gould. (2000). *Toronto Street Names*, p. 122.

84 Austin Seton Thompson. (1980). *Jarvis Street: A Story of Triumph and Tragedy*, p. 86.

[85] Leonard Wise and Allan Gould. (2000). *Toronto Street Names*, p. 133; J.R. Robertson. (1896). *Landmarks of Toronto,* Vol. 2, pp. 705, 1022.

[86] Jennifer Parsons and Kevin Lillian. (1995) *Toronto 1837: A Model City*, p. 113.

[87] Leonard Wise and Allan Gould. (2000). *Toronto Street Names*, p. 123.

[88] Mike Filey. (1996). *Toronto Sketches 5: "The Way We Were."* This land was part of the parcel that Ewart bought from Samuel Jarvis in May 1843. Today that parcel comprises the block between Carlton and Maitland streets on the west side of Jarvis Street. Austin Seton Thompson. (1980). *Jarvis Street: A Story of Triumph and Tragedy*, p. 108.

[89] Murray H. Nicolson's "Peasants in the Urban Society: The Irish Catholics in Victorian Toronto" in Robert F. Harney. (1985). *Gathering Places: Peoples and Neighbourhoods of Toronto, 1834-1945*, pp. 50-52.

[90] Margaret and Merilyn McKelvey. (1984). *Toronto: Carved in Stone*, p. 15.

[91] Marion MacRae and Anthony Adamson. (1975). *Hallowed Walls: Church Architecture of Upper Canada*, p. 84.

[92] Henry Scadding. (1873). *Toronto of Old.* Abridged and edited by F.H. Armstrong (1966), p. 141; Jesse Edgar Middleton. (1923). *The Municipality of Toronto: A History*, p. 719.

[93] Marion MacRae and Anthony Adamson. (1975). *Hallowed Walls: Church Architecture of Upper Canada*, p. 84.

[94] Donald Jones. (1992). *Fifty Tales of Toronto*, p. 86.

[95] Marion MacRae and Anthony Adamson. (1975). *Hallowed Walls: Church Architecture of Upper Canada*, pp. 83-84.

[96] We have already seen how his lowest bid won him the competition to build York General Hospital. W.G. Crosbie. (1975). *The Toronto General Hospital 1819-1965*, p. 10.

[97] Marion MacRae and Anthony Adamson. (1975). *Hallowed Walls: Church Architecture of Upper Canada*, p. 84.

[98] Stephen Otto. (1983). *Toronto: No Mean City*, p. 46.

[99] Dendy and Kilbourn. (1986). *Toronto Observed: Its Architecture, Patrons, and History*, p. 60.

[100] Leonard Wise and Allan Gould. (2000). *Toronto Street Names*, p. 161.

[101] Edith Firth. (1966). *The Town of York 1815-1834*, p. 223.

[102] Ontario Archives, Minutes of the Magistrates of the Home District Quarter Sessions, 17 May 1823.

[103] Angela Carr. (1995). *Toronto Architect Edmond Burke*, p. 170 taken from Jones' *Grammar of Ornament.*

[104] Marion MacRae and Anthony Adamson. (1983). *Cornerstones of Order: Courthouses and Town Halls of Ontario*, p. 41.

[105] Ontario Archives, Minutes of the Magistrates of the Home District Quarter Sessions, 17 May 1823.

[106] Marion MacRae and Anthony Adamson. (1983). *Cornerstones of Order: Courthouses and Town Halls of Ontario, 1784-1914*, pp. 39-40. Supporting documentation: Ontario Archives, Minutes

of the Magistrates of the Home District Quarter Sessions, 27 August 1823 – "Account of John Ewart for £25 for plans approved."

[107] Jennifer Parsons and Kevin Lellian. (1995). *Toronto 1837: A Model City*, p. 13.

[108] Marion MacRae and Anthony Adamson. (1983). *Cornerstones of Order: Courthouses and Town Halls of Ontario*, p. 41.

[109] Lucy Booth Martyn. (1982). *The Face of Early Toronto: An Archival Record 1797-1936*, p. 14.

[110] Dr. W.W. Baldwin is sometimes listed alone or listed first when referring to work he did with Ewart (i.e., the Courthouse and Jail, Osgoode Hall, Bank of Upper Canada, Third Parliament Buildings). This is more likely because he was one of York's most prominent citizens, rather than because he did most of the collaborative work. As Dr. Baldwin was a physician, lawyer, part-time architect, and legislator it is more likely that John Ewart, the full-time architect and builder, did the lion's share of the architectural designing with knowledgeable and practical designs and input from Dr. Baldwin.

[111] J. Ross Robertson. (1896). *Landmarks of Toronto*, Vol. 1, p. 81.

[112] Marion MacRae and Anthony Adamson. (1983). *Cornerstones of Order: Courthouses and Town Halls of Ontario*, footnote 7, p. 14.

[113] *The Firebrand: William Lyon Mackenzie and the Rebellion of Upper Canada*, p. 6.

[114] Lucy Booth Martyn. (1982). *The Face of Early Toronto: An Archival Record 1797-1936*, p. 14.

[115] Eric Arthur. (1964). *Toronto: No Mean City*, p. 39.

CHAPTER 3
Building Upon a Respected Reputation (1825-1829)

Founding Trustee of
Strangers' Burial Ground – "Potters' Field" (1825)
Bank of Upper Canada (1825-1827)
Workers' Residence in London, Upper Canada (1826)
London Court House and Jail (1827-1830)
Moss Park (1827-1829)
Coffin Block (c 1828-1830)

The four years between 1825 and 1829 were defining ones for John Ewart's reputation in York and in London, Upper Canada. His reputation was built upon a combination of his architectural and building work and his emerging role as a community leader in York.

During this relatively short period of time, Ewart would help establish the first non-sectarian cemetery for York. He would work on projects such as the building of London's first public works buildings, especially the courthouse and jail as well as York's Bank of Upper Canada and William Allan's home, *Moss Park*.

The population of the provincial capital had not yet reached 2,000 people. It was just a small percentage of Upper Canada's population of almost 158,000. Lower Canada, especially around Montreal and Quebec City, was three times bigger at 479,000.[116]

However, Thomas Radcliff wrote his family back in Great Britain at the time that in "Upper Canada the people live much better than persons of a similar class in Britain; and to have proof of this, it is only necessary to visit almost any hut in the backwoods. The Interior of it seldom fails to display many substantial comforts, such as immense loaves of beautiful bread, entire pigs hanging round the chimney, dried venison, trenchers of milk, and bags of Indian corn."[117]

The labour wages per day near the end of this decade, "with diet, were 2s. 6d. with working hours from light to dark in winter, from six o'clock to dusk in summer."[118] Workers on the land found only 646 cultivated acres of farmland in Upper Canada. They would help multiply that figure to 3,706 acres by 1851-52 with much of the land used for wheat, oats and barley.[119] Recreationally, the town's inhabitants followed the sports of their homelands: hunting, fishing, and as early as 1829, curling enjoyed by the Scots on the Don River.[120] Ewart's sons George and John Jr. would later play this sport.

Although many of the immigrants were British, there were sufficient regional and national differences in how they built their homes or cottages that for the observant traveler it was not difficult "to tell what nation the natives of the houses 'hail from,' if we are aware of any of the whims and conceits that characterize them."[121]

One's impression of the town might be of a loose association of immigrants making a go of it in the 'colonies' without all of the rules and laws they might find 'back home.' This was not the case. People still enjoyed going to the theatre, eating delicacies from around the world imported into the provincial capital. Although "Muddy York's" roads were impassable after the Spring and Fall rains, speeding and parking laws appeared soon after the War of 1812. One law stated that no person should "gallop, or ride or drive a horse or horses at an unreasonable rate in the streets of the Town or on the Bank or Beach in front of the Same." It was also illegal to leave a "Wagon, Cart or Carriage of any description standing in the street for more than 24 hours."[122]

Although many of Ewart's greatest buildings would only begin by the end of this decade, there are a few noteworthy exceptions, especially the London Court House and Jail. However, before we return to his design and construction work, we must look at one of his community projects. The founding of "Potters' Field" has left an historical legacy that has lasted longer than most of his buildings.

Founding Trustee of Strangers' Burial Ground (1825)

("Potters' Field" – the original *Mount Pleasant Group of Cemeteries*)

Up until 1825, only Anglicans and Roman Catholics could be buried in York within the cemeteries of their respective churches. Other people, aside from a few private cemeteries, 'were out of luck.'[123] John Ewart, his friend Thomas Carfrae[124], William Lyon Mackenzie (newspaper owner and Toronto's first mayor in 1834) and several others decided this situation was unfair.

1. Thomas Carfrae (left) was a wealthy Scottish merchant, customs collector for York, politician and philanthropist.
[TPL T-16701]

2. William Lyon Mackenzie was the publisher and principal writer of the *Colonial Advocate* newspaper and later became Toronto's first mayor in 1834.
[TPL T-31909]

Carfrae was as staunchly Tory as William Lyon Mackenzie was a Reformer. On the matter of a public cemetery, at least, the Tory and Reformer agreed. "A meeting of the inhabitants of York friendly to the purchasing of a public burial place for all classes and sects, was held at the Masonic Lodge. Mr. Patrick having been called to the chair, and Mr. Mackenzie named as secretary. Mr. Carfrae from the select committee appointed to purchase a burying ground, reported that they had selected and bought six acres on Yonge Street about a mile from the town [from Mrs. Elmsley's farm at the northwest corner of Yonge and Bloor Streets for £75[125]. Messrs. Peter Paterson, John Ewart, Thomas Carfrae, Thomas Helliwell, and Doctor Morrison were then appointed trustees"[126] for life.[127] These five businessmen and professionals ran the cemetery for most of its 30 years.

Beside Carfrae and Ewart's professions, we know that Dr. T.D. Morrision was a physician, Paterson a wholesale and retail ironmonger (one who sold tools and household implements) and Helliwell and his brother Joseph were both brewers on the Don River at Todmorden.

The cemetery was formally instituted in February 1825 and the Act of Parliament that incorporated it passed on January 30, 1826. "It has a neat Sexton's house built close by the gate: the name of the Sexton is John Wolsencroft, who keeps a Registry of every person buried therein. Persons of all creeds and persons of no creeds are allowed burial in this cemetery, fees to the Sexton 5 shillings."[128] Burials started almost immediately. Among the first ten graves dug in the cemetery, five were for members of Thomas Carfrae's own family (4 children and his mother).[129]

At the nearby St. James' Church, a survey of the 161 burials done in 1838 outside the garrison chaplaincy shows the bulk of the burials were "obscure, the most humble being 'a man unknown."[130] Of those whose ages are known, 29 were infants, 43 children, nine teenagers, 63 adults, and nine what we would call seniors. Members of well-known families were not spared grief in that year as members of the Boulton, Powell, Ridout and Robinson families also had deaths.[131]

By the time of its closing in 1855, Potters' Field had about 6,000 graves. The town of Yorkville was growing and needed the land at Yonge and Bloor for commercial and residential purposes. It was decided by the trustees to secure 15 acres of land at the end of Winchester Street on the hill overlooking the Don River Valley.[132] This site, now known as The Necropolis, would also be the cemetery where John Ewart and many of his family would later come to rest.

Such was Ewart's contribution to the York General Burying Grounds that one of two chapels in the present day Mount Pleasant Cemetery's Mausoleum is named in his honour—the other, for Thomas Carfrae.

During this same period, men were at work on two other significant projects that would soon include Ewart. They are the only two known buildings on which Ewart worked that still stand in Toronto: the East Wing of Osgoode Hall and the Bank of Upper Canada. On February 28, 1825, the same month that the cemetery was instituted, the Bank of Upper Canada bought the Honourable William Campbell's lot at the corner of Adelaide and George Streets for £500[133] securing a prestigious location for their second bank building in York. Across town, the Law Society of Upper Canada ordered their treasurer, "sometime architect Dr. William Warren Baldwin to draw up plans and elevations for the new buildings" of Osgoode Hall.[134]

Bank of Upper Canada (1825-27)

3. Sketch by W.J. Thomson, reproduced in the *Evening Telegram,* of The Bank of Upper Canada on the northeast corner of Adelaide Street East and George Street. After 1872 it became the De La Salle Institute and is currently an office building. [TPL T-10484]

The Bank of Upper Canada was York's first financial institution[135] and it "surely impressed the small pioneer society it served. Founded in 1822, the bank initially had quarters in a nearby house. It was a measure of the burgeoning wealth of the little town, the capability of its architect, and the influence of the bank's shareholders—mostly members of the ruling oligarchy—that this classically inspired spectacle could have been so quickly achieved. Imagine this finely cut limestone structure standing on the edge of the frontier town, a town composed of little more than muddy streets and wooden houses. With a virtual monopoly in the province, the Bank of Upper Canada prospered. It enhanced its headquarters with a new brick wing and Doric porch while at the same time erecting country branches across the province. This over extension of its assets led to the ultimate failure of the bank in 1866."[136]

The bank was started by some of the leaders of the Family Compact. John Strachan was the leader of the group that first sought the bank's charter[137]. William Allan was its first president (until 1835) and the directors were D'Arcy Boulton Jr., Henry John Boulton, and Dr. W.W. Baldwin. "For eleven years the Bank held a monopoly in Upper Canada, issuing paper currency, handling the credit accounts that allowed merchants in York to prosper, and mortgaging the lands that represented the wealth of the Family Compact."[138]

The Bank of Upper Canada bought its land from the Honourable William Campbell on 28 February 1825 for £500. The bank's reputation was greatly enhanced by being Campbell's next door neighbour at the corner of Adelaide and George Streets.[139]

The difficulty in crediting the proper architect of this building is that many of the papers relating to the bank were destroyed when it failed in 1866. Often smaller banks were taken over by larger ones so that the 'parent' company saved the records. The Bank of Upper Canada was not taken over—it stopped doing business. Its papers were destroyed when they were sold in the 1870s at $20 a ton to a paper manufacturer. "Doubtless many private and public figures breathed a sigh of relief after the sale"[140] as their private records of financial transactions would not become public.

The question of who designed the bank, therefore, has been debated in recent decades. Dendy and Kilbourn argue that W.W. Baldwin was the designer. "One of the key elements in the creation of important architecture is patronage. Simply paying for a building does not amount to patronage. It requires active participation in the design process that determines the character of the building, its significant details and materials, and often its interior fittings. When the Bank of Upper Canada was built, William Warren Baldwin [already 50 years old] was a director involved in the planning for the new building and thus one of its patrons; he extended his influence to the drawing board and, working with the builders, became its designer."[141] They further argue that Baldwin's design "makes it a fitting introduction to bank architecture, which holds a central position in the history of Canadian architecture and architectural patronage."[142] "Freestanding town homes and villas of fashionable Regency England inspired the bank, like those in pre-1850 Britain. Most banks were family companies and former homes were used for offices."[143]

Stephen Otto writes that "[a]nother civil engineer, Francis Hall, was responsible in 1826 for the proposal of a 'Provincial Building Contemplated at York' and may have had a hand the year before in the design of the Bank of Upper Canada on Duke (now Adelaide) Street. Contemporary accounts said the building would exhibit a combination of Doric and Tuscan orders. It appears today, though, that the plans must have been revised and simplified during construction. The occasion for this may have been Francis Hall's resignation as the contractor, long before the building was completed. New plans could have come from either the obliging Dr Baldwin, one of the bank's directors, or John Ewart, a York builder who often worked in association with Baldwin but was quite capable of producing good designs on his own. Ewart arrived in town before 1820 and was involved in one way or another in most of the public buildings erected in York before the arrival of Thomas Young and John G. Howard in the early 1830s. They soon secured the greater portion of architectural commissions in the new city."[144]

Sheldon and Judy Godfrey, the present owners of the building, write that "[t]radition has credited W.W. Baldwin with being the architect of the bank based on the statement in Roswell's Toronto City Directory, (1850-51) that 'we believe the building was designed by the Right Hon. Dr. Baldwin'. It is likely that Dr. Baldwin had at least responsibility as a consultant for the plans of the bank's new head office. The plans were, by all accounts, initiated by Thomas Gibbs Ridout, the bank's cashier or general manager. Ridout was linked to Dr. Baldwin philosophically and by family ties…Even more likely is the possibility that the architect originally engaged for the bank building was also its contractor, Francis Hall (1792-1862) a trained architect, born in Scotland….Hall moved to Nova Scotia and Kenney, Kidd and Co. took over but they were inexperienced immigrants, "unaware of the pitfalls when the bank directed a change in the specifications from brick to cut stone." They stopped work in 1826 but finally concluded they wouldn't get paid at all if they did not finish. They ended up losing over £1,000."[145]

If speculation is correct that W.W. Baldwin was the principal designer, then Marian MacRae concludes, "that if Baldwin was involved, probably Ewart was too."[146] Patricia McHugh makes the same assumption in her book.[147] Stephen Otto credits MacRae to drawing his attention to the possibility that Ewart was the actual designer: "Another candidate for the honour of designing the Bank is John Ewart, based on stylistic similarities common to the Bank, his York County Courthouse of 1825-6, and the original Osgoode Hall, now incorporated in the east wing, which he designed in 1829."[148]

MacRae goes further: "Ewart's smooth, spare trim still curves around the original entrance [of Osgoode Hall]. Trim of the same plasticity, so characteristic of his work, also informs the doorway of the Bank of Upper Canada begun at the corner of Duke (Adelaide) and George streets in 1825. This is probably another result of the successful collaboration between Ewart, who understood the design of buildings, and Baldwin, who recognized the architectural needs of York."[149]

4. The Bank of Upper Canada circa 1872 shortly after the extension on the right was added by De La Salle College.[150] A stylistic feature in common between the bank and Osgoode's East Wing are the paneled parapets.[151] [TPL T-10485]

5. Today's Bank of Upper Canada building and its restored adjacent buildings (1980s). The First York Post Office is on the far right. This 2004 view looks at the northeast corner of Adelaide and George Streets. The old bank building is listed as a National Historic Site, but today is largely forgotten, evidence of which can be seen in the overgrown trees and cracked staircase. [JEF]

The Bank of Upper Canada went through several renovations and additions after the initial building was completed. The portico was added in 1843-4 by John G. Howard; with further additions in 1850-1 by F.W. Cumberland and Thomas Ridout. In 1871 and 1876 further renovations were completed by Henry Langley.[152] Sheldon and Judy Godfrey restored the building from 1980 to 1982 and it is now used as commercial office space.[153]

The most likely conclusion is that Dr William Warren Baldwin and John Ewart worked on the design of this building together while several contractors did the work, including Francis Hall. How much work Ewart himself performed on the building is unknown. Stephen Otto's research led him to conclude that Ewart was likely involved in the design of the Bank of Upper Canada.[154] Otto further states that there "are stylistic similarities between Moss Park and the Bank that may lead to a conclusion that Ewart did both. Dr. Baldwin gets a lot of credit for the Bank and for Osgoode Hall but the Minutes of the Law Society bear out that Ewart did the work."[155]

At the same time as work was being done on the Bank of Upper Canada, Ewart was busy commuting to the town of London working on opening up the town, building the Workers' Residence in order to get ready for the construction of the London Court House and Jail.

Workers' Residence in London, Upper Canada (1826) London Court House and Jail[156] (1827-31)

6. London Court House and Jail (2004) at the Forks of the Thames River. [JEF]

If you look at a map of the London District at the turn of the nineteenth century, you would find the town of London centred on the site where the two main branches of the Thames River meet. Someone travelling to this area, however, would have seen only "land around the capital site that was swampy, portions were subject to spring flooding, dense bush covered the remainder, and there were no settlers." Colonel Talbot, of the famed Talbot Settlement, and others "undertook the colossal task of creating a judicial centre in this virgin terrain."[157]

In 1793, Lieutenant-Governor John Graves Simcoe had selected this site for the capital of Upper Canada. However, as we learned in Chapter 1, Home Secretary Henry Dundas overruled his decision in 1794 in favour of York because of York's secluded harbour and distance from the American border. London, therefore, was not built and the land "lay undeveloped until its selection in 1826 as the judicial and administrative centre of the London District. A court-house and gaol (1829) and homes for the government officials were built, stores and hotels were opened, and by 1834 the community contained over 1100 inhabitants."[158]

The London and Middlesex Historical Society concluded that the "construction of the court house definitely marked the founding of London."[159] To this day, the brick and stucco castle-like building is an important feature of the London downtown.

7. Colonel Thomas Talbot (1771-1853) [TPL T-16586]

John Ewart was commissioned to design and build the courthouse and jail on four acres of elevated land, but before construction could be started he had to create a road into the area and a house for the labourers and tradesmen who would have to be brought in. The story of this courthouse is the story of the founding of London. John Ewart had taken a forest and built a town. To understand this tale, however, one must know something of Colonel Thomas Talbot, the leading businessman in the district. Talbot had been a career officer in the British army and an aide-de-camp to John Graves Simcoe. He returned to Upper Canada at the age of 29 to settle along the shore of Lake Erie and would eventually be the head of the Talbot Settlement in southwestern Ontario. An Irish aristocrat who grew up in Malahide Castle, Dublin, he was a supporter of the British status quo in Upper

Canada and a staunch Tory.[160] The settlement he owned and created grew to 650,000 acres of which 98,700 were cleared. His acreage was equivalent to 2,664 square kilometres of land, or the size of just over 4 modern-day Torontos.[161] There were about 50,000 inhabitants near the end of his life.[162] He died a bachelor and left his entire estate to his servants, which reinforced his reputation as an eccentric and benevolent despot.[163]

Mrs. Robert Jamieson[164] wrote of her visit to Talbot when he was 65 years old: "The reports I had heard of his singular manners, of his being a woman-hater, who had not for thirty years allowed a female to appear in his sight, I had partly discredited, yet enough remained to make me feel a little nervous…I was prepared to meet the old buffalo in his lair…My welcome was not only cordial, but courtly. The Colonel, taking me under my arm, and ordering the boy and his horses to be well taken care of, handed me into the hall or vestibule, where sacks of wheat and piles of sheepskins lay heaped in primitive fashion; thence into a room, the walls of which were formed of naked logs. Here no fauteuil, spring-cushioned, extended its comfortable arms…Colonel Talbot held all such luxuries in sovereign contempt."[165]

Ten years before Mrs. Jamieson's visit, Talbot led a commission to build London's first civic building—the courthouse and jail. "The Commission agreed at a meeting on March 6, 1826 in St. Thomas to advertise for plans and estimates. On April 9, 1827, the Commission accepted the proposal[166] of Master Builder and Architect John Ewart[167] of York for a building 'of Gothic Style, 100 feet long, 50 feet wide and 50 feet high, having an octagonal tower fourteen feet in diameter at each corner.' The foundation and basement cells were to be of stone and the upper structure of brick, mortared over to give the appearance of stone. Cost was £4,000, later increased to £4,050 when certain alterations were included."[168] In May and June, Mahlon Burwell, a naval surveyor, laid out

Dundas, King and Ridout Streets as the north, south and east boundaries of the Courthouse Square. The river was the western boundary.[169]

MacRae and Adamson wrote that the "plans came in before the money, as it happened, but the commissioners were accustomed to that sort of thing and went ahead without it. At the second meeting of the Commission, convened by order of the president, 9 April 1827, the secretary recorded that the Ewart scheme was comprehensive. He provided the plans, specifications and estimates for the London Court House and undertook to build it. Since the operation would be lengthy, and the need for a courthouse and jail urgent, the district was to get a temporary building at the north-east corner of the four-acre site as part of the Ewart package. Peter van Every was the schoolmaster and served as the interim jailer until his school was ready.[170] When the new courthouse was finished, the temporary one would be hoisted out of the jail yard, set on rollers and trundled down to a spot diagonally opposite at the south-west corner of the reserve, where the obliging architect would convert it for use as a grammar school."[171] All of these provisions were included in Ewart's £4,000 fee.[172]

8. "The Old Log Court House" was the temporary London District Court House and Jail. Rough-hewn logs were used to enclose the cells. The building became a district grammar school, a private residence and lastly a storehouse for the Public Utilities Commission. [University of Western Ontario, Regional Collection]

To get into the building site "was a colossal undertaking in a wooded wilderness with severe winters, no roads, no skilled workmen and no materials. Log roads were built, stones gathered from the surrounding area, clay deposits located, kilns built, bricks produced and trees cut for the timber supports and roof. The opportunities for employment attracted settlers and London soon had 300 residents living in cabins and huts scattered around the construction site. Ewart must have been a very reputable man and a Master Builder indeed, for he completed the immense project by the spring of 1829. The Commission's accounts show that Ewart received £550 initial payment on October 1, 1827 and £150 a month until completion. There are no indications in the records of any dissatisfaction with the quality of workmanship or any disagreement over payment[173], unlike the problems which delayed the completion of later courthouses in the district. The hand-written accounts are neatly balanced at the sum of £4,050."[174] Ewart earned seven percent commission, or £280, for his work as both architect and building contractor.[175]

To house some of the workers coming into London to build the courthouse, Ewart built a workers' residence which was 50 feet long by 30 feet wide and 20 feet high. When the courthouse was completed, Ewart sold the house and lot for £625.[176] "Thomas Parke, father of the later Police Magistrate, was his foreman or partner, and had charge of the work. He became a citizen of the new town. One of the employees was Robert Carfrae…The brick for the building, as I am informed by Hon. Freeman Talbot, was manufactured by a York man, William Hale, who also became a resident of London. There were two brickyards—one at the rear of the present Robinson Hall, and the other in London West on land subsequently belonging to Walter Nixon."[177]

Once these buildings were complete, Ewart could start erecting the courthouse. "It was not an easy job. There were no bulldozers to dig the foundations and no trucks to deliver the lumber, concrete and brick. Stones dug up during the excavation were mortared together for the foundation, trees were cut down and sawed into planks, and one William Hale made bricks on the site."[178] But in September 1828 George Gurnett, a visiting English journalist, was able to report: "the courthouse is in a state of forwardness, the walls being carried up near three storeys and when completed, will be the handsomest building of the kind in the province."[179] It was ready for occupation in 1829, although Ewart was still adding finishing touches until 1831. The complete structure was "100 feet long, 50 feet wide and 50 feet high, with large octagonal towers at the four corners. A bay projected to the west to form an imposing riverside entrance."[180]

The design of the courthouse and jail was something new for Ewart. It would introduce the Early Gothic Revival to public buildings in Upper Canada.[181] Rather than using the two-building style used in his York Courthouse and Jail, Ewart designed a romantic medieval style castle partly based on Talbot's home castle of Malahide, in Ireland.[182] The courthouse has other influences as well, according to noted architectural historian Marion MacRae. "James Wyatt's Royal Military Academy, built in Woolwich in 1808, may have inspired the form and placing of its octagonal towers and the generous use of lancet windows."[183] It also matched "exactly William the Conqueror's Norman tower of 1097 in the length of its river façade, and in its original colour—for both castles, in the days of their youth, were covered with white lime mortar."[184] The east façade is based on Colonel Talbot's ancestral Irish home of Malahide near Dublin and O'Reilly's Ballinlough, in West Meath. The west façade is Scottish in form similar to the shape of 14th century Tantallon[185], the most storied castle he had ever known. This fortress on the North Sea anchored its heavy curtain-walls at the ends by towers and strengthened the centre with a "truly massive tower projecting as a polygonal bay."[186] The battlements of the London Courthouse were intended to be purely decorative but in 1838 they were used "to serve their original defensive purpose. It was after the abortive rebellion of December 1837"[187] when men with rifles were placed on the rooftops as a visible deterrent to any rioters thinking of entering the courthouse or jail.

Nancy Tausky and Lynne D. DiStefano, authors of *Victorian Architecture in London and Southwestern Ontario*, wrote that the "design did combine several major influences in nineteenth century architecture. The castellated form and pointed windows were borrowed from the Gothic Revival style popularized in

England, but the plainness of the east façade, the simple string courses (projecting horizontal bands along the wall), the window surrounds, and the polygonal shape of the western bay owed more to the Italian Palladian tradition. Inside, the shape of the towers was repeated in the second storey courtroom, where 'Elliptical arches' in the corners formed an octagonal ceiling. The judge sat at the west end on his elevated chair backed by a wooden screen, a massive painting of the royal coat of arms (completed by 'Craig, painter' for 11 pounds, 11 shillings in 1830), and three tall Gothic windows. Facing him at the other end was a raised spectators' gallery. In between, was the prisoner's box, with access by a trapdoor for the lawyers, all divided from the spectators by the 'bar,' a wooden railing."[188]

9. Early photo of the courthouse and jail. [Ontario Archives ACC 3619 S 12569]

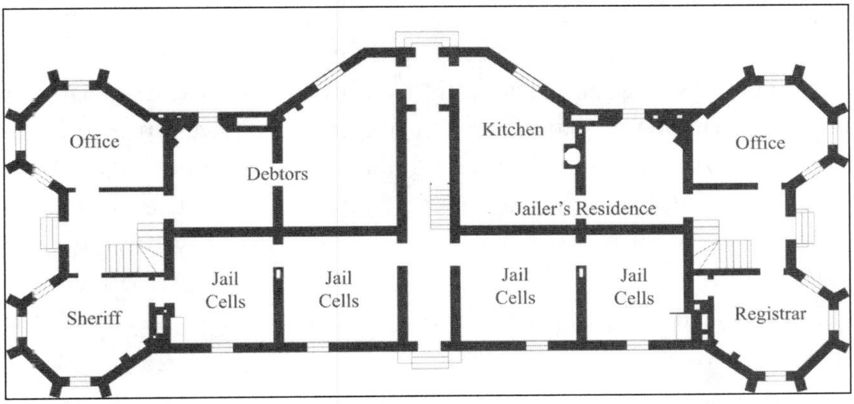

10 First floor plan [DH]

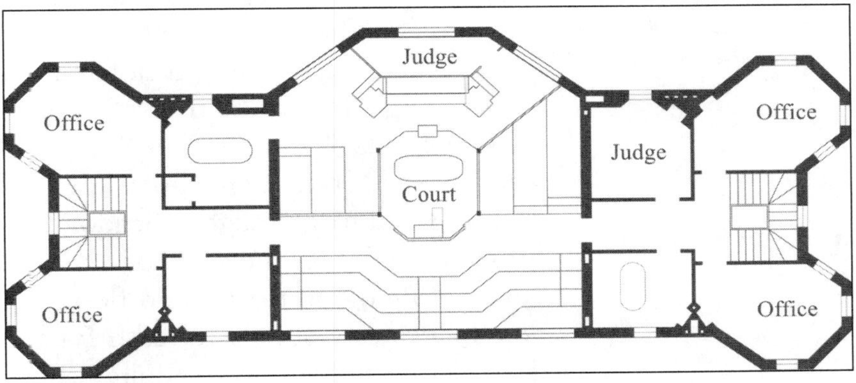

11. Second floor plan. [DH]

The courthouse was used for its original purpose continuously for over 145 years.[189] It has not existed without drama or controversy, however. In 1830, Cornelius Burley was the first person hanged at the jail. The first attempt failed due to a faulty rope; the jailers had to search through the crowd of 3,000 to hang the hapless prisoner a second time. In 1838 during the Rebellion, 18 men were tried in London. Six were hanged and the rest were transported to Van Dieman's land in Tasmania.[190] One of the surviving rebels, E.A. Theller wrote: "I was thrust into a small cell with three others. This cell was about seven feet square…the only ventilation was through a small diamond-shaped hole in the door, through which the scant fare which the prison rules allowed was handed to us. The only place for relieving the calls of nature was a corner of our cell, and for many days and nights together we endured the suffocating odour of its fetid exhalations. Day and night were undistinguishable to us, except for a few hours of the afternoon when the descending sun would cast a slanting ray through the grated windows of the corridor"[191]. Prisoners slept on coarse blankets in these cramped quarters with a dingy gray wall for company.[192]

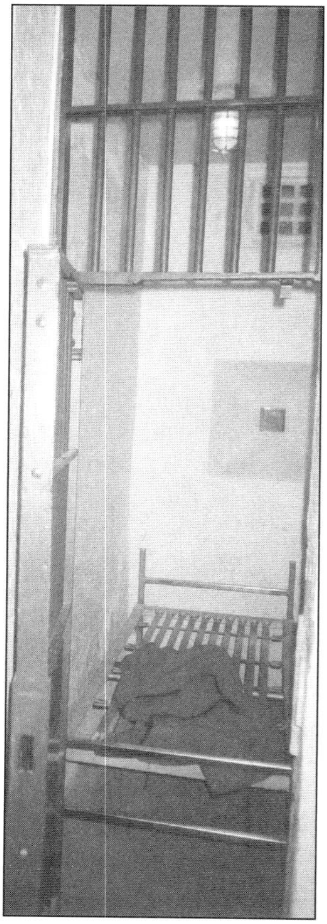

12. London Court House jail cell (2004 photo). [JEF]

The Commissioners and Ewart did not anticipate the degree of subversive activities in the very small town of London and, therefore, did not build a large enough facility to hold the many prisoners taken during the Rebellion. The ground floor plan shows the jail cells open onto a straight corridor that runs through the shortest axis of the building. Being on the ground floor, the possibilities of a successful dash for the door by a felon were quite good. Additionally, the use of small soft bricks shows that the Commissioners were not worried that the odd debtor or troublemaker would try to escape or 'bust out.' But escapes did occur.[193]

The interior of the courtroom has remained relatively unchanged. The room's Gothic style has been preserved, with six windows surmounted by elliptical arches supported by pillars nearly 20 feet high. Arches also from four of the pillars come toward the centre creating an octagon ceiling.[194] Today, the old jail is used as a military museum for the 1st Hussars Regiment. The courthouse is open to the public with some of the rooms rented out for special events.

Moss Park (1827-29)

13. Sketch in John Ross Robertson's *Landmarks of Toronto*, (Vol. 1, p. 560) owned by William Allan. The house is located on the west side of Sherbourne Street south of Shuter. His estate occupied a sizable portion of what is now downtown Toronto.[195] [TPL T-30698]

Moss Park was the first example of Greek Revival architecture in York. It was also considered to be the first museum in Toronto with its dining room decorated by stuffed birds and other specimens in glass cases.[196] Allan was the economic strategist and financial wizard behind the Family Compact. He immigrated to Montreal from Huntley, Aberdeenshire in 1789 and worked his way to York in 1795. He opened a store and invested in property and business ventures and became the President of the Bank of Upper Canada.

The house was erected on Park Lot No. 5, a two-hundred acre block of previously undeveloped pine forest that extended north from Richmond to Bloor Street along the west side of what is now Sherbourne Street. Allan purchased this property in 1819, with land to the east owned by the Ridouts and that to the west by Samuel Peters Jarvis. The Jarvis and Allan properties were separated by a small stream that ran southeast into Toronto harbour.[197] Ewart had worked on Jarvis's home *Hazelburn* in 1824 and 1825.

Although there is not an architect on record, Stephen Otto's research of the home and gardens led him to conclude that Ewart was likely involved in this design.[198] As we recorded earlier in this chapter, Otto concluded that there "are stylistic similarities between *Moss Park* and the Bank that may lead to a conclusion that Ewart did both."[199] Mary Allodi and Stephen Otto go so far as to say that it "was probably Ewart, a Scot like Allan, who was responsible for designing and constructing Allan's last and most luxurious home, Moss Park."[200]

Pleasance Crawford and Stephen Otto describe *Moss Park* as "the town's first major building in the Greek Revival style…a two-storey brick dwelling with an impressive portico on the south side that was in full view from the public road. Its main entrance, on the less imposing east side, faced a private avenue. The nearest neighbour lamented the presence of 'twelve windows in the…side next to us,' while a former chief justice's wife called the house 'a Palace.'" [201]

Allan's only surviving son, George William Allan, inherited *Moss Park*. We know that George became Mayor of Toronto (1865), President of the Senate (1867), President of the Royal Canadian Institute, President of the Ontario Association of Artists and of the Art Union of Canada; President for 25 years of the Horticultural Society of Toronto and President of the Upper Canada Bible Society. He is best known, however, for donating Allan Gardens to the City in 1857 and "through the greenhouses, he invited his fellow citizens to share with him his lifelong love of flowers."[202]

14. *Moss Park* photo from circa 1897. The vast estate originally covered a large portion of modern downtown Toronto. [TPL T-33502]

Of all of Ewart's works presented in this book, *Moss Park* is the most tenuous link to his design and building work. There were few records kept for the construction of homes, particularly by an architect and builder such as Ewart, who did not pass along his drawings or business papers to his heirs. None of his sons joined in his architectural work nor was there a desire in those early years for most people to keep old papers and business notes. Although Ewart could certainly have designed the house, we cannot be certain. *Moss Park* is included in this book as an area for further research.

Coffin Block (circa 1828-1830)

15. The Coffin Block circa 1860s. Toward the back of the block (west end) was Ewart's office and home (three storey building). The eastern end was the stagecoach office. [TPL T-12553]

York's street layout was designed on the rectangular grid system imposed by Lieutenant-Governor Simcoe's surveyor. Because this system did not incorporate the changing slope of the waterfront or the location of rivers and other obstacles, there were several places in town where the streets could not be laid out in a perfect grid. One of these unique corners was the 'Coffin Block,' bounded by Wellington Street to the north and Front Street on the south with Scott Street on the west. Today the Gooderham building exists at the eastern tip.

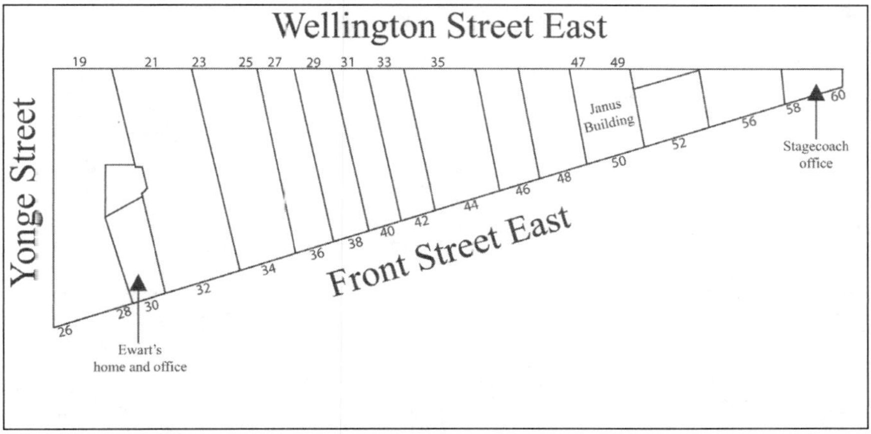

16. This map shows the Coffin Block with Ewart's own home and office at number 30. He lived here until his death in 1856.[203] He also owned the Janus building west of the stagecoach office at number 50.[204] [DH]

Ewart bought The Coffin Block land on March 1, 1826 from the estate of Thomas Scott through Scott's executors John Strachan and William Allan. During his lifetime, Ewart sold all but the most westerly portion of the block. His three-storey brick building on the Front Street frontage was both his home and office. After his death Montreal Telegraph Company took over the building.[205] In the following print of the fish market in 1840, you can clearly see the Coffin Block on the right. Ewart's home and office is the three-storey building in the eastern end of the block.

Today's Ewart's home and office are replaced by Berczy Park across the street from the St. Lawrence Centre for the Arts.

17. The Old Fish Market circa 1840 was located south of Front Street to the east of Wellington. Lake fishing was an important commercial activity in York and the trade enriched Ewart's Wharf, which was just south of the Coffin Block off Church Street.[206] [TPL T-32138]

Like so much architecture of the 1820s and 1830s, there are no records of who was the block's architect. Without citing sources, Lucy Booth Martyn (a former archivist with the Archives of Ontario) contends that it was Ewart. "This narrow triangle was the site of the Ewart Building, nicknamed the Coffin Block because its shape resembled that of early coffins, tapering from a wide end to a narrow foot. The Coffin Block was three storeys high, painted yellow, with wide eaves. The narrow end facing east was for many years the headquarters of various stage-coach lines….With the nearby fish market on the shore to add atmosphere, there was always a bustle as passengers and freight were loaded….In the 1840s a fashionable dance academy had rooms upstairs, and there was a restaurant in the basement. Later the two upper floors became the annex of the Wellington Hotel on the northwest corner of Wellington and Church streets."[207] Parsons and Lillian write that "Ewart's coffin block was demolished in 1891 so that Gooderham (of Gooderham and Worts Distillery) could construct the 'flatiron' building which stands in its place today."[208]

18. This photo shows the eastern end of the block that forms the triangle by the stagecoach office where Wellington and Front Streets meet. [CTA Fonds 1478 Item 15 cropped to highlight Coffin Block]

Located close to the wharves, the Coffin Block was the centre of stagecoach travel and figured as a natural point of reference for many early travelers to Toronto. From 1828 to 1830, George Playter's stagecoach line could be found at the end of the block, succeeded by William Weller's line from 1830 through to 1835.[209] Weller offered stages to areas east and west of York, with the principal run between York and Hamilton. The line's run between York and Montreal was scheduled for 35 hours and 40 minutes, which remained the quickest method until train travel took over. As well, given the generally poor road conditions, it was usually considered safe to travel by coach from late fall to early spring before the rains turned the roads to mud.[210]

In the 1840s the Wellington Hotel converted the two upper floors of the Coffin Block into an annex.[211] Many of the officers from Fort York had their separate quarters here as there was insufficient space at the fort. James Scott's store was on the main floor and Bannerman's restaurant was in the basement.

"All of these businesses flourished under the patronage of the militia."[212]

By the end of the 1820s, Ewart's respected position in York was firmly entrenched. His work was well received and led to the subsequent four years being the busiest and most important of his career. Within such a short span of time he would work on the design and/or construction of Upper Canada College, the Third Parliament Buildings, Osgoode Hall, his own wharf, the Emigrants' Asylum and St. Andrew's Presbyterian Church.

---

116 Canadian census figures for 1825.

117 John Howison. 1825. *Sketches of Upper Canada.* 3rd Edition, reprinted in Edwin C. Guillet's (1933). *Pioneer Days in Upper Canada*, p. 270.

118 Thomas Radcliff. (1953). *Authentic Letters from Upper* Canada p. 191.

119 *Ontario statistics*, p. xiv.

120 Edwin C. Guillet's (1933). *Pioneer Days in Upper Canada*, p. 209.

121 John MacTaggart (1829) from *Three Years in Canada* (1829). Reprinted in Edwin C. Guillet's (1933). *Pioneer Days in Upper Canada,* Vol. 1, p. 308; the original book's p. 1.

122 Bruce West. (1967). *Toronto*, p. 94.

123 Mike Filey. (1999). *Mount Pleasant Cemetery: An Illustrated Guide*, p. 14.

124 In fact, Carfrae asked Ewart to be the executor of his will.

125 Edith Firth. (1962). *The Town of York 1815-1834*, pp. 103-104, 311-312.

126 *Ibid*, p. 311. The above quote reproduced in this book is from the *Colonial Advocate*, December 8, 1825.

127 Henry Scadding. (1873). *Toronto of Old*, abridged and edited by F.H. Armstrong (1966), p. 299.

128 George Walton. (Compiler). (1833-34). *The York Commercial Directory.*

129 *Ibid.*

130 William Cooke. (1998). *The Parish and Cathedral of St. James', Toronto 1797-1997*, p. 32.

131 *Ibid*, p. 32.

132 Mike Filey. (1999). *Mount Pleasant Cemetery: An Illustrated Guide*, p. 14.

133 Sheldon and Judy Godfrey. (1984). *Stones, Bricks and History: The Corner of Duke and George, 1798-1884*, p. 7.

134 Dana Johnson and Leslie Maitland. "Osgoode Hall and the Development of Public Architecture in Canada" in *14 SSAC BULLETIN 4:85 December 1985*, pp. 14-15.

135 It is also the oldest bank building still in existence in Canada. Margaret and Merilyn McKelvey. (1984). *Toronto Carved in Stone*, p. 12.

136 Patricia McHugh. (1989). *Toronto Architecture: A City Guide*, p. 29.

137 Edith Firth, *The Town of York 1815-1834*, p. xxviii, p. 45: "In 1815 there were no banks in Canada. An economy of promissory notes, permeated slightly by British paper money during the war, led to two early petitions to the House of Assembly for banking institutions. Kingston petitioned in 1817, and a year later York did the same under the leadership. of Rev. John Strachan. After some deliberation, the 1821 charter was granted to York."

138 William Dendy and William Kibourn. (1986). *Toronto Observed*, p. 24.

139 Sheldon and Judy Godfrey. (1984). *Stones, Bricks and History,* p. 7. The Godfreys restored the bank building plus the adjacent De La Salle School and York's First Post Office in the 1980s.

140 Peter Baskerville. (ed.) (1987). *The Bank of Upper Canada: A Collection of Documents.* p. vix

141 In the eighteenth and early nineteenth centuries a gentleman's interest in and knowledge of architecture was taken for granted. In many cases landowners, prosperous farmers, professional men, and clerics made up for the dearth of professional architects in the period by stepping in to design houses and farm buildings for themselves and their friends, as well as occasional churches and such public buildings as courthouses. Using one of the many large and small architectural pattern books published during the period as sources for the basic patterns, decorative motifs, and other details, they relied on skilled local craftsmen for execution. This approach was well established in Britain, where the results in numerous houses and small public buildings are virtually indistinguishable from the work of more highly trained professional architects of the period. William Dendy and William Kilbourn. (1985). *Toronto Observed*, p. 25.

142 William Dendy and William Kibourn. (1986). *Toronto Observed*, p. 24.

143 *Ibid*, p. 26.

144 Stephen Otto. (1983). *Toronto: No Mean City*, pp. 75 & 80.

145 Sheldon and Judy Godfrey. (1984). *Stones, Bricks and History,* p. 7.

146 Marion MacRae. *Dictionary of Canadian Biography*, VIII, pp. 280-282.

147 Patricia McHugh. (1989). *Toronto Architecture: A City Guide*, p. 29.

148 Stephen Otto. (22 March 1983). "Architects of the Bank of Upper Canada: Francis Hall" monograph. Toronto: The Town of York Historical Society.

149 *Dictionary of Canadian Biography.* Vol. VIII, p. 281 "John Ewart", by Marion MacRae.

150 Willliam Dendy and Willliam Kilbourn. (1986). *Toronto Observed*, p. 25.

151 Stephen Otto, letter to Janet Ewart FitzGerald, June 23, 2001; and interview for this book on April 16, 2004.

152 *Ibid,* p. 27.

153 Sheldon and Judy Godfrey. (1984). *Stones, Bricks and History*, Introduction.

154 Stephen Otto, letter to Janet Ewart FitzGerald, June 23, 2001; and telephone interview for this book on April 16, 2004.

155 Stephen Otto telephone interview for this book on April 16, 2004.

156 The University of Western Ontario, Regional Collection, vertical file 412 has the papers relating to the construction of the Court House and Jail.

157 William E. Corfield. (1974). *Towers of Justice*, p. 1.

158 *The Founding of London* plaque at the forks of the Thames by the Ontario Heritage Foundation, London Ontario.

159 London and Middlesex Historical Society (Ontario). (1908). *Programs of the London and Middlesex Historical Society: Transactions 1902-1907.*

160 Robert Bothwell. (1986). *A Short History of Ontario*, p. 49.

161 Toronto, in 2004, is 636 square kilometres according to the Public Information and Referral Service for the City of Toronto.

162 John Bentley Mays. (2002). *Arrivals: Stories from the History of Ontario*, p. 216.

163 Robert Bothwell. (1986). *A Short History of Ontario*, p. 49.

164 The former Miss Anna Brownell Murphy of Dublin wrote travel books to secure her sufficient income because her marriage to Robert Jamieson, magistrate in York, was unsuccessful. Her books on Europe's artists and writers were intended to help middle-class tourists enjoy the churches and museums they would visit. Her *Winter Studies and Summer Rambles in Canada* (1838) was "a remarkable testament to the natural beauty of Ontario in the early nineteenth century and a witness to the surprise many urbane European visitors felt upon first encountering the wilderness of the New World; dense, magnificent, seemingly endless. John Bentley Mays. (2002). *Arrivals: Stories from the History of Ontario*, p. 206.

165 John Bentley Mays. (2002). *Arrivals: Stories from the History of Ontario*, p. 211.

166 Marion MacRae (1983) wrote that the secretary of the minutes reported that: 'The proposal of Mr. Ewart of the Town of York was accepted' (*Cornerstones of Order*, p. 95.)

167 Nancy Zwart Tausky and Lynne Delehanty DiStefano. (1986). *Victorian Architecture in London and Southwestern Ontario, Symbols of Aspiration*, p. 12 writes about Ewart: "one of the most talented architects then in Upper Canada."

168 William E. Corfield. (1974). *Towers of Justice*, p. 2.

169 *Ibid*, p. 1.

170 Marion MacRae and Anthony Adamson. (1986). *Cornerstones of Order*, p. 97.

171 *Ibid*, p. 95.

172 Pat Morden`s chapter on the courthouse in Edward Phelps. (1989). *Middlesex: Two Centuries*, p. 26.

173 In fact, at the beginning the commissioners asked Ewart to design the building with only £250 in hand [MacRae (1983), p. 95] and later were unable to secure enough subscriptions from local municipalities to pay Ewart so Colonel Talbot put in £600 of his own funds from his Bank of Upper Canada account "so that Ewart would be paid on time." William E. Corfield. (1974). *Towers of Justice*, p. 3.

174 *Ibid.*

175 Marion MacRae and Anthony Adamson. (1983). *Cornerstones of Order*, p. 121.

176 *Courier of Upper Canada*, 28 April 1832, c2 reprinted from a lost issue of the *London (UC) Sun*.

177 London and Middlesex Historical Society (Ontario). (1908). *Programs of the London and Middlesex Historical Society: Transactions 1902-1907*.

178 In 1838 Hale was arrested with other "hapless rebels and innocent farmers alike" and imprisoned in the London gaol. Pat Morden`s chapter on the courthouse in Edward Phelps. (1989). *Middlesex: Two Centuries*, p. 30.

179 *Ibid*, p. 27.

180 *Ibid*, p. 27.

181 Harold Kalman. (1994). *A History of Canadian Architecture*, Vol. 1, p. 275.

182 "It is no secret that Talbot had long wanted to build himself a castle in Port Talbot, his Lake Erie home…Ewart's willingness to follow Talbot's wishes would seem to be borne out by the Commissioner's recommendation that Ewart be given a lot of his choice, 'as he appears liberal in his views of building the Gaol and Courthouse.'" Harold Kalman. (1994). *A History of Canadian Architecture*, Vol. 1, p. 275 citing a letter from Talbot to George Hillier 24 April 1827, cited in Tausky and DiStefano's *Victorian Architecture*, p. 45. The only specification was that "particular attention will be given to free ventilation through the building." Phelps. (1989), p. 26.

183 Marion MacRae and Anthony Adamson. (1983). *Cornerstones of Order*, pp. 96-97.

184 *Ibid*, pp. 96-97.

185 Within 20 kilometres from Tranent, East Lothian where Ewart grew up.

186 Marion MacRae and Anthony Adamson. (1983). *Cornerstones of Order*, pp. 96-97.

187 Pat Morden`s chapter on the courthouse in Edward Phelps. (1989). *Middlesex: Two Centuries*, p. 30.

188 Nancy Tausky and Lynne D. DiStefano. (1986). *Victorian Architecture in London and Southwestern Ontario*, p. 27.

189 William E. Corfield. (1974). *Towers of Justice*, p. 4.

190 *Welcome to Middlesex County* brochure in the author's collection.

191 Phelps, Edward. (ed.). (1989). *Middlesex: Two Centuries*, p. 30.

192 Punishment by imprisonment was considered less severe for prisoners than the public floggings that were common until the mid-19th century. ["Middlesex Court House and Jail: A study in proposed future uses" (1973), p. 10.]

193 Marion MacRae and Anthony Adamson. (1986). *Cornerstones of Order*, p. 97.

194 "The Middlesex Court House", undated in the private collection of William E.C. Colter, pp. 7-8. Justice Colter presided over this courtroom for many years.

195 Mary Allodi and Stephen Otto. (Spring, 2001). "Landmark Sketches: Two Drawings Preserve the Likeness of the 1830s Home of One of Toronto's Wealthiest and Most Influential Citizens" in *Rotunda: The Magazine of the Royal Ontario Museum*, p. 18.

[196] Jennifer Parsons and Kevin Lillian. (1995). *Toronto 1837: A Model City*, p. 115.

[197] William Dendy. (1993). *Lost Toronto: Images of the City's Past*, pp. 92-94.

[198] Stephen Otto, letter to Janet Ewart FitzGerald, June 23, 2001; and interview for this book on April 16, 2004.

[199] Stephen Otto interview for this book on April 16, 2004.

[200] Mary Allodi and Stephen Otto. (Spring, 2001). "Landmark Sketches: Two Drawings Preserve the Likeness of the 1830s Home of One of Toronto's Wealthiest and Most Influential Citizens" in *Rotunda: The Magazine of the Royal Ontario Museum*, pp. 18-23.

[201] Pleasance Crawford and Stephen Otto. (Fall, 1997). "Andre Parmentier's 'Two or Three Places in Upper Canada' in *Journal of the New England Garden History Society*, 5:1-8, p. 4, Footnote 20: Mrs. S.P. Jarvis, letter to W.D. Powell, 5 March 1828, and Mrs. W.D. Powell, letter to George Murray, 15 January 1832, Powell Papers, Toronto Public Library.

[202] Eric Arthur. (1964). *Toronto: No Mean City*, p. 53.

[203] *The Globe and Mail*. Saturday, September 20, 1856. "Death Notice" p. 2, c. 8.

[204] July 24 1885 Catherine Ewart and W.S. Thompson re: the agreed upon use of the common wall between the Janus buildings and one just east of it where Thompson planned to erect a building three stories high. Document #4788 SE Land Registry Ontario Archives.

[205] *Ibid.*

[206] J.M.S. Careless. (1984). *Toronto to 1918*, p. 47.

[207] (1982). *The Face of Early Toronto: An Archival Record 1797-1936*, p. 37.

[208] (1995). *Toronto 1837: A Model City*, p. 10, footnote 11.

[209] Lucy Booth Martyn. (1982). *The Face of Early Toronto: An Archival Record 1797-1936*, p. 37.

[210] Jennifer Parsons and Kevin Lillian. (1995) *Toronto 1837: A Model City*, p. 9.

[211] *Ibid*, p. 10, Footnote #10 Dendy, *Lost Toronto*, p. 53.

[212] Jennifer Parsons and Kevin Lillian. (1995) *Toronto 1837: A Model City*, p. 9.

CHAPTER 4
Constructing a New City (1829-1833)

Upper Canada College (1829-1831)
Third Parliament Buildings (1829-1832)
Osgoode Hall (1829-1832)
Ewart's Wharf (1829-1831)
Emigrants' Asylum (1830)
Mechanics' Institute (1830)
St. Andrew's Presbyterian Church (1830-1831)
Wholesale Grocer's Store (1833)

By 1830, Ewart had been in York for 12 years. The town's population had climbed to nearly 4,000 with half the population under sixteen years of age.[213] Almost 60% of the population were males but within ten years that figure would even out to 50%[214] as the settling families became more established.

Over 100 books published during the 1830s in London, Dublin, Edinburgh, and Glasgow described Upper Canada's features and benefits to potential immigrants. People "seized on any book describing Canada or the United States in the hope that perhaps this latest volume might answer their questions about immigration."[215]

Newspapers were also full of information on the town. The advertisements were particularly helpful in describing what was available to townspeople. John Ewart would have walked by James F. Smith's grocery store at the corner of Church and Front Street on his way to his wharf. Smith's ad in the *Upper Canada Gazette* had such luxuries listed as "oysters, lobsters, mackerel, north shore herring, salmon (pickled and smoked), imported wines and liquors, 'sugar-double, single refined and moist', tea of every description, sauces, pickles, East Indian preserves, candied lemons, citron and orange peel; anchovy paste and fresh curry, codfish of various kinds, English cheese, tobacco, snuff, Havana cigars and pipes."[216]

A *Brockville News* article in October 1833 speculated that York was growing faster than any other town in North America. The year before, nearly 300 buildings were erected as part of Upper Canada's effort to absorb 60,000 new immigrants. In 1833 another 400 were built or under construction in the area. Many of these buildings stretched along King Street.[217] The *Kingston Chronicle* of 29 August 1830 updated its readers on the construction work being done in York. The paper describes, in note form, four projects involving John Ewart[218]:

Minor College Establishment

Rapid expansion of the town with many new brick buildings. In December, Upper Canada College's five buildings with one central one. The walls done and ready for the roof. Students will move in by October 1 and the buildings completed by January 1, 1831. Priestman had the contract but failed and now taken over by Kennedy and White.[219] [Ewart drew the plans for the college and contracted to build the four boarding-house buildings.]

Parliament House

Parliament House [The Third Parliament Buildings] and two wings for post offices attached to the government. Will form together, decidedly the most elegant structure in Upper Canada, 132x88 feet and each wing 90x55 including a public library. Messrs Ewart and Parks expect to have the west wing finished by first of January. The Parliament House was also to have been finished by the same time, but in consequence of some failure on the part of Mr. Priestman, the original contractor, the work has been somewhat delayed. It is now placed, however, under the superintendence of Mr. Ewart, who we understand, intends to make every possible exertion to get it completed in January.[220]

The Emigrants' Asylum in York

The Emigrants' Asylum; or the Building—by whatever name it is to be called—for the accommodation of destitute Emigrants and

Strangers; the foundation being already laid and the bricks and other materials for the super-structure being on the ground. Built on the hospital grounds and will be 90 x 20, 1 storey high, 6 tenements or apartments. Contractors also Messrs Ewart and Sparks and expected to be done by October 1830.[221]

The Law Society Hall [later called Osgoode Hall]

...to be completed by New Year's Day. It is 66 feet in front by 40 in depth and exclusive of the sunk or partly underground apartment—which is to be occupied by the Housekeeper—is three stories high...this building erected from the funds of the Law Society, under the management and superintendence of Mr. John Ewart.[222]

Ewart also did other building work at this time that, although less noteworthy, still contributed to the physical integrity of important buildings. For example, in the Schedule of Accounts sent to the House of Assembly on 2nd February 1831, there is a notation of payment to "John Ewart for repairs to Government House, and office." The Honourable James Baby is noted as Inspector General,[223] and we know him as the Chair of the building committee for St. Paul's Catholic Church that Ewart designed. A sample of Ewart's fee for such work is recorded in the Public Accounts "To Whom Paid and for What Service" of the Inspector General's Office, 7th January 1831: "Mr. John Ewart, being the amount of his account for repairs & to the Government Office in the years 1827 and 1828, audited in Council, 23rd February 1830; namely, £15 4s."[224]

How much was Ewart's £15 4s. worth? A pound was divided into 20 shillings and the shilling divided into 12 pennies. Therefore, one pound equalled 240 pennies.[225] To get a sense of what a one pound note was worth in the early 1830s, we can use Thomas Radcliff's[226] list of costs in the late 1820s and early 1830s. In the construction field, for example, the wages were, from highest to lowest:

> Bricklayers, 7s. 6d. to 8s. 9d. or 12s. 6d. to 15s. per thousand bricks laid.
>
> Stone Masons earned from 6s. 3d. to 7s. 6d. per day
>
> Carpenters and Joiners, 6s. 3d. per day
>
> Blacksmiths, 5s.
>
> Labourers and Farm Servants, 3s. 9d. a day

Once Ewart was paid, he would have used the money to buy items in shops such as:

> £1 to the tailor for making a coat, 5s. for trousers, and 5s. waistcoat. The shoemaker would receive 22s. 6d. for making a pair of top boots; 13s. 9d. for a pair of Hessian boots, and 12s. 6d. for Wellington boots

Again, as a comparison for what £1 would be worth in the early 1830s, these 1832 rates of travel to York provide a useful comparison.[227]

	Steerage	Cabin
From Liverpool to New York	£5 0 0	£30 0 0
From Liverpool to Quebec	From £2-£4 10	From £12-15

In other words, with 20 shillings to a pound, the 15£ that Ewart earned for repairs to Government House could have paid for a steerage trip from Liverpool to New York plus buy a tailor-made coat, 4 pairs of trousers, a pair of good shoes and Wellington boots, boots with enough left over to hire five labourers to work on a construction project for six days. In today's dollars that would be the equivalent of about four to six thousand dollars.

Ewart's high productivity coincided with the rapid expansion of the building trade in York. We now come to some of York's most important building projects just before its incorporation as the City of Toronto in 1834.

Upper Canada College (1829-31)

1. Upper Canada College Lithograph by Thomas Young in 1835 showing the King Street Campus. [TPL T-30087]

Upper Canada College is probably the best known private boys' schools in Canada, and certainly one of the most prestigious. From it have graduated many of the most powerful and well-connected men in both business and the arts. The College did not become a private school until 1900, nine years after it had moved to its Deer Park campus on Avenue Road above St. Clair from its original site on King Street.[228]

The college was founded by Royal Charter in 1829, granted by King George IV. The first school buildings were set back 100 feet from the north side of King Street near Simcoe in the heart of Toronto's New Town. Its neighbours included the Lieutenant Governor's home, Government House (1815-1862, 1866-1912) and the Third Parliament Buildings (1829-1900) that Ewart also worked on.[229] The college's location led, years later, to the King and Simcoe Streets intersection being called the Four Nations Corner: Education, Legislation, Salvation, and Damnation,[230] representing Upper Canada College,

Government House, the second St. Andrew's church (after 1876) and the British Hotel and Tavern respectively.

John Ewart was paid to make drawings[231], and following the prescriptions of Colborne's organization of the college, he planned a grouping with the main administration block at the centre[232], flanked by four houses for masters that would also function as boarding houses for students. All were built in red brick (possibly dug on the site)…There was no architectural grandeur, and it is difficult to see where the money went.[233] Ewart took up the contract for building the four boarding-house buildings; Matthew Priestman won the contract for the centre block. According to the sources, (some of which can be traced to J.G. Chewett himself), Chewett was the Surveyor-General of Upper Canada and manager of the project and probably involved as he had been at the legislature.

Upper Canada College opened in temporary quarters on January 4, 1830 and by the autumn of 1831[234] its new buildings on King Street West were completed. The school was made possible due to the patronage of Sir John Colborne (1778-1863), the Lieutenant Governor of Upper Canada from 1828 to 1836. He wanted "a private boys school geared to teach the sons of the Anglican ruling class."[235] Colborne arrived in York with a laudable career in the military. William Leake of Queen's College in Cambridge England had served under Colborne at Waterloo and published a two-volume work, *Lord Seaton's Regiment at the Battle of Waterloo*. He gave Colborne credit for having won the final battle at Waterloo, for which he was knighted for his bravery.[236]

Colborne modelled the school on Elizabeth College in England. At the time Upper Canada College incorporated the Royal Grammar School and was the only government-supported school in the Home District. It was public but not free, however, with families having to pay £3 a year for the day school, or £25 if the student boarded. There were 89 boys in the first term.[237] The boarding school was built in the late Georgian style. It was to have separate 'houses,' each led by a 'master.' The school was to offer room and board to the boys. Masters were hired in England, and they were to arrive in York in early November 1829.

Colborne's plan must have included the donation of Russell Square[238] by the town to the college, and he implicitly defined the architectural form for the new college."[239]

As a builder of some reputation and influence, Ewart was able to enrol his boys in Upper Canada College. His second eldest son, Thomas, became the second Head Boy of the school, while his younger son, John Jr., became the fourth Head Boy two years later.[240]

2. Upper Canada College took up a great deal of the streetscape for the time and would have been an imposing sight for all these boys (circa 1860s). [TPL T-31168]

All the buildings [renovated and enlarged] were demolished in 1900, except for the one section of the boarding house that was converted to a warehouse—and still stands on the southwest corner of Adelaide and Duncan streets.[241] One of the new buildings erected on the site is the Royal Alexandra Theatre.

Third Parliament Buildings (1829-32)

3. This 1835 Thomas Young lithograph (similar to his work on the Courthouse and Jail) includes Bishop Strachan's home (*The Palace*) in the centre of the illustration. The Third Parliament Buildings were located on Front Street just north of the lake. The lithograph includes a portico of four columns that was never built. Eric Arthur calls this an unfortunate mistake because the portico's absence exposes a marked difference in scale between the doorways and the windows of the chambers.[242] [TPL T-10249]

Upper Canada (Ontario) has had four sets of Parliament Buildings, with the present Queen's Park Legislature being the fourth. Lieutenant-Governor Simcoe's first brick Parliament buildings were burned during the American raid on York in 1813.

The second set of buildings built on that same site at the bottom of Berkeley Street were accidentally burned down on Christmas Eve 1824. The legislators set up quarters in Ewart's recently completed York General Hospital and stayed for the next five years until June 3, 1829.[243]

The Third Parliament Buildings were built on the designs of Thomas Rogers of Kingston. Rogers was not the original winner of the design competition. There were four original entrants: Ewart, Baldwin[244], John Ford (a Scottish carpenter who settled in York in 1819) and Joseph Nixon.[245] Nixon's design won out but it was never used. In 1828, Rogers was asked to prepare his own design and had his estimate pared down from £7,000 to only £5,400. "Through various political, financial and contractor difficulties, the buildings were opened in 1832 'at a nearly crippling cost of more than £10,000.' It was the largest building in town."[246]

Eric Arthur, who researched this complicated project thoroughly, explained how the costs ballooned to £10,000:

> *An advertisement in the Loyalist produced a successful [contracting] bidder—Matthew Priestman. A contract was drawn up between him and the Commissioners [process originally started in 1825 by appointed Commissioners William Allan, William Thompson and Grant Powell] to the effect that he find all materials, and erect the building for £5,400 with January 31, 1831 for occupancy by the Legislature. He carried with him into bankruptcy his two subcontractors, Turton, the mason and Crowther, the carpenter. He disappears from the scene soon after his financial failure. Mr. Nixon reappears with new plans and offers to do the work in stone or brick -- £15,000 for the former and £11,000 for the latter. The two Houses approved his proposal but delayed on account of the state of the revenue at the time. In this confused state of affairs, John Ewart, the architect, was appointed to tidy things up and superintend the work already begun. He, no doubt, was useful in advising the commission on the settlement with the trades. It turned out that Priestman had been paid £1,000 before he failed, and in the settlement Turton wanted £6,000 more than he had already received and Crowther demanded an extra £1,750. These figures would indicate the government was no longer haggling over the old figure of £5,400, but even so, Turton's request for £6,000 would seem equally unrealistic. In addition, Priestman made a claim for £1,889. To settle that item, a special committee was set up composed of Alexander McDonnell, James FitzGibbs and David*

McNab. They allowed him £1,654. Very puzzling is the fact that Turton, the mason, was asked to continue in his subcontract. Eventually some settlement was made and work proceeded on a day-to-day basis under a new superintendent, Duncan Kennedy.[247]

After the process was settled, Ewart and Mr. Parke were the contractors for building the west wing of the Parliament buildings in 1830.[248]

When the provinces of Upper and Lower Canada were united in 1841, the Front Street buildings were turned over to King's College for medical school purposes until 1849. Then the buildings were used for various activities: as an insane asylum (1849 to 1851),[249] again as the parliament buildings (1856 to 1859), military barracks (1861-1867) or were otherwise vacant. The buildings returned to their original purpose on the birth of Ontario in 1867 and remained the legislature for another 25 years until Premier Sir Oliver Mowat (John Ewart's son-in-law) moved the government into Queen's Park in 1893[250]. The Third Parliament Buildings were demolished in 1903 and today the Metro Hall, the CBC Headquarters and Workmen's Compensation are the main buildings on the site.

4. Third Parliament Buildings in the late nineteenth century. [CTA Fonds 1498 Item 10]

Osgoode Hall (1829-32)

5. Osgoode Hall in 1857 shows Ewart's East Wing after the portico was added and the central and west wings built. The photo is by Armstrong, Beere and Hime taken a few months before the domed centre section was demolished in 1357 during the Cumberland and Storm reconstruction. You can see the side of the East Wing stands apart from the later Romanesque law school added behind it,[251] and the original wooden fence (replaced in 1866 with current wrought iron fence with 'cow proofing' gates. [CTA Fonds 1498 Item 9]

Given the construction dates of the London Court House and Jail (1827-1831), Upper Canada College (1829-1831), and the Third Parliament Buildings (1829-1832), it is a wonder that Ewart found the time and creative energy to take on the longest-lasting of his buildings in Toronto: Osgoode Hall. All of these buildings were erected between 1827 and 1832 and in two cities over two hundred kilometres apart from each other.

The architectural history of Osgoode Hall has been anything but consistent or complete. Various authors have attributed the work to John Ewart, as we shall see, but only in recent years. Other architects such as the Montreal firm of Hopkins, Lawson & Nelson and the Surveyor-General of Upper Canada, J.G. Chewett, were credited with the design, with John Ritchie credited as the builder.[252] Eric Arthur wrote that Osgoode's architect's "present identity is shrouded in some mystery."[253] Stephen Otto, in upgrading Arthur's book *Toronto: No Mean City*, 19 years after its first edition, concluded: "The wing was begun in 1829 and finished in 1832. The architect, John Ewart, was allowed none of the Gothic whimsy that marked the court house he built overlooking the forks of the Thames in the distant London District."[254]

Osgoode Hall is the home of the Law Society of Upper Canada, founded in 1797 in Niagara-on-the-Lake as the regulatory body for lawyers and to provide teaching and examination for prospective lawyers. An act of the provincial parliament in 1822 allowed the society to own land to construct its future home. Originally, the hall was planned for Russell Square, which eventually became the site of Upper Canada College. Instead, the benchers[255] decided in 1828 to buy six acres from John Beverley Robinson's[256] park lot (on the north side of Queen Street) for £1,000.[257]

The site was important because Robinson had sold one-half of his park lot to King's College, the predecessor of the

University of Toronto. Part of it was to be the formal carriage way (now University Avenue) up to the College, where Queen's Park now stands. "The location of Osgoode Hall, beside the gates to the drive, took advantage of the grand scale of the College's plans in order to underline its own public importance and its association with education."[258] Ironically, the construction of Osgoode Hall was also in part because Archdeacon John Strachan wanted lawyers trained in his King's College, as they were becoming the most powerful professionals in Upper Canada. Strachan felt lawyers should be properly educated in British ways, but under his Church of England supervision. So, to prevent the law school moving to the university, some of the benchers felt the Society must have its own building to provide a place for the education, qualification and supervision of Upper Canada's lawyers. With Baldwin's return as Treasurer[259] in July 1825, there was a new push for the hall by the Reform benchers. Some of the Tories amongst the benchers opposed the building.[260]

Dendy and Kilbourn write that "[p]lanning for the hall to be named after the first Chief Justice of Upper Canada, William Osgoode, began in earnest in 1829 when the Society retained as architect John Ewart, who was then working on buildings for Upper Canada College on King Street West, and for the Legislature on Front Street West."[261] MacRae and Adamson add that the benchers, as reported in their minutes, wanted a hall "'in a manner worthy of the province and of the seat of government.' To that end they retained John Ewart to design a hall for them appropriate to a body whose august traditions stemmed from the Honourable Societies of the Inns of the Courts of England."[262]

Planning had actually started earlier in 1825 when the Society ordered their treasurer, "sometime architect Dr. William Warren Baldwin[263] to draw up plans and elevations for the new buildings. His proposed elevation was approved by

Convocation[264] on 3 October 1827, his rough plans and estimates in January of 1828....A change of site—to a six-acre plot on Queen Street – forced a reorientation in the project, from Baldwin's north-south axis to one east-west." A five-man building committee, including [Robert] Baldwin, became responsible for the final construction of the hall. "The available records of the Law Society place in some doubt the authorship of the plan actually constructed, for after the appointment of John Ewart as superintendent of the construction itself in June of 1829, the secretary refers to Ewart as both superintendent and architect. Credit for the design must presumably be shared; the prominent role of Dr. W.W. Baldwin in the early planning, and as a member of the Building Committee, suggests strongly that it was his approved 1828 plan, perhaps reworked by Ewart to conform to a new site and a reduced budget, which formed the final design. Nor should the partnership be a surprise, for the two had earlier collaborated on the Home District Court House and Jail."[265]

All doubt seems to be corrected in the Minutes of the Law Society. On Saturday June 20, 1829 the minutes record: "At several meetings during this term the benchers deliberated respecting the Hall proposed to be erected for the use of the Society—Mr. John Ewart, the architect attended and it was at length resolved that he should procure the necessary materials and provide and superintend the workmen...The Society are to supply the necessary funds and pay Mr. Ewart a remuneration of 7 ½ per cent upon the whole expense."[266]

Marion MacRae records other minutes for her assertion that Ewart was the architect of the East Wing: "Christopher Hagerman moved in Convocation November 1831 that "the architect Mr. Ewart be informed that a committee has been appointed to receive and examine the accounts when the building is completed." Also in 1831, "Hagerman noted that Ewart's estimate for a two-storey building (a single pavilion) was

'£1,869.4.9d. With the additional storey, an extra £397.17.6.d. was needed making a total of £2,238.1.3d.' on which he was to receive a commission of seven and a half percent for planning, supervising and contracting."[267] Hagerman further had five mechanics review the work and estimate the value of work done. They felt it was higher than necessary at which point bencher Robert Baldwin explained that the building committee, of which he was a member, "had asked Ewart to use better materials than those specified." Baldwin concluded his summing up in a rousing style: Mr. Ewart has fully justified the confidence reposed in him, wrote Baldwin, adding that the work "has been performed in a manner highly creditable to Mr. Ewart and on terms most advantageous to the Society." The Hall opened February 6 and 7, 1832.[268]

The need for a third storey became evident after the Society decided it did not have the resources to build Ewart's complete "master plan,"[269] so they decided to build one pavilion. "The architect was asked to increase its capacity by adding a third storey for the accommodation of students. This first unit of Osgoode, finally three storeys in height, made its architectural statement for the Law Society with dignified simplicity."[270] The third floor attic contained an apartment for the secretary and bedchambers for the nine students who came from outside York to study law. The students sat on the backbenches of the courtrooms and took notes on cases being argued. This was the earliest formal aspect of the Society's law school's curriculum.[271]

To put Ewart's building in perspective, the Palais de Justice in Brussels cost £2,000,000 while the original Osgoode Hall cost £3,550, including the land. "The comparison may seem foolish because one building is but a fragment of the other in size. The comparison is made only to show that each architect sought, in his own way, to demonstrate the dignity of one of our most treasured democratic institutions. It was no mean feat to achieve it in Toronto with so limited a purse."[272]

Ewart's final design was similar to his Second Courthouse and Jail (on which he worked with Baldwin) and Baldwin's own design for the Third Parliament Buildings. Baldwin "had drawn plans for a complex of three linked pavilions…in which the Law Society and the courts would each occupy a wing and the lawyers' chambers would fill the central block. John Ewart, a well-established local designer and builder who had collaborated previously with Baldwin, followed a similar plan for Osgoode Hall…Instructed to have the work 'done in the plainest manner still consistent with the permanent stability of the building,' he started construction in the summer of 1829, hoping to be finished in just over a year."[273]

Originally the hall was a U-shaped two-storey building facing Queen Street at the top of York Street so that everyone in town would see the glorious new building at the outskirts of town. A wide pediment on panelled pilasters would ornament the centre block and on either side, house-like blocks with separate entrances were connected to the centre by long wings. By the time construction began in 1831, the project had been cut back to only one three-storey pavilion built of red brick[274], later referred to as the East Wing.

Johnson, Dana and Maitland, Leslie in "Osgoode Hall and the Development of Public Architecture in Canada" wrote that the "intended tripartite subdivision of Osgoode Hall was typical of Toronto, but was then found nowhere else in Canada. The first known example was the first Parliament Buildings in York (1794-97)…Even more marked an example was Ewart's Upper Canada College, where five separate units were arranged in a connected row. The Home District and Jail (1825) varied the pattern; here two identical structures were placed on a public square, but lacked the usual linking structure."[275]

Osgoode Hall's closest parallel was probably Carlton Place in Glasgow, by Peter Nicholson (like Ewart, also from East

Lothian, Scotland).[276] "In the first decades of the nineteenth century, Regency planning—Regent Street in London is perhaps the best example—revelled in long vistas punctuated with outstanding buildings. It drew inspiration from the English landscape-design tradition and from seventeenth- and eighteenth-century France. In the 1820s the taste of lieutenant governors, such as Maitland and Colborne, and the knowledge of architectural amateurs, such as William Warren Baldwin, and of a growing body of architectural professionals, such as John Ewart, Thomas Rogers, and John Harper, brought Regency ideas to York. Spadina Avenue, University Avenue north of Queen and Wellington Place with Clarence Square—and a new vision for York Street—were the results…[Osgoode Hall] was planned to align with York Street to terminate a long vista up the gentle slope from the harbour, turning York Street into another Regency 'avenue'."[277]

6. 1857 panorama looking north up York Street with Ewart's East Wing at the top of the street. Compare the striking pose of Osgoode Hall relative to the wooden homes and businesses that line the street. [CTA Fonds 1498 Item 16]

The financing for the hall was as insecure as the financing for the London Court House. By the end of 1831 the treasurer's and the society's funds were still not separated. A committee decided it was better to have regular accounting books because the society was unable to say how much money it held. It "was desperately selling stock and arranging bank loans to pay Ewart's bills"[278] This situation almost led some of the benchers to win a motion disposing of the hall and building a smaller, or temporary headquarters for the Society. The Baldwins and others barely won a decision to keep the Hall under construction.[279]

When the east wing was finished in 1832, "at a cost of just over £2,000, Ewart's building[280] was similar to a large aristocratic house, with a centre-hall plan: a kitchen, service rooms, and students' dining-room in the basement; on the main floor the Benchers' dining-room on the west side, and a library and administrative office across the hall; on the second floor the Convocation room, above the dining-room and offices; and more offices on the third floor. In 1833 the building was extended to the northwest with a three-storey wing of offices and student rooms. Designed by W.W. Baldwin, who intended that it should conform to Ewart's masterplan, it was awkwardly arranged, difficult to heat, and never really satisfactory,"[281] and ultimately demolished to make room for grander additions.

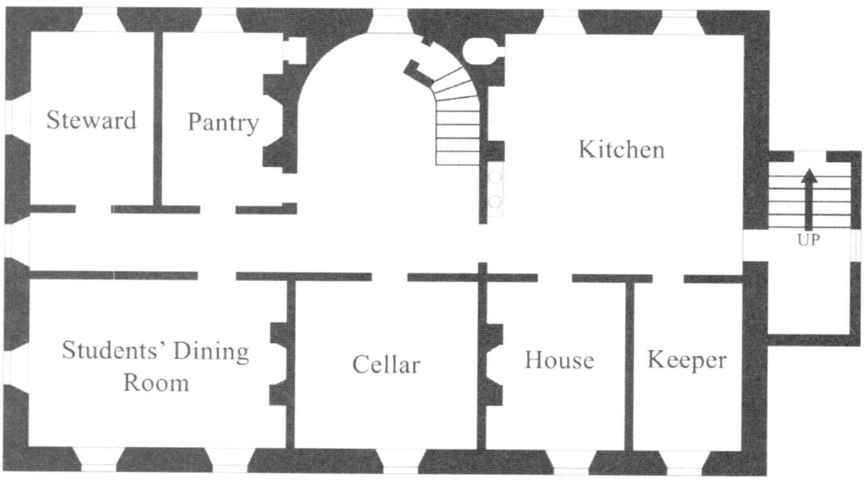

7. Basement floor plan. [DH]

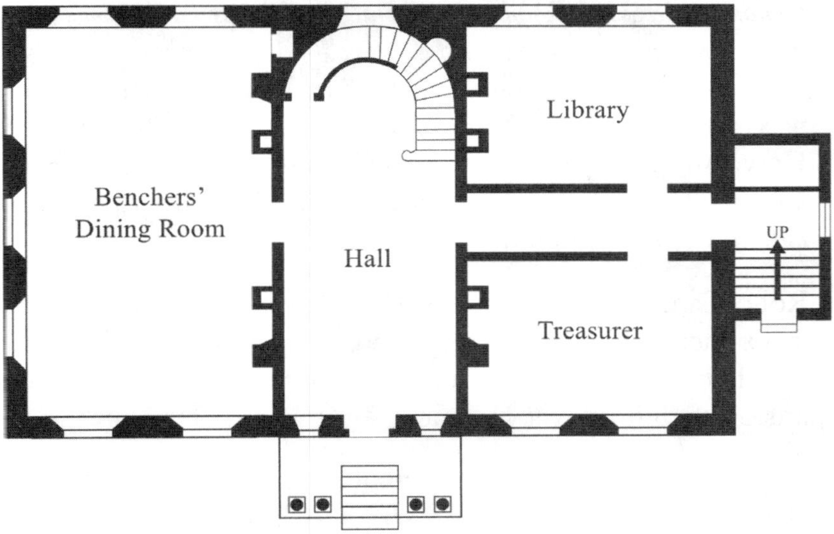

8. First floor plan including entrance way from Queen Street. Note that Ewart's original East Wing did not have the portico shown at the bottom of this illustration with the four pillars. [DH]

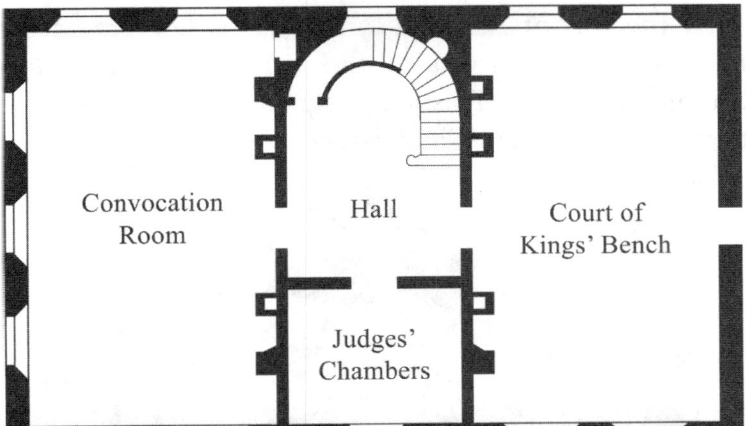

9. Second floor plan. The Judges' Chambers window looked south onto York Street with the lake visible on the horizon. [DH]

Diarist James Lesslie, shown the building days after the first meeting of the benchers held at the new Hall, wrote:

Conducted by Mr. [Rolph] through all the Rooms of 'Osgoode Hall' and admired the workmanship much—The Convocation Room particularly elegant."[282] *Justice Sir William Campbell* (whose home was moved across from Osgoode on the other side of University Avenue in 1972) *made a special effort to visit the new building. It was during the last frail year of his life (he was 76 years old), and he was as similarly impressed as Lesslie.*[283]

Rollo Campbell wrote in his *Two Lectures on Canada* in 1857: "The public buildings are very fine, and upon a scale which shows that their projectors anticipated for the city a greater expansion than it has yet obtained."[284]

Another feature of importance that came with the construction of Osgoode Hall was the laying of York's first sidewalk. "The town was frequently referred to as "Muddy York", and on turning north from King Street up York Street, one might have been mired if the Society had not laid, along the west side of York Street to the Hall, the first sidewalk in the town."[285] At the top of the Hall's front steps lawyers used a boot scraper to remove most of the mud from their shoes before entering the Hall. This boot scraper remained on the steps for over a hundred and sixty years.[286]

10. This disabled bread wagon on Bloor Street in 1909 shows that road conditions did not improve in "Muddy York" for well over 100 years. [CTA Fonds 1244 Item 31]

Osgoode Hall went through various renovations and additions. There were three main expansions. W.W. Baldwin's 1833 additional wing onto Ewart's building expanded the student quarters (as mentioned) but never really fit the needs of the Society. The 1844 additions by Henry Bowyer Lane were "his finest work. Retaining the basic materials of both the Ewart and Baldwin buildings and the layout proposed in Ewart's masterplan, Lane added to the front of the Ewart building a monumental portico of Ohio stone—inspired by the Palladian traditions of eighteenth-century English architecture—with two-storey fluted Ionic columns supporting a pediment, raised on an arcaded ground floor of channelled masonry. Across the front were fluted pilasters between the central windows, unfluted ones at the corners of the block, stone window-frames, and a full Ionic cornice and parapet extending around the block. The entire scheme was repeated in a new building attached to the west end of the Baldwin building that was designed to house the new superior courts. Porticoes such as Lane designed—raised high on arcaded 'basements'—were originally used as the dominant features of large country houses for the British landed aristocracy, and these associations with established power led them to be adapted for English courthouses; in Canada in the 1830s and 1840s they were instantly recognized symbols of the Law, and of the court-houses in which it was administered."[287]

One wonders what Ewart's role, if any, might have been in the 1833 and 1844 expansions or what his opinions might have been about changes to his master plan. Certainly he would have seen the ongoing work and known the people involved in the design and construction of the central block and west wing.

The last major expansion in the nineteenth century was by Cumberland and Storm (1857). Baldwin's central wing was demolished and replaced with a new central block that included offices, storage areas for records, facilities for Common Pleas and Queen's Bench and a library.[288] The central block exists today and remains an impressive structure. "Osgoode Hall at no time established new trends in public design, nor did it even influence directly any known public building. Rather, Osgoode Hall is a particularly rich embodiment of the diverse trends which affected public architecture in early Canada."[289]

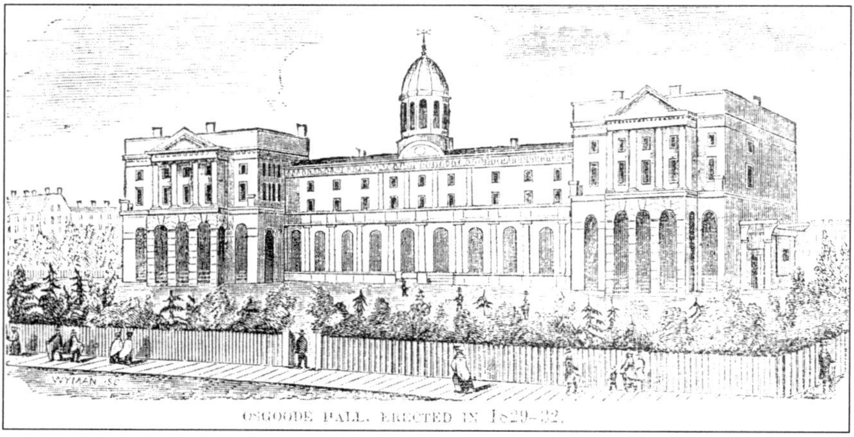

11. Toronto Public Library wood engraving by F.E. Wyman, published in the *Globe Pictorial Supplement* shows the 1844 additions including a wooden fence and boardwalk. [TPL T-33830]

Of Ewart's original east wing, only pre-portico exterior and interior walls appear to be original. There were extensive renovations to the rooms and more elaborate decorations and furniture. A modern-day tour of the building cannot erase, however, the thoughtfulness of the overall design and the grandeur of its opening day in 1832.

12. Osgoode Hall in 1868-69 photo after the addition of the 'cow gates' which prevented the nearby farm animals from entering the beautifully landscaped grounds. [TPL T-12016]

Ewart Wharf (1829-31)

When John Ewart landed in York as a new resident, the first likely thing he did was to secure several water lots. J. Ross Robertson lists the following additional water lot patents[290] in his Landmarks of Toronto:

Lot D John Ewart All of it registered September 11, 1828

Lot D John Ewart Some Part registered 3-10 June 1, 1832

Lot E D'Arcy Boulton, Jr. All of it 3-10 June 1, 1832.

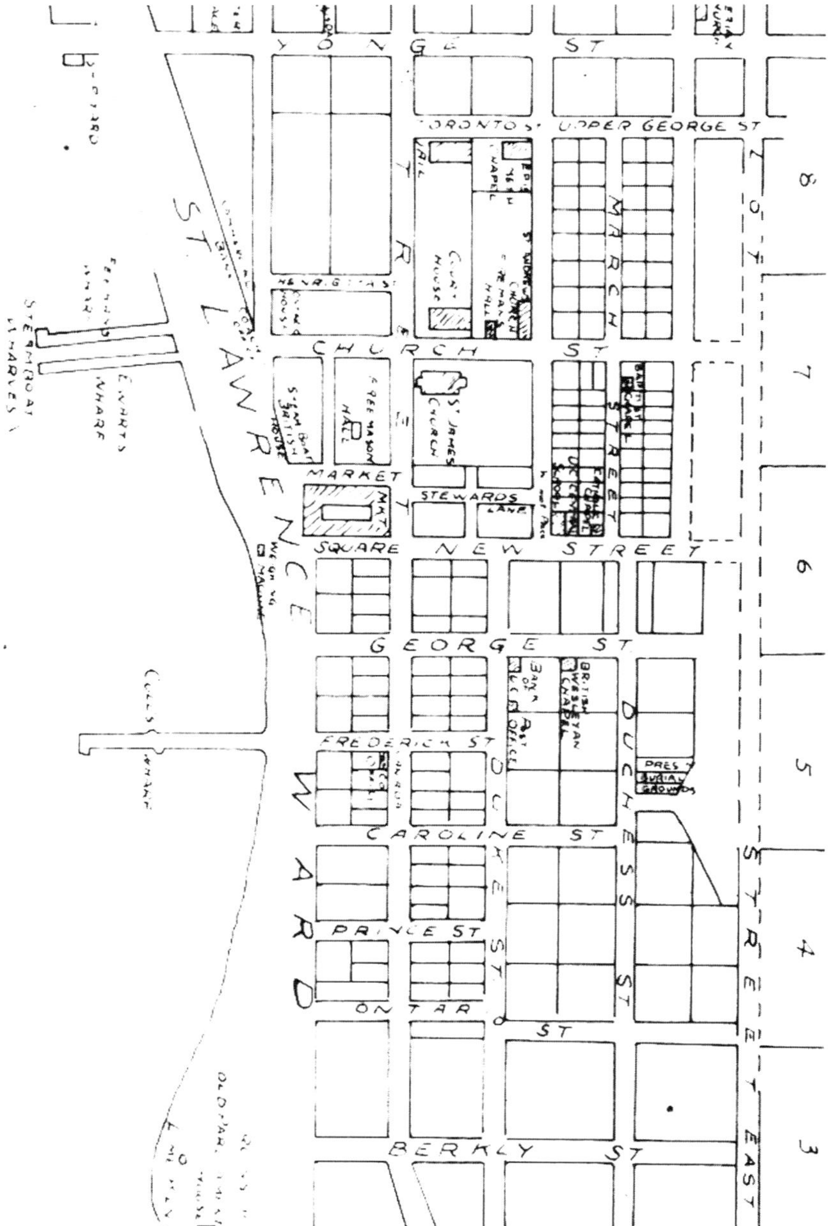
YONGE ST
TORONTO ST
UPPER GEORGE ST
CHURCH ST
MARKET
SQUARE
NEW STREET
STEWARDS LANE
MKT
GEORGE ST
FREDERICK ST
CAROLINE ST
PRINCE ST
ONTARIO ST
BERKLY ST
PARLIAMENT ST
LOT STREET EAST
MARCH STREET
DUKE ST
DUCHESS ST
ST LAWRENCE WARD
ST JAMES CHURCH
COURT HOUSE
FREE MASON HALL
BRITISH WESLEYAN CHAPEL
POST OFFICE
PRES. BURIAL GROUNDS
STEAMBOAT WHARVES
EWARTS WHARF
8
7
6
5
4
3

13. You read in Chapter 1 that Ewart had two water lots: the "Custom's House Reserve" lot at the bottom of Yonge Street, and the water lot on the east side of Church Street just west of the one owned by D'Arcy Boulton Jr. (owner of *The Grange*). The map on the previous page shows the actual wharf that Ewart built between 1829 and 1831 which was suitable, as the map indicates, for steamboats. [TPL City of Toronto Map (east) 1834 cropped to highlight area shown]

As a harbour town, it was important to have wharves for both commercial and passenger travel. The first wharf in York was not built until ten years after Simcoe's arrival, an 1803 structure by William Allan that became the Merchants' Wharf. "The second was the King's or Navy Wharf between John and Peter streets before 1818. The third the Commissariat Wharf[291] at the bottom of Peter Street. Then Cooper's Wharf at the bottom of Church street about 1815-16. Between 1818-1834 there were only 3 new wharves: one of them was Ewart's at the bottom of Church street east of Cooper's. He received the patent to the water lot on August 15, 1828 and probably built the wharf that year."[292]

14. Maitland's Wharf (circa 1845) as engraved by W.H. Bartlett. Ewart's wharf may have been similarly built of wood with a long pier to handle larger steam ships. Below is Ewart's petition to deepen the water level by his wharf, extend its length and add a wood yard to store wood needed by the steam ships. [TPL T-32137]

On October 13, 1831 Ewart petitioned Lieutenant-Governor Peregrine Maitland for modifications to his wharf:

> *That your petitioner is the proprietor of the water lots lettered D and E, in front of the Town of York that the lot D was granted to your petitioner and lot E purchased by him from D'Arcy Boulton junior esquire to whom the same was also sold at a government sale by auction and which no patent has yet been made out.*
>
> *That having understood encouragement having been held out by your excellency for the creation of a wharf for the use of steam boats, your petitioner has commenced a wharf intended for such purpose, but finds that the water at the extremity of the usual length granted, namely 10 chains*[293] *is not sufficiently deep, your petitioner prays that Lot E may extend to 13 Chains in depth and that your petitioner may receive on such terms and may (some unclear words omitted here) an extension to the lot D of three chains in depth.*

That your petitioner is also desirous to purchase an additional water lot of 4 chains in front by 13 chains in depth west of and adjoining the water lot granted to William Cooper for the purpose of making a wood yard for the use of the steamboats, an accommodation much wanted wherefore your petitioner prays your excellency will be pleased to authorise the same to be sold to him on such terms as your excellency may think fit.

And your petitioner will ever pray, John Ewart, Oct. 13 '31.[294]

His letter to Maitland introduces us to his desire to open up a wood yard for the steam ships but, likely, also for the construction trades in York. Ewart's understanding of the needs of a growing town highlights his entrepreneurial spirit. Land and water lots were valuable tools in acquiring a degree of wealth in a growing town, and Ewart acted upon it. His ability to purchase lots suggests that he arrived in York at the age of 30 with over a decade of working experiences, and sufficient capital to invest in his new community.

15. York Harbour in 1828 by James Gray, from Gibraltar Point on what is now Toronto Island shows St. James steeple to the right and a modern steamer. Ewart understood that steam travel would increase the use of the harbour and the need for wharves that provided wood to stoke the fires. By 1834 the *Cobourg* (418 tons) could reach 24 kph on its three-hour crossing to Niagara. [TPL T-10339]

Emigrants' Asylum 1830

As we read in the August 29, 1830 *Kingston Chronicle* article earlier in this chapter, John Ewart was involved in the construction of The Emigrants' Asylum in York. This facility was "for the accommodation of destitute Emigrants and Strangers; the foundation being already laid and the bricks and other materials for the super-structure being on the ground." Ewart built the asylum on the hospital grounds. The building was 90 feet x 20 feet, 1 storey high with 6 tenements or apartments. Ewart did the work with another contractor, Mr. Sparks, and expected the work would be done by October 1830.[295]

An outbreak of disease amongst immigrants and newcomers to York triggered the need for the asylum. The largest outbreaks occurred after the asylum was opened, but it could not deal with the cholera epidemic among the city's residents. Cholera is a summer disease that arrived in North America from Europe. The first major outbreak was in June and July of 1832, a second in July and August 1834 and, finally, the "worst immigrant generated epidemic in history" in 1847. It killed 2,000 people in Kingston and Toronto alone.[296] To help cope with these diseases, Dr. W.W. Baldwin was appointed President of the Board of Health of York in 1832. This new duty was added to his role as a judge of the Surrogate Court (1812-1836).[297]

The actual design of this 1830 building has not been found. We can presume that the building was made in a compatible design to that of Ewart's York General Hospital.

Mechanics' Institute 1830
(Forerunner of *Toronto Public Library*)

16. The Mechanics Institute as it appeared in the 1870s, years after its founding. Ewart would have been present to participate in discussion about the design and construction of the building but was not on record as being a commissioner on the project.[298] [TPL T-11997]

By the early 1830s there were a few shops in York carrying books, but there were no lending libraries, especially for those tradesmen who wanted to increase their knowledge and skills. The Mechanics'[299] Institute movement began in Edinburgh in 1821 and in London in 1824[300] and soon spread to North America. Its aim was to teach workers the applied technology behind new methods of manufacturing and craftsmanship introduced during the Industrial Revolution.[301] The Institute was also referred to as the Society for Mutual Improvement in the Arts and Sciences[302] and was "dedicated to the concept of the education and basic dignity of the working man."[303]

John Ewart, J.H. Dunn, Joseph Bates and James Lesslie thought that a similar institute would benefit York and placed the following notice in the *Colonial Advocate* (William Lyon Mackenzie's newspaper): "The residents of York and its vicinity are respectfully informed, that a public meeting will be held for the purpose of forming a Mechanics' Institute, having for its object the mutual improvement of its members in useful Scientific knowledge. It is to be conducted (as far as practical) on the principles of the Mechanics' Institute of the United Kingdom of Great Britain and Ireland. A Library of reference and circulation will be formed, Lectures delivered and classes established for instruction in various branches of useful study. Subjects connected with Religion and Politics will be carefully excluded, and every means resorted to that will tend to eradicate a spirit of party. Mechanics are earnestly requested to attend. Suitable accommodations will be provided for the Ladies. N.B. The time and place of meeting will be made known in a few days." [304]

Edith Firth records that the meeting was held on December 24, 1830 with J.H. Dunn "chosen as patron and John Ewart president. Joseph Bates and James Lesslie, its most active founders, were appointed secretaries." Also involved in the early days were Dr. Baldwin, Dr. Rolph, Dr. Dunlop, Ex-Sheriff Jarvis, Jesse Ketchum, and David Paterson.[305]

The Institute followed through on its advertised goals. It strictly controlled the learning agenda to concentrate on practical knowledge and skills. It purposely excluded lectures or discussions of a religious or political nature to prevent the educational purposes of the institute being overridden by religious or political parties. The founders wanted a learning institute, not a new political body to influence public policy.

James Lesslie explains: "The Mechanics' Institute is viewed with suspicion by some of our Gentry & some of its professed & warmest friends to be influenced by them. The intelligence of the lower Classes they and their system would if possible keep under their Lord and Slave system is not to be grafted upon the people of U.C. and their favourite maxim 'Ignorance is Bliss' which was this day defended by one of them shows clearly the principle from which their opposition to the dissemination of knowledge arises."[306]

Ewart was part of a 12-member group of petitioners that took a more drastic step in promoting the education of many of York's boys. They asked Lieutenant-Governor Colborne to reduce the fees for some boys attending Upper Canada College so that sons of tradesmen could get a non-classical education.

> *The Petition of the undersigned inhabitants of the Town of York and its vicinity, Respectfully Showeth,*
>
> *That they highly appreciate your Excellency's measure for the promotion of Education in this Province, that they rejoice in the rapidly increasing success which has hitherto attended those measures, that at the same time they humbly represent to your Excellency that the benefits dispensed by the Upper Canada College might, in their opinion, be greatly extended in favour of the Children of many families in this Town and vicinity whose parents do not desire to have them instructed in the Classics, by admitting them upon less expensive terms, and to receive an English Education only.*
>
> *Wherefore they pray that your Excellency will be pleased to cause such alterations to be made in the regulations and changes [i.e. charges] of the College as will enable your Excellency's Petitioners and others in similar circumstances to have their sons Educated in the College in such branches of an English Education as will qualify them for discharging with efficiency and respectability, the scientific and other business of Tradesmen and Mechanics.*

And our Petitioners will ever pray.

(Signed) Daniel Brooke, John Murchison, Thomas Moore, John Ewart, Jacob Latham, R.C. Horne, L. Fairbanks, H. Richardson, Jas. E. Small, Robert Baldwin, J.S. Baldwin, F.T. Billings.[307]

Colborne's refusal of this petition illustrates the 'suspicion' that Lesslie referred to above. Colborne wanted the highest class of students from across the province to attend the school, recognizing that they would be the future leaders of Upper Canada. E. McMahon, Colborne's Secretary, replied on his behalf this way: The request is denied because: (1) "the general interests of the Province have been considered more than the convenience of any Town or Township", (2) [UCC] "wanted new students to be attracted to the school's high standards", (3) "it needed to provide a higher education for university preparatory work, therefore, including the classics and two modern languages," (4) "it needed the revenues as the government's £500 per year was not enough to keep and attract good teachers."[308]

The Institute met on Colborne Street, near Church Street, on the second floor of the Masonic Hall. The Hall was a wooden building with a cupola (the first building in York with such a decoration). The first public lectures were held here.[309]

The early years did not go smoothly for the institute. Diarist James Lesslie recorded on January 21, 1832: "…Mr. Ewart called today requesting that a meeting should be called of the "Mechanics' Institute" to get it established on a firmer basis.— It has been almost defunct but hopes are entertained of its yet meeting with liberal Countenance even altho' it should only be a good Library of Scientific Works and such articles of Apparatus as might amuse as well as instruct…"[310] Within a month, Ewart's active participation led to this Lesslie extract from February 27th, 1832: "…Attended Committee Meeting of the Mechanics' Institute preparatory to the General Meeting on

Monday night.—A young man was present and introduced by the Chairman, Mr. Ewart, as a fit person to undertake the tuition of a Drawing Class—the specimens of his work were certainly most superior."

Despite this shaky start, the Institute had a long and useful life. In a description of the Mechanics' Institute in the City Directory it states: "The Library contains 800 volumes of books, and is open for distribution and reference every Monday and Thursday evenings. Public Lectures on Wednesday Evenings, during the winter season."[311] The institute had such a reputation that the original Toronto Board of Trade, (founded in 1845) had its first offices in the building until 1866.[312]

The *Free Library By-law* of January 1883 led to the merger between the Mechanics' Institute and the new Toronto Public Library.[313] The Library took over the institute's building and it became the first library branch.

St. Andrew's Presbyterian Church (1830-31)

17. St. Andrew's Presbyterian Church as drawn by John G. Howard in 1840 after having added the tower and spire to Ewart's original building. [TPL T-10706]

The second Presbyterian church in York was located on the southwest corner of Church and Adelaide Streets, across from the future Mechanics' Institute, and "designed by congregation member John Ewart, with a spire added in 1840 by John G. Howard".[314]

The entire block of land bounded by Toronto, Adelaide, Church and King Streets, "was granted by the Crown on 29th April 1819 to Grant Powell, Darcy Boulton, and Alexander Macdonald in trust for a Gaol and Court House. The Court House was built facing on Church St., near King Street. The corner was purchased by the Trustees of St. Andrew's Church."[315] The property cost "about £500."[316]

The original plan, however, had been to build the church where the "later Parliament House in the Park Reserve East adjoining the Town of York, together with Seven or Eight Acres adjoining the same."[317] The request was denied, so the congregation bought the Church Street lot instead.

Included as founding members were William Lyon Mackenzie,[318] Dr. W. Dunlop, Hon. William Morris and Ewart's friend from their work together on Potters' Field, Thomas Carfrae, Jr.[319]

Ewart chaired a meeting on March 3, 1830 to discuss the building of St. Andrew's Church.[320] It was eventually agreed that Ewart would design the church. He had already designed St. Paul's Catholic Church and was busy working on the Third Parliament Buildings, Upper Canada College and Osgoode Hall.

First, funding had to be secured. William Lyon Mackenzie's *Colonial Advocate* reported on Thursday, March 18, 1830 that "We have understood that Sir John Colborne has promised the Scots Presbyterian Kirk, proposed to be erected here, £100 yearly for five years[321], but have not heard what fund it is to be paid out of. We are told that Mr. Ewart, the builder has subscribed £50; Mr. Hugh Carfrae £50; Hon. W. Allan £25; Mr. Morris of Perth £10; Mr. McLean of Stormont £10; Hon. D. Cameron and Chief Justice Robinson £20 each."[322] Further funds were donated through the Glasgow Colonial Society, the 71st and 79th Highland Regiments and Presbyterians in Montreal and Kingston.[323] As well "Dr. Strachan (a former Presbyterian)…and other Anglicans subscribed to the building fund."[324]

A report of a similar but subsequent meeting took place on, Thursday, May 20, 1830:

> *A meeting of the subscribers was held in Bradley's Hotel on Tuesday last. They have £750 subscribed and are as we understand to proceed with the building forthwith. Messrs. J.F. Smith, John Ewart, Jacob Latham, Walter Rose, Thomas Carfrae, Jr., and Alexander Murray are appointed Trustees of the Church.*[325]

With funds in hand, Thomas Carfrae laid the cornerstone in June 1830 and one year later the church was completed.[326] "St. Andrew's, as built in 1831, was a handsome, dignified structure in brick, stuccoed and lined in imitation of ashlar.[327] It had all of the monumentality of St. Paul's in the treatment of its masonry, and had in addition—as became a more costly structure—a little discreet detailing in the manner of Soane. Ewart, while working in London in 1812, had become acquainted with the architectural designs of John Soane, either through simple observation—a designer's intense interest in all that was being built—or because he was employed as a mason on some of Soane's projects."[328]

Writing in January 1831, trustee Dr. Dunlop stated that they "cannot proceed till April, for from the unprecedented quantity of building going on in York, we cannot get the Church walls plastered until the Spring, as our hard frosts preclude the possibility of doing it in winter."[329] The building faced Church Street and was 67 feet along the front and 97 feet down the side. The interior was well lit by double height windows and a gallery around three sides of the church was furnished with long wooden pews. The ground floor also had box pews, which enclosed the seated parishioners within a low wall and a door that opened onto the aisle. The gallery was reached by stairways on either side of the main entrance and the pulpit by steps on either side as well. The pulpit occupied the west wall of the building and was positioned above the Precentor's[330] seat. In 1831 the pulpit was an open platform without a sounding board above it, an omission that caught the attention of William Lyon Mackenzie. Writing in the *Colonial Advocate* he states: "the pulpit wants a top, and old Roman decoration which might have been as well continued."[331]

Although MacRae refers to St. Andrew's Church as part of the Regency style, Harold Kalman judges it as "adopting a consistent Georgian style, as might be expected by the manner in which the Toronto establishment embraced Georgian for its houses and public buildings. The style is seen at St. Andrew's Church of Scotland…designed and built in 1830-34 by John Ewart… St. Andrew's was built of brick, stuccoed and scored to imitate stone. The tower was placed at the entrance, but the entablature and the pilasters supporting it were continued around it so that the lower portion appeared to be a central projection of the façade (as on a Georgian house). Tall and elegant round-arched windows—separated by pilasters—illuminated the nave, and a square-headed door and window, with carefully detailed classical surrounds, were inserted into the entrance bay. These details around the entry may be considered to be Neoclassical features, but the overall intent was not one of reviving a lost classical past, but rather of continuing an eighteenth-century building tradition."[332]

The history of the building of the church is easier to present than that of the congregation's. This was the second Presbyterian congregation in York. The first was founded on the principle of absolute separation of Church and State and it later became the Knox Presbyterian Church.[333] "The Irish Secessionist Presbyterian Reverend James Harris (1793-1873) came to York in 1820 and soon after began to organize a congregation. Jessie Ketchum, Harris' future father-in-law, donated a church and lands in 1821. The congregation consisted of about 400 Irish and American tradesmen and artisans."[334]

As part of the United Synod of Upper Canada, the Harris church did not support state-funded religion[335] as did St. Andrew's Church, where Colborne had pledged £500 over five years to cover fifty percent of the minister's wages. Conflicts continued between Harris' church and St. Andrew's until 1834, when some of St. Andrew's members joined with the former Harris congregation to create the Free Church.[336] "Radicals, like William Lyon Mackenzie, were quick to leave St. Andrew's for Knox over these issues. All of this tension added to the unsettled nature of Toronto prior to the 1837 Rebellion."[337]

Oliver Mowat wrote to his mother in October 9, 1844 about the secession from St. Andrew's congregation of many of the leading members of the church, including John Ewart, his father-in-law.[338] Whether Ewart ever rejoined the congregation is unclear, but he did return to St. Andrew's at least once to see his daughter, Jane, marry Mr. Mowat on May 19, 1846.

Wholesale Grocer's Store (1833)

In reviewing the limited documentation of early York and Toronto, it becomes apparent that Ewart was probably involved in many projects for which we have no records. For example, in examining early newspapers, we have the following:

> *Among the most splendid single buildings we may notice at that corner of King and Yonge Streets erected by Ridout and brothers, hardware merchants, which is a magnificent building; and so are those immediate opposite built by Mr. Ewart and [one] occupied by Mr. Ware,*

wholesale grocery merchants. Grocery stores including that of Mr. Ware, comprise in the extensive assortments, all the ordinary articles such establishments carry, with almost every luxury in the articles of wines, fruits, etc. which can be obtained from the four corners of the globe.[339]

The design and/or construction of stores would not have been a major commission for Ewart. It does suggests, however, that even at the apex of his influence as an architect and builder, he took on projects that meant a great deal to his clients, if not to the larger circle of powerful and wealthy men of the town. Alas, we have not found any surviving drawings or photos of these buildings.

Ewart's remaining twenty years in Toronto were filled less with building large projects and more with building his community. He entered politics, was instrumental in founding and directing several key organizations in the new city of Toronto and acted as commissioner on several projects including the work on the Provincial Lunatic Asylum.

---

213 J.M.S. Careless. (1984). *Toronto to 1918*, p. 202.

214 *Ibid*, p. 200.

215 Thomas Radcliff. (ed.). (1953). *Authentic Letters from Upper Canada*, p. v.

216 Edwin C. Guillet. (1933). *Pioneer Days in Upper Canada*, p. 50: *Upper Canada Gazette*, March 25, 1830 ad.

217 *Brockville Recorder*. Friday 11 October 1833, Vol. XIII, No. 41 p. 2, c. 5 and a reprint of same article from *Colonial Advocate*, October 3, 1833, "Growth and Trade in the Town of York".

218 The following are quotes from the newspaper article but not the complete texts.

219 *Kingston Chronicle* 29 August 1830 p. 2 c. 3.

220 *Ibid*, p. 2 c. 3 & 4.

221 *Ibid*, p. 2 c. 4.

222 *Ibid*, p. 2 c. 4.

223 Upper Canada Schedule of Accounts sent to the House of Assembly, the 2d February 1831. www.canadiana.org/ECO/PageView/9_00942_7/0018?id=04f58050bf5990e7.

224 Public Accounts of the Inspector General, 7 January 1831. www.canadiana.org/ECO/PageView/9_00942_7/001?id=04f58050b:5990e7

225 Paul Gaines, personal correspondence.

226 Thomas Radcliff. (Ed.) (1953). *Authentic Letters from Upper Canada*, p. 206.

227 *Ibid*, p. 205.

228 Lucy Booth Martyn. (1982). *The Face of Early Toronto: An Archival Record 1797-1936*, p. 99.

229 Patricia McHugh. (1989). *Toronto Architecture: A City Guide.* (2nd ed.), p. 48.

230 William Kilbourn. (1956). *The Firebrand: William Lyon Mackenzie and the Rebellion in Upper Canada*, p. 5.

231 A modest two and a half percent commission on the cost. Lucy Booth Martyn. (1982). *The Face of Early Toronto: An Archival Record 1797-1936*, p. 99.

232 Included the administrative offices, classrooms and chapel at 80 x 82 feet, radiating out from a central hall on both stories. The four houses, each divided into two separate units, contained dormitories for a total of 120 boys. John Ross Robertson. (1896), *Landmarks of Toronto*, Vol. 1, p. 150.

233 Stephen Otto expands this point in *Toronto: No Mean City* (1983), p. 64: "at more than £17,000 easily the most expensive of any building project undertaken before York's incorporation as Toronto. John Ewart was paid for drawing plans and when the contractor failed, for building the four boarding houses."

234 William Dendy. (1993). *Lost Toronto*, p. 59 gives the completion date as fall of 1831 while John G. Howard's journals gives the opening date of the new buildings as January 30, 1833 "built in Russell Square to plan by John Ewart," Vol. 1, p. 19 footnote.

235 Leonard Wise and Allan Gould. (2000). *Toronto Street Names.* Wise and Gould also note that John G. Howard was Colborne's protégé and began his career in York as a drawing instructor at Upper Canada College.

236 Donald Jones. (1992). *Fifty Tales of Toronto*, p. 68.

237 Lucy Booth Martyn. (1982). *The Face of Early Toronto: An Archival Record 1797-1936*, p. 99.

238 A government square set aside by provincial administrator Peter Russell early in his term.

239 William Dendy. (1993). *Lost Toronto*, p. 59.

240 James FitzGerald. (1994). *Old Boys, p. xviii.* Thomas Ewart and John Ewart Jr.'s names are inscribed high up on the walls of Laidlaw Hall with the other Head Boys at U.C.C.

241 William Dendy. (1993). *Lost Toronto*, p. 59.

242 *Toronto: No Mean City*, p. 49.

243 W.G. Crosbie. (1975). *The Toronto General Hospital 1819-1965*, p. 10.

244 William Dendy. (1993). *Lost Toronto*, p. 52.

245 National Archives of Canada, Upper Canada Sundries, RG-5, A 1, pp. 43443-43446, 12 December 1826: Report of the Commissioners for Parliament Buildings to the Lieutenant

Governor recommending Joseph Nixon's plan and appending proposals of Baldwin, Ford and Ewart. (Originally, Stephen Otto provided us with this citation.)

246 William Dendy. (1993). *Lost Toronto*, p. 52.

247 Eric Arthur. (1964). *Toronto: No Mean City*, pp. 45 & 46.

248 National Archives of Canada, RG 1, E3, Executive Council papers, Vol. 64, pp. 166-227; Vol 65, pp. 7-61. Also, Jesse Edgar Middleton. (1923). *The Municipality of Toronto: A History, Vols. 1-3*, p. 167.

249 Ewart was involved later in his career with the development of the Provincial Lunatic Asylum as a commissioner supervising the work of John G. Howard.

250 Mike Filey. (1994). *Toronto Sketches 3*, pp. 6 & 7.

251 Stephen Otto. (1983). *Toronto: No Mean City*, p. 103.

252 Eric Arthur. (1952). "The History and Architecture of Fabric" in C.H.A. Armstrong's (1952). *The Honourable Society of Osgoode Hall*, pp. 50 & 51.

253 Eric Arthur. (1964). *Toronto: No Mean City*, p. 65.

254 Stephen Otto. (1983). *Toronto: No Mean City*.

255 Benchers are members of the governing body. Based on the term 'reserved benches' in the dining halls of English Inns of Court for same body of men. Christopher Moore. (1997). *The Law Society of Upper Canada and Ontario's lawyers 1779-1997*, p. 343.

256 The future chief justice of Upper Canada.

257 Marion MacRae and Anthony Adamson. (1983). *Cornerstones of Order*, p. 45.

258 Dendy and Kilbourn. (1986). *Toronto Observed*, pp. 71 & 72, footnote.

259 Treasurers are the administrative, volunteer head of the society. In the early history of the Law Society, they also handled the money. Christopher Moore. (1997). *The Law Society of Upper Canada and Ontario's lawyers 1779-1997*, p. 343.

260 Christopher Moore. (1997). *The Law Society of Upper Canada and Ontario's Lawyers 1779-1997*, pp. 78 & 79.

261 William Dendy and William Kilbourn. (1986). *Toronto Observed*, pp. 71 & 72.

262 Marion MacRae and Aanthony Adamson. (1983). *Cornerstones of Order*, p. 45.

263 Dr. W.W. Baldwin was Treasurer for four different terms: 1811-1814; 1820; 1825-1828; and 1832-1835. Christopher Moore. (1997). *The Law Society of Upper Canada and Ontario's lawyers 1779-1997,* p. 345.

264 Meetings of the society including those that examined and conferred degrees on students-at-law. Christopher Moore. (1997). *The Law Society of Upper Canada and Ontario's lawyers 1779-1997*, p. 343.

265 Dana Johnson and Leslie Maitland. (December 1985). 'Osgoode Hall and the Development of Public Architecture in Canada,' in *14 SSAC BULLETIN* 4:85, pp. 14-15; John Honsberger (2004). *Osgoode Hall: An Illustrated History*, p. 116.

266 John Honsberger (2004). *Osgoode Hall: An Illustrated History*, pp. 117 & 118.

[267] Stephen Langmead, Professor (retired 2004) in the Department of Architectural Science, Faculty of Engineering and Applied Science, Ryerson University and a registered architect in Ontario (retired 2002) explains that architects up to the 1960s received a similar 7% fee for their work. Since then a fee scale is used based on five categories of work and the amount of money invested in the project (equals a reverse scale of about 4% of the total cost). 60% of that fee goes to the architect and 40% to mechanical and electrical consultants.

[268] Marion MacRae and Anthony Adamson. (1983). *Cornerstones of Order*, p. 47. Christopher Moore's footnote in (1997). *The Law Society of Upper Canada and Ontario's Lawyers 1779-1997*, p. 82.

[269] William Dendy and William Kilbourn. (1986). *Toronto Observed*, pp. 71 & 72.

[270] Marion MacRae and Anthony Adamson. (1983). *Cornerstones of Order*, p. 47.

[271] John Honsberger (2004). *Osgoode Hall: An Illustrated History*, pp. 123 and 124.

[272] Eric Arthur. (1952). "The History and Architecture of Fabric" in C.H.A. Armstrong's (1952). *The Honourable Society of Osgoode Hall*, p. 49.

[273] Christopher Moore. (1997). *The Law Society of Upper Canada and Ontario's Lawyers 1779-1997*, p. 82 footnote 26: LSUCA, Minutes of Convocation, Vol. 1, 24 June 1829 (Ewart's contract), and 1829-32 *passim*, on the construction. In February 1832 the building was said to have been completed fourteen months behind schedule due to the additional third storey, changing from oak to walnut interior trim and a few other changes.

[274] William Dendy and William Kilbourn. (1986). *Toronto Observed*, pp. 71 & 72.

[275] Ewart's own design for Upper Canada College followed this tripartite subdivision. Johnson, Dana and Maitland, Leslie. "Osgoode Hall and the Development of Public Architecture in Canada" in *14 SSAC BULLETIN 4:85* December 1985, p. 15.

[276] Marion MacRae and Anthony Adamson. (1983). *Cornerstones of Order*, p. 47.

[277] William Dendy. (1993). *Lost Toronto*, p. 6.

[278] Christopher Moore's footnote in (1997). *The Law Society of Upper Canada and Ontario's Lawyers 1779-1997*, pp. 83 & 84: LSUCA, Minutes of Convocation, Vol. 1:228, 17 November 1831.

[279] Christopher Moore's footnote in (1997). *The Law Society of Upper Canada and Ontario's Lawyers 1779-1997*, pp. 83 & 84, footnote 32: LSUCA, Minutes of Convocation Vol. 1, 20 April, 3 November and 8 November 1830.

[280] Angela K. Carr in "Hopkins, Lawford & Nelson at Osgoode Hall: The Debacle of 1855" in *17 SSAC BULLETIN*, 4:88, pp. 17-25 writes that Ewart built the east wing. She did her master's degree at U of T on the architecture of Osgoode complete with diagrams of 22 changes to the buildings over the decades. Her work may be considered authoritative.

[281] William Dendy and William Kilbourn. (1986). *Toronto Observed*, pp. 71 & 72.

[282] Edith Firth. (1962). *The Town of York 1815-1834*, p. 335, January 10, 1832.

[283] Christopher Moore. (1997). *The Law Society of Upper Canada and Ontario's Lawyers 1779-1997*, p. 82, regarding Campbell's letter to Convocation, Vol. 1, 23 April 1833.

[284] Margaret and Merilyn McKelvey. (1984). *Toronto: Carved in Stone*. p. 14.

---

285 C.H.A. Armstrong. (1952). *The Honourable Society of Osgoode Hall.* p. 30.

286 John Honsberger (2004). *Osgoode Hall: An Illustrated History*, p. 121.

287 William Dendy and William Kilbourn. (1986). *Toronto Observed*, pp. 71 & 72.

288 *Ibid.*

289 Dana Johnson and Leslie Maitland. "Osgoode Hall and the Development of Public Architecture in Canada" in *14 SSAC BULLETIN* 4:85 December 1985, p. 18.

290 (1896). Landmarks of Toronto, Vol. 1: p. 343.

291 Military department wharf for securing food supplies.

292 Jesse Edgar Middleton. (1923). *The Municipality of Toronto: A History, Vols. 1-3*, p. 440.

293 A chain is a unit of measurement of land equalling 66 feet or approximately 20 metres

294 Archives of Ontario E 17/9

295 *Kingston Chronicle.* 29 August 1830, p. 2 c. 4.

296 W.G. Crosbie. (1975). *The Toronto General Hospital 1819-1965*, pp. 18, 26, 28.

297 The W.W. Baldwin Papers in the Baldwin Room at Toronto Public Reference Library, (1954) *The Guide to the Manuscript Collection*, p. 9.

298 Stephen Otto. (1983). *Toronto,* p. 115.

299 The word "mechanics" is used not to refer to a job description but as the processes by which something is done or functions.

300 J. Ross Robertson. (1896). *Landmarks of Toronto*, Vol. 1, p. 398.

301 Heritage Plaque outside the old Institute's 1854 Cumberland and Storm building at Adelaide and Church Street.

302 J. Ross Robertson. (1896). *Landmarks of Toronto,* Vol. 1, p. 398.

303 William Dendy. (1993). *Lost Toronto*, p. 137.

304 Edith Firth. (1962). *The Town of York 1815-1834*, pp. 324 & 325.

305 *Ibid,* p. 325.

306 *Ibid,* p. 325.

307 *Ibid,* p. 167. *Canadian Freeman*, September 15, 1831.

308 *Ibid,* p. 168.

309 J. Ross Robertson. (1896). *Landmarks of Toronto,* Vol. 1, p. 398.

310 Edith Firth. (1962). *The Town of York 1815-1834,* p. 334.

311 Toronto Public Library digital directories circa 1830-1860: http://mtrl.toronto.on.ca:80….ge.html:sessionid=01-6233-41995397 This item must be before 1850 as Robertson reports that in that year the library had 1,300 volumes, was open every evening to members and had a subscription rate of 7s 6d. (1896). *Landmarks of Toronto,* Vol. 1, p. 398.

312 William Dendy. (1993). *Lost Toronto*, p. 28.

---

[313] J. Ross Robertson. (1896). *Landmarks of Toronto*, Vol. 1, p. 399.

[314] Stephen Otto. (1983). *Toronto: No Mean City*, pp. 46 & 47.

[315] Reverend Stuart C. Parker. (1930). *The Book of St. Andrew*, pp. 5 & 6.

[316] *Ibid*, p. 6.

[317] Petition of St. Andrew's Church to the Lieutenant Governor, signed by Chairman John Ewart and James Newbigging, Secretary. Edith Firth. (1962). *The Town of York 1815-1834,* p. 199.

[318] Harold Kalman. (2000). *A Concise History of Canadian Architecture*, p. 149.

[319] Reverend Stuart C. Parker. (1930). *The Book of St. Andrew*, p. 5.

[320] Jesse Edward Middleton. (1923). *The Municipality of Toronto: A History*, p. 703.

[321] To cover half the £200 annual stipend for the minister. Lucy Booth Martyn. (1982). *The Face of Early Toronto: An Archival Record 1797-1936*, p. 66.

[322] Reverend Stuart C. Parker. (1930). *The Book of St. Andrew*, p. 3.

[323] Edith Firth. (1962). *The Town of York 1815-1834,* p. lvii.

[324] Lucy Booth Martyn. (1982). *The Face of Early Toronto: An Archival Record 1797-1936*, p. 66.

[325] Reverend Stuart C. Parker. (1930). *The Book of St. Andrew*, p. 4.

[326] *Ibid*, p. 6.

[327] Masonry made of square-cut stones.

[328] Marion MacRae and Anthony Adamson. (1975). *Hallowed Walls*, p. 86.

[329] Reverend Stuart C. Parker. (1930). *The Book of St. Andrew*, p. 7.

[330] The person who leads the singing of the church's congregation.

[331] Reverend Stuart C. Parker. (1930). *The Book of St. Andrew*, p. 8.

[332] Harold Kalman. (2000). *A Concise History of Canadian Architecture*, p. 149.

[333] Edith Firth. (1962). *The Town of York 1815-1834, p.* lvii.

[334] Lucy Booth Martyn. (1983). *A View of Original Toronto: The Fabric of York/Toronto Circa 1834*, p. 36.

[335] Frederick Henry Armstrong. (1988). *A City in the Making: Progress, People & Perils in Victorian Toronto*, p. 172.

[336] Lucy Booth Martyn. (1982). *The Face of Early Toronto: An Archival Record 1797-1936*, p. 67.

[337] Edith Firth. (1962). *The Town of York 1815-1834,* p. lviii.

[338] C.R.W. Biggar. (1905). *Sir Oliver Mowat: A Biographical Sketch.*

[339] *Brockville Recorder.* Friday 11 October 1833, Vol. XIII, No. 41 p. 2, c. 5 & 6 and a reprint of same article from *Colonial Advocate*, October 3, 1833 "Growth and Trade in the Town of York".

CHAPTER 5
A New Era for the Growing City (1834-1856)

Ewart's Politics
Life in the New Toronto
St. Andrew's Society of Toronto (1836)
City of Toronto and Lake Huron Railroad Company (1836)
St. James' Church/Cathedral (Rebuilding after the Fire of 1839)
Great West Railroad Company (1845)
Ewart's Position on Boards of Directors and Commissions
Provincial Lunatic Asylum (1846-1850)
Ewart's Diverse Interests
Family Life
John Ewart's Death (1856)

The town of York was incorporated as the City of Toronto in 1834. What was this new city like? What might Ewart have seen and experienced in the town-turned-city that he helped to build?

Eric Arthur presented Dr. Henry Scadding's memory of the town in the 1820s, noting that "the intersection of the future Queen and Yonge was so remote from York that travellers found it difficult to locate the few houses in the area, and that it was quite possible to be lost in the surrounding woods and swamps."[340]

T.A. Reed in Eric Arthur's book, *Toronto: No Mean City*, observed that in 1833, the corner of King and Yonge Streets was still "'far westward of the town proper, the venture of a store…in 1833 being described as 'wild and foolish'."[341] He continues: "There were neither sidewalks, drains nor sewers, no water supply except from wells, no attempt at street lighting, nothing indeed that placed the city above the average of any frontier town. When an enquiry was made into the causes of the cholera epidemic of 1832, a disaster that was repeated in 1834, these primitive conditions were blamed, together with the universal practice of allowing garbage to accumulate on the vacant lots and the curse of strong drink. During these epidemics, business came to a standstill, the streets were deserted, 25 per cent of the population were attacked and one in ten died."[342]

The 1834 population was 9,254, with assessed values of the new city's property totalling £3,450. Within seven years that assessment would rise to £81,610 and a population of 14,249.[343]

"By 1834…lordly classical pediments of a two-storey brick courthouse and similar-looking jail were self-confidently pronouncing order and civility for the little settlement of 9,000 while Renaissance stone St. James's Cathedral pontificated God's assuring presence."[344]

Architecture is the only form of fine art that is available to everyone in a community. Ewart's buildings to date—York General Hospital, *Hazelburn*, St. Paul's Roman Catholic Church, the Courthouses and Jails of York and London, the Bank of Upper Canada, *Moss Park*, the Third Parliament Buildings, Upper Canada College, Osgoode Hall, St. Andrew's Presbyterian Church and his own wharf—were all architectural examples of what J.C. Loudon called the "fine art open to the inspection of all and interesting to all."[345]

Marion MacRae believes that after "1830, Ewart abandoned active design work."[346] Her assessment is a bit premature as he did both St. Andrew's Presbyterian Church and the Wholesale Grocer's building after that date. However, his design work clearly slowed down and, in part, due to the reasons that MacRae gives: "The architectural styles best known to him were becoming increasingly unfashionable and he may have begun to suffer from the bane of many builders, hardening of the leg arteries. He nevertheless maintained a building yard and a wharf until his death. His highly lucrative construction trade was probably carried out by subcontractors, an arrangement which evidently enabled him to return frequently to Great Britain and to New York on business."[347]

One can evaluate Ewart's position in Toronto by comparing his 1833 property assessment with that of other well known citizens.[348] This comparison also provides a useful measuring stick to evaluate the relative value of one pound earned in income compared to one pound of assessment. In Ewart's case, for example, his earnings for the "planning, supervising and contracting"[349] of the East Wing of Osgoode Hall were £168, which surpassed the £140 assessed value of his home.

The roll for 1833 gives the lowest assessment as £19—for owning 2 horses and one cow. The largest assessment was for Jesse Ketchum who owned 15 city lots, 14 wooden framed homes less than two storeys, one brick two-storey home with nine fireplaces, six horses, two cows, and one pleasure wagon equalling £1,439. Ewart's friend on the Potters' Field cemetery project was Thomas Carfrae Jr. who had four city lots, one framed house under two storeys, one brick two-storey home with two fireplaces equalling £415. William Allan, the owner of *Moss Park*, had an assessment of £510. The Bank of Upper Canada was assessed at £160. William Lyon Mackenzie was assessed at £95 for one town lot, one framed wooden house and one extra fireplace. Chief Justice John Beverley Robinson's assessment was £462. The 'Honourable And Venerable John Strachan was assessed £593 for *The Palace.*

John Ewart's property assessment was £140 for his one town lot on Queen Street and one brick house with 3 fireplaces. He paid £1 7s. and 6d. in taxes that year. It appears that Ewart moved to his Front Street property in 1834 as his assessment actually went down to £138 to cover his town lot, two-storey brick home with three fireplaces, his horse and even his dog.[350] Given his property holdings in Toronto as well as the large property in present day Beaches, Ewart was a man of considerable wealth even compared to some of the members of the Family Compact described above.

Ewart's Politics

There is little to be found about John Ewart's politics. We do know that he ran unsuccessfully as a Tory in the January 1835 City Council election. The general election that year was a major loss for the Reform candidates, many of whom had won the year before, sitting on Toronto's first city council. In 1835, the seesaw of municipal politics saw the Tories win in every riding but St. Andrews. John Ewart happened to be the Tory's one losing candidate for alderman. He campaigned against John Harper (Reformer) who received 65 votes, Dr. Thomas D. Morrison (a major Reform candidate with 63 votes), Robert Stanton (Tory with 59) and Ewart with 53. However, the returns for St. Andrew's ward were invalidated. A new election was held and the four Reformers won by increased majorities.[351]

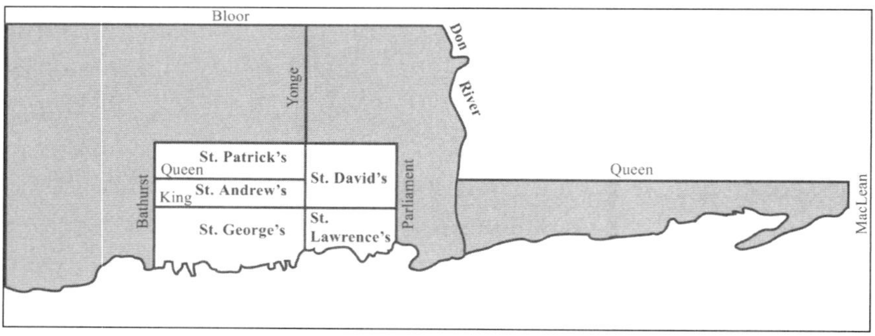

1. Political boundaries from 1834 to 1880.[352] The darker areas are the "Liberties" or suburbs that were also taxed. The Liberties were abolished in 1859. [DH]

There were only 120 voters (with two votes each) in the St. Andrew's riding. The voting list was a short one and, therefore, it was relatively easy to address each voter before an election.[353] To run for office was limited to only a few. According to the Act of Incorporation, Section 16, the requirements for an alderman were "...to have been resident householder for one year next before the election, to be so resident at the time of the election, and to be possessed of real property within the City or Liberties[354], rated at two hundred pounds."[355] Ewart's property in the Liberties (just outside the city) would have increased his assessment above the £200 mark.

In three short years the control of council went from Reform to Tory and back again. Ewart lost out on the Tory wave of 1835 but still represented what Armstrong contended were the real Tories of the new city, namely, those from the merchant rather than administrative classes, as might have been expected.[356] The administrative classes had ruled the town and much of Upper Canada to this time through the Family Compact. The city's incorporation brought out a new voting class that voted unpredictably.

Ewart's son George had greater success at the polls. Although we know little of his wholesale business dealings or his actual politics, we do know that he ran successfully six times for city alderman in St. Lawrence Ward between 1858 and 1867. He may have run unsuccessfully at other times. George's first election saw him following his brother-in-law Oliver Mowat as the alderman for St. Lawrence Ward (Mowat was the alderman in 1857). George switched wards only in 1867 when he ran successfully during Canada's Confederation year.[357]

Although John Ewart ran as a Tory he was equally comfortable in his business dealings with both Reformers and Tories. His working relationships had him working closely with leaders of both parties.[358] For example, soon after his election defeat, Ewart joined a dozen men (both Tories and Reformers) in paying for, and presenting, a plaque to honour the proud Tory leader of the Family Compact, Rev. Strachan, for his efforts during the two outbreaks of the Asiatic Cholera epidemics. The plaque was placed in St. James' Church in 1835.[359]

Life in the New Toronto

What would Ewart have seen in his day-to-day life in Toronto? There are many excellent primary sources of information about this period in Toronto's life. Here are two examples of how people viewed the young city in its first decade.

Perhaps the most uncomplimentary description of the young city was by Mrs. Jameson[360] who wrote in 1836: "[Toronto is]…most strangely mean and melancholy. A little ill-built town…some government offices, built of staring red brick, in the most tasteless, vulgar style imaginable; three feet of snow all around; and the gray, sullen, wintry lake, and the dark gloom of the pine forest bounding the prospect…' 'Two years ago' (she wrote in 1837), 'we bought our books at the same shop where we bought our shoes, our spades, our sugar, and salt pork! Now,' she had to acknowledge, 'we have two good booksellers' shops, and at one of these a circulating library of two or three hundred volumes of common novels.' She felt that a 'reasonable person' might be happy in Toronto if he or she could tolerate the flies and frogs in summer and the 'relentless iron winter.' On another occasion, she wrote of the infrequency of the mails: 'It is now seven weeks since the date of the last letters from my dear far-distant home. The archdeacon told me, by way of comfort, that when he came to settle in this country, there was only one mail-post from England the course of a whole year, and it was called, as if in mockery, 'The Express'…."[361]

Eric Arthur explains one reason why Jameson might not have enjoyed Toronto very much. She was a highly educated, talented woman, but her views may have been prejudiced by her unhappy marriage to the Attorney-General of Upper Canada whom she later left behind upon her return to Great Britain.[362]

The city now had a population of over 14,000, of which 47% were Anglican, 17% Roman Catholic, 14% Methodists (of all types), and 14% Presbyterian.[363] Although conservative in nature, special events brought out the best and worst in people. On Queen Victoria's birthday, April 2, 1840, an ox was roasted in the streets of Toronto and "everyone invited to come and slice off a piece for himself."[364] Ewart would also have seen people drink impressive quantities of liquor at this and other gatherings. A drinker was considered moderate if he or she did not "exceed four glasses in the day."[365] "People attended bees, weddings, auction sales, and other social assemblies merely for the purposes of drinking; liquor was frequently taken to revival camp-meetings and consumed by those who came to scoff but did not remain to pray. Even funeral wakes were not exempt from strong drink, and on at least one occasion 'so hilarious did the participants become that the corpse was offered a share of the beverage.'"[366]

In 1842 these types of scenes provided England's best known writer, Charles Dickens with this view: "...the town itself is full of life and motion, bustle, business and improvement."[367] Dickens continued:

The streets are well paved, and lighted with gas, the houses large and good; the shops excellent. Many of them have a display of goods in their windows, such as may be seen in thriving country towns in England; and there are some that would do no discredit to the metropolis itself. There is a good stone prison here; and there are, besides, a handsome church, a Court-house, public offices, many commodious private residences, and a Government Observatory for noting and recording the magnetic variations. In the College of Upper Canada, which is one of the public establishments of the city, a sound education in every department of polite learning can be had at a very moderate expense; the annual charge for the instruction of each pupil not exceeding nine pounds sterling. It has pretty good endowments in the way of land, and is a valuable and useful institution. The first stone of a new college

[King's College] had been laid but a few days before by the Governor General. It will be a handsome, spacious edifice, approached by a long avenue [University Avenue], which is already planted and made available as a public walk. The town is well adapted for wholesome exercise at all seasons, for the footways in the thoroughfares which lie beyond the principal street are planked like floors, and kept in very good and clean repair.[368]

On the reverse side, he was shocked into writing a friend 'the wild and rabid Toryism of Toronto, is, I speak seriously, appalling.'[369]

2. A streetscape of King Street looking east in 1847 gives a sense of the growing city as Ewart would have seen it. It was published in the *Illustrated London News*, in an article about one of the colonies' growing cities. You can see St. James Cathedral and the increased size of homes and businesses in the downtown area. [TPL *Illustrated London News*, January 30, 1847, Vol. 10, p. 68]

3. Similar streetscape to above but looking west. [TPL *Illustrated London News*, January 30, 1847, Vol. 10, p. 68]

St. Andrew's Society of Toronto (1836)

Ewart was a founder of the St. Andrew's benevolent society in 1836.[370] The St. Andrew's Society of Toronto was created to assist immigrant Scots just arriving in the new city. Its mandate has been to keep a keen interest in Toronto's Scottish people and their activities. Aid was originally given only to individual members of the Scottish community, who would be interviewed by a committee. The Society expected people receiving aid to repay the society when they could. The society continues to this day.[371] His son, George, would later become a President of the society.

The City of Toronto and Lake Huron Railroad Company (1836)

On July 11, 1836, a group of 39 men came together committed to raising subscriptions for a railway to extend from Toronto to Lake Simcoe. They were the leading Tory and Reform politicians and business people in Toronto, and leaders of the provincial government. Beside the now familiar John

Ewart, William Allan, William Ketchum, Joseph Bloor, John Elmsley, George Taylor Denison and William Henry Draper, there were also men of no particular political affiliation, such as the hatter Joseph Rogers, undertaker John Ross, retired general merchant Alexander Wood and silversmith William Stennett. "In the end, some of the gentlemen must have lost their enthusiasm because papers later noted that only £1,500 had been paid by some 29 subscribers."[372]

The railway did proceed, however, and was incorporated by an Act of Parliament. The company had capital of £500,000 in 100,000 shares at £5 each. The Board of Directors elected on July 14, 1845 were: The Hon. William Allan, President; George P. Ridout, Vice-President and the fellow board members: Clarke Gamble; William B. Jarvis, Sheriff of the Home District; John Ewart, The Hon. Henry Sherwood, Solicitor General; William H. Boulton, Toronto Mayor; William Proudfoot, President of the Bank of Upper Canada; Frederick Widder, Commissioner of the Canada Company; George Ridout; William Atkinson. The Bank of Upper Canada is listed as the Banker.[373] Ewart was on the board for 10 years.[374]

The route was expected to be a popular one and people were anxious for the line to be completed. The worldwide depression or 'panic of 1837,' slowed the process down and made construction difficult. Work began again in 1844 with the return of prosperity,[375] and on October 15, 1851, with 20,000 citizens looking on, Lady Elgin, wife of the Rt. Hon. James, Earl of Elgin and Kincardine, governor-general of British North America turned the first sod of the Ontario, Simcoe and Huron Railway. The ceremony took place in front of the Old Parliament Buildings on Front Street, just west of Simcoe Street. Less than two years later, on May 16, 1853, history was made in Toronto when the little steam engine *Toronto*, pulling three passenger cars and a freight car undertook the first scheduled railway trip out of the young city.

4. The *Toronto* was the first locomotive manufactured in Canada West, in May 1853 [TPL T-13602]

The destination was Machell's Corners (now Aurora), and the trip was completed successfully in a little over two hours. Within a few weeks the tracks of the O.S.&H. (known affectionately as the Oats, Straw and Hay and soon to be renamed the Northern Railway of Canada) had been pushed through to Bradford, then Allandale (now part of Barrie) and by January of 1855, to Collingwood on Georgian Bay. Further extensions took the Northern to Orillia, Gravenhurst, Muskoka Wharf and on a spur out of Collingwood to Meaford.

With the opening of the Northern Railway to Collingwood, it became possible to transport grain from the mid-Western United States that arrived in Collingwood by barge direct to the 37,000 hungry citizens of Toronto by train. This saved on time and money incurred if one shipped via Georgian Bay, the Detroit and St. Clair Rivers, Lake Erie, the Welland Canal and Lake Ontario—a trip of at least three weeks even with favourable winds. In 1888, the Northern became part of the Grand Trunk empire which in turn re-emerged in 1923 as part of the Canadian National Railway System.[376]

The line was "one of the most successful Canadian railways" and "one of the major factors in the rapid commercial and industrial expansion of the city."[377] Ewart would live to see the line's extension to Collingwood.

St. James' Church/Cathedral
(Rebuilding the Church after the 1839 Fire)

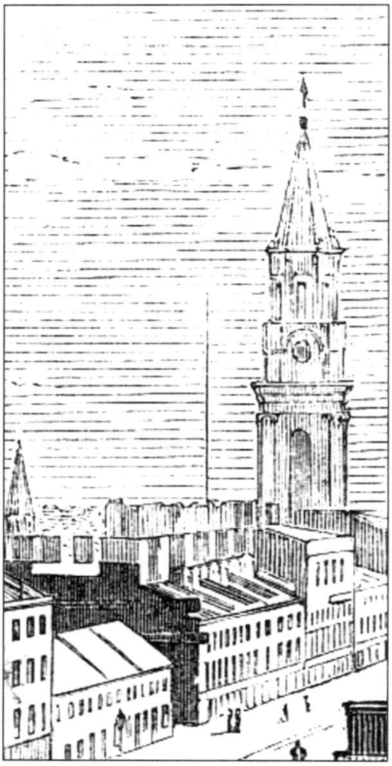

5. Cropped to show St. James Cathedral as Ewart rebuilt it in 1839 before the great fire of 1849. [TPL *Illustrated London News*, January 30, 1847, Vol. 10, p. 68]

John Ewart was contracted by Reverend Strachan to rebuild St. James' Church of England after the 1839 fire. Along with St. Paul's Roman Catholic and St. Andrew's Presbyterian Churches, Ewart had now worked on the three most important church buildings in York and early Toronto.

"In January 1839 the 'exceedingly beautiful Church', as Dr. Strachan described it, was partially destroyed by fire. Only the walls remained. The loss of the recently installed organ was a bitter blow. The proposed tower and bells had not yet been added."[378]

J.S. Buckingham, in his work *Canada, Nova Scotia, New Brunswick*, published in 1843, writes about Toronto's churches: "The largest and handsomest is that for the Established Church of England. This was partially destroyed by fire a few years since and has been recently rebuilt from the subscriptions of the inhabitants. Nearly all of the more wealthy families here belong to the Establishment....The Kirk of Scotland, also an Established church in the colonies stands near it, and though smaller is a fine building. The Roman Catholic Church in size and rank of architecture comes next to the two named. The three churches (which had been named in reverse order of construction dates) were all the work of John Ewart, the first architectural designer of demonstrable merit to appear in York...He rebuilt the 1839 version of St. James' Church of England on King Street."[379]

The year after its fire, the Anglican Diocese of Toronto was created and the Rev. John Strachan made its first Bishop. He had the church rebuilt as a cathedral that survived until the Great Fire of 1849.[380]

MacRae and Adamson describe Ewart's "unenviable task at St. James' had been to rebuild that edifice following its destruction by fire in 1839. He had been instructed to reproduce the preceding building but to give it a higher ceiling, greater length in the nave, and a different pulpit[381]...It was very much a church designed by the building committee, and the grateful sigh with which its builders turned over completion of the bell tower to John G. Howard carries down the years. Howard does not appear to have fared much better at the hands of the building committee; the abridgement of a spire, which incurred James Buckingham's censure, was his contribution."[382]

Any artist will tell you that working on a project with a committee is tantamount to cause for quitting the job. While one member recommends one course of action, another will recommend the opposite. To please everyone means pleasing no one and the final work is rarely what the architect or builders had recommended from the start.

St. James' Cathedral stood for only ten more years. Another great fire consumed the rebuilt cathedral church. Its replacement still stands today.[383]

Great West Railway Company (1845)

Although John Ewart was already on the boards of the City of Toronto and the Lake Huron Railroad Company, he believed that another railway line was needed to enter Toronto from the west. The Great Western Railway was the second company to link with Toronto. First chartered in 1834 by Sir Allan MacNab, it was reorganized in 1845 to serve Western Ontario from Windsor to Niagara.[384] In London, Colonel Talbot was the guest of honour at the groundbreaking, just two years before his death.[385]

Randall White describes how the "Canadian canal system, begun in the 1820s to support Montreal's empire of the St. Lawrence, was completed in 1848 with the opening of the new canals on the upper St. Lawrence River. But railways were the new transportation technology. Four major lines completed in the 1850s brought the age of steam to Canada West and began to transform economic and social life in the region. By 1855 the Great Western Railway had linked Windsor (and Detroit), and Hamilton, while a branch line also linked Toronto, Hamilton, and Niagara. In the same year the Northern Railway was completed, linking Collingwood on Georgian Bay with Toronto, thus reviving in a new form the old Toronto Passage. It brought grain from the upper lakes of the American Midwest and a tremendous lumber trade to Toronto. The British-backed Grand Trunk Railway had linked Montreal and Toronto by 1856 as well as Toronto and Sarnia in 1859. Early in 1858 Buffalo interests completed the Buffalo and Lake Huron Railway, linking Goderich on Lake Huron with Fort Erie on the Niagara River."[386]

6. Sir Allan MacNab was speaker of the House of Assembly and helped suppress the Rebellion of 1837. [TPL T-13738]

To help raise money for the building of the Great West Railroad Company, Ewart joined Sir Allan MacNab, future Coalition Premier of Canada East and West (1854) and owner of Dundurn Castle in Hamilton, on a trip to England in 1845. MacNab was the archetype of the Upper Canadian Tory.[387] As Speaker of the Legislature, MacNab "ruled that no motion should be put in the French language. Having thus embarrassed his colleagues and comforted his enemies [who thought him opposed to all francophones], he went happily off to England with John Ewart to sell stock in the Great Western Railway."[388]

Marion MacRae writes in *MacNab of Dundurn* that "Mr. Ewart and Sir Allan made a forceful team. Sir Allan had limitless faith in Canada. John Ewart was one of that growing company of men of enquiring mind and technical skill who cannot contemplate a river or an ocean without setting to work at once that they may bridge the one or float ships on the other. Ewart gave devout thanks for James Watt, Matthew Boulton and George Stephenson who made possible tidy, organized rapid land travel. The bridge building would be endless; the miles of steel could go on and on; the switches, the signals, the shops….Marvelous!…The persuasions of MacNab and Ewart were most effective and they were jubilant. Fifty-five thousand shares of stock in the Great Western had been sold to eleven investors."[389]

Throughout this process, the 48-year old MacNab and Ewart (now 57) became friends. For example, MacNab and Ewart may have collaborated on the dining room mantelpiece at Dundurn Castle.[390] Another example occurred when MacNab was Speaker of the legislature in Montreal in 1846. His daughter Sophia writes about a family trip to witness a military review on June 18. "Mr. and Mrs. Ewart, Papa, Minnie and I went in the Dalys' carriage. Lord Cathcart and his staff were there. Mrs. and Miss Campbell were striding about the battlefield with the Governor and his staff. There was a sham fight in simulation of the Battle of Waterloo."[391]

The Great Western Railway line was opened from its origins in Hamilton to Toronto in 1854. The company used the First Union Station at Front and York streets until its own station could be built.[392]

In 1882, the Great Western amalgamated with the Grand Trunk to form the line that eventually became Canadian National. [The station] was destroyed by fire on May 17, 1952.

7. View of the Great Western Railway Station by Frederic V. Poole as seen in the *Canadian Illustrated News* in its issue of 2 April 1870. Ewart helped found this railway link to Toronto beginning in 1845. [TPL T-12182]

Ewart's Positions on Boards of Directors and Commissions

There is very little information about the details of John Ewart's involvement in the various organizations we have mentioned. The following list of organizations comes to us through City Directories. No dates are given on the digital records of the Toronto Public Library's City Directory listings but they are clearly after incorporation of the city in 1834 up to Ewart's death in 1856. Some of the information would come from George Walton, the compiler (1833-34) of The York Commercial Directory, York. It includes information on his personal holdings. For example, there is a notation about "Ewart's Wharf on Bay Shore, John Ewart, builder, at 30 Front

Street and William Ewart also at 30 Front Street (the family home)."[393]

The following list of eight organizations provides evidence of Ewart's activities in the business community in the latter part of his life. We can presume that his contacts within the community, his own business dealings, his political connections and his social standing all contributed to his being sought after to help with organizations, whether old or new.

Building and Loan Society

In 1844 Ewart joined a group of other builders and architects (including Henry Bowyer Joseph Lane, Thomas Storm, and William Thomas) on a committee chaired by William Henry Boulton to form a building and loan society.[394]

British America Fire & Life Assurance Company

Incorporated by an Act of Parliament, this corporation had capital of £100,000 in shares of £12 10s. each. Its Board of Directors were: John William Allan, Governor; J.S. Baldwin, Deputy Governor; D'Arcy Boulton, Alexander Burnside, John Ewart, Mr. Sheriff Jarvis, Alex Hamilton, James Newbigging, Peter Patterson, William Proudfoot, George P. Ridout, Simon Washburn, Charles Stotesbury, George Duggan, Jr., Dr. Deihl, John Ellah, and Thomas Helliwell. The Trustees were Alex Burnside, John Ewart and William Proudfoot. The Bank of Upper Canada is listed as the Bank. This company had offices on Adelaide Street opposite the Bank of Upper Canada.[395]

The Bible Society

Located at 23 Yonge Street, the Bible Society was under the patronage of His Excellency Sir Charles T. Metcalfe, the Governor General of Canada. The Honourable John Henry Dunn was President. The Vice-Presidents were: Dr. Baldwin, Hon. Robert Baldwin, John James E. Small, Jesse Ketchum,

Hon. L.P. Sherwood, Rev. Dr. Harris, Charles C. Small, George Monroe, Col. Philpotts, John Ewart, Rev. William Rintoul, Rev. J.J. Grasett, Rev. John Ross, Rev. W.T. Leach, Rev. William Ryerson, Rev. James Richardson, Rev. Dr. McCaul, Peter Paterson, Rev. James Harris, Thomas Champion, and the Hon. J.S. Macaulay.[396]

Court of Requests

The Court of Requests came under the Home District legal process and related to matters of debts owed. The No. 3 Division represented the City of Toronto and the Townships of York and Scarborough. The Commissioners were: John Ewart, George Gurnett, Peter Paterson, William Stennett, Alexander Burnside and George Duggan, Jr. The Clerk was George Walton and the Bailiffs were William Higgins and Thomas Metcalf. The Court sat on the first and third Saturday in every month and the office was open daily from 10:00 a.m. to 3:00 p.m.[397]

The Toronto Bowling Club and the Toronto Cricket Club

Ewart was the President of both of these clubs in 1840.[398]

Toronto Curling Club

Ewart was a manager of the Toronto Curling Club along with Thomas Aitkin, Robert Mitchell, George Denholm, Robert G. Anderson, John Helliwell. The President in this City Directory listing (undated) was Dr. F.S. Primrose with Angus Morrison and Alex. Badenach, Vice-Presidents.[399]

Ewart's sons, Thomas and John Jr., were avid curlers. In a match on February 5, 1840 they played against their counterparts from Scarborough on Toronto Bay. There were 24 players aside on three rinks with one stone each. The game was for 93 shots or for the greatest number at half-past four o'clock. Scarborough won that match by 40 shots. "His Excellency the

Governor General was on the ice, and appeared to take much interest in the progress of the match, entering into conversation with the players regarding the game. His Excellency, Sir George Arthur and suite were also present part of the day."[400]

Toronto General Hospital

8. Toronto General Hospital (1854 to 1921) was at the corner of Gerrard, east of Parliament. This photo was taken in 1868. [TPL T-10971]

Ewart was a trustee along with: Hon C. Widmer (President), Rev. J.J. Grasett, James F. Smith, J.A. Armstrong, William Ross, George P. Ridout, Clarke Gamble, Thomas D. Harris and Alex. Dixon, Esquires. Mrs. E. Cooper was the Head Nurse or Matron.[401] As designer and builder of the first York General Hospital, we do not know if he was involved in discussions on the design and construction of this impressive, much larger building during his term as trustee.

Provincial Lunatic Asylum (1846-1850)

"In the early days of York-Toronto the insane were confined in jail,[402] in a wing of the Front Street Parliament Buildings[403] and in King's College. In 1841 John Ewart, Robert Sympson Jameson, Dr. William Charles Gwynne and William Botsford Jarvis were named to a board to supervise the province's temporary lunatic asylum.[404]

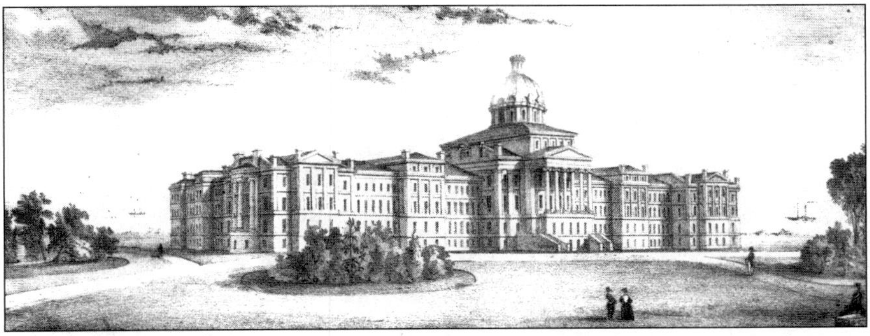

9. The Provincial Lunatic Asylum as originally proposed. In Mr. Howard's diary he states on September 28, 1846 that "Mr. Ewart and Johnstone came about lithographing the perspective view of the Asylum."[405] The cupola on the roof was designed to hold water with gravity providing the pressure to permit running water throughout the building. [TPL T-10262]

On August 3, 1844 John G. Howard submitted a request to General Metcalfe to be named architect for the Provincial Lunatic Asylum. He won the competition for this building in part due to the "joint testimonial from John Strachan, Christopher Widmer and John Ewart."[406] Another reason for the success of the design of Canada's first Mental Asylum was the new idea of treating 'lunatics' as patients in a hospital….John Howard's grandiose plans, as in the lithograph pictured above, were not entirely carried out due to problems with the budget. The Greek portico and flanking wings had to be abandoned, but it still became the largest building in Canada when completed in 1858....The central dome, covered by glittering galvanized iron which could be seen for miles, contained a huge water tank which provided the luxury of running water[407]. A spectacular spiral staircase rose through the dome to the cupola above."[408]

10. John G. Howard as drawn by George D'Almaine with Howard's own drawing of the Third Parliament Buildings in the background. This was done during the time that Howard was surveying the harbour (circa 1835). [TPL T-13710]

Howard writes in his journal that Ewart "shewed him the Plan for the Reservoir". Ewart had suggested a reservoir and waterworks for supplying the asylum and city with fresh lake water.[409] Ewart also helped get approval for the plans by going with Howard and James G. Chewett to Montreal to present plans for the asylum to Colonel C.B. Holloway, commanding officer of the Royal Engineers.[410]

11. Imposing 1868 photo by famous Montreal photographer, William Notman, of the asylum on Queen Street West, known for years as "999", north of the Garrison and opposite Ossington Avenue. [TPL T-10966]

Ewart's Diverse Interests

Ewart's curiosity never seemed to diminish. In his Journals of John G. Howard 1833-1849, Howard provides us with a chronological sketch of his evolving working relationship with Ewart, who is mentioned in each volume.

The two men had grown close professionally, with the older Ewart encouraging the work of the younger Howard. Howard was one of the few Torontonians to keep notes that survive. Here is a sampling of the entries that testifies to Ewart's diverse interests. His spelling and punctuation have not been corrected.

February 23, 1836
"2 hours of the time Measuring for Mr. Ewart at his wharf. Mr. Chewett came. Staid [sic] till 7. At Ewart's Plans till 10."[411]

September 21, 1841
"Mr. Ewart likewise wrote in it recommending me to them at Kingston to work the Plans for the New University."[412]

May 11, 1843
"…then to Mayor's office. Saw a model for a Block Pavement submitted by Mr. Ewart."[413]

March 12, 1844
"Mr Ewart came and gave me a job to design a house for him."

March 27, 1844
"took Mr. Morrison and Ewart's sketches to them."[414]

August 3, 1844
Howard submitted a request to be named architect for the Provincial Lunatic Asylum "accompanying his letter with a joint testimonial from John Strachan, Christopher Widmer and John Ewart." [this document is in the Public Archives of Canada RG5 C1 Vol. 133][415]

October 7, 1844
"met Ewart re: Toronto General Hospital where Ewart was a trustee."[416]

There are 45 citations to Ewart in the Index for 1845 including April 18 when Howard, Ewart and Chewett went to Montreal to present plans for the asylum to Colonel C.B. Holloway, commanding officer of the Royal Engineers.[417]

June 4, 1846
"met with Ewart to discuss site of 'proposed New Potters' field burial

ground. On June 15th met Ewart at Necropolis site and then they went to the asylum construction site together."[418]

June 4, 1847
re: survey of Ewart's Kingston Road property with his house on the property.[419]

June 4, 1847
"Mr Ewart came. Gave me instructions to prepare Plans and Specifications for a Temporary Hospital" [in his role as trustee for Toronto General Hospital][420]

February 21, 1848
"Mr Ewart called to day about making him a Plan of a Gun for which he talks of taking out a Patent. He staid [sic] ½ an hour."[421]

Family Life

The year 1846 was a happy time for Ewart, for other reasons. Jane, his youngest daughter, married Oliver Mowat[422] on May 19 at St. Andrew's Presbyterian Church with Rev. Dr. Jennings officiating.[423] Mowat began his courtship of Jane on visits to the Ewart home to visit one of his closest friends, Jane's brother Thomas.[424] Oliver met and fell in love with Jane during these visits. "Gracious, attractive, and accomplished, she was quite different from the 'unthinking, unintelligent' girls whom he so much disliked. Her background was similar to his own in many ways.[425] C.R.W. Biggar writes of these meetings this way: "In this household he found the helpmate of his life, and wooed and won the youngest daughter of the house, the 'beautiful Miss Ewart' as she was commonly called."[426]

12. Jane Ewart portrait by Théophile Hamel in 1852 when she was 28 years old. [ROM 991.181.2]

13. Sir Oliver Mowat who would become Canada's longest serving Premier (of Ontario, October 1872-July 1896) and then Lieutenant Governor. [JEF]

The Mowats started their married life in a rented brick house, part of a three-storied row on the east side of Bay Street south of King. As a wedding present, John Ewart gave his daughter "in consideration of five shillings and natural love and affection" the land for their future home, *Northfield*. At the time of the gift, Jarvis was just a dirt road with a small creek on one side and a narrow plank sidewalk on the east side.[427]

Northfield would later be a substantial house and with it "Mowat led the way in the development of upper Jarvis Street, and provided early proof of the first category mentioned in Sam Jarvis's advertisement that his lots would be found 'peculiarly eligible for the residence of private families' as well as for men of commerce or 'mechanics.' Mowat's *Northfield* was among the first houses built on Jarvis Street that attained the grace and style of a so-called private family residence…It had a frontage on Jarvis Street of nearly 1,200 feet, and Mowat and his brother-in-law George Ewart subdivided it in 1861. Their registered plan extended from Carlton Street to Maitland Street.[428]

14. View of *Northfield* today. [JEF]

"Jane's father," according to Margaret Evans, "like John Mowat[429] in Kingston [Oliver's father], took a prominent part in the general life of early Toronto. He was a founder of St. Andrew's Church in connection with the Church of Scotland, the first president of the York Mechanics' Institute, a middle-class society for continuing education. He was a petitioner in 1831 for extension of the benefits of an education at Upper Canada College to sons of less well-to-do families through lowered fees and a modified curriculum."[430]

There was another wedding in 1846. Ewart's son, Thomas (aged 27), married Catherine Skirving (aged 26). They would have three children: Jane Emily (b. 1847) from whom my family line would eventually evolve; John Skirving (b. 1849); and Louise (b 1851). Thomas was a law student with Oliver Mowat and the two formed a law firm together after graduation. Of

Thomas, Mowat wrote to his brother, John, on November 12, 1840: "Among the Toronto law students that I have met with, a son of John Ewart, Esq., a retired merchant and staunch 'kirker' is decidedly the most sensible and studious."[431]

15. Thomas Ewart [JEF]

16. Catherine Skirving Ewart [JEF]

Thomas, born in 1819, went into a thriving law practice with Messrs Mowat and Helliwell. His family was growing with two young children and a loving wife. All of this was shattered in his early 30s by a diagnosis of tuberculosis.

Thomas Ewart's granddaughter, Mabel Ewart (Steele) Grubbe, described in family notes some of the details of Thomas' illness. Together with his father and brother George, Thomas travelled south from Toronto in January 1850 to find relief from his condition in the warmer climate of the southwestern U.S. "From New York they sailed on the steam vessel *Southerner* for $25 each to Charleston. Another steamer took them to Savannah in 4 or 5 hours and then another to Jacksonville, Florida. The party stayed over several days in

Savannah, a city which exports large quantities of cotton and rice. Roses were in full bloom and ripe oranges on the trees. They went horse back riding. Steamer *St. Matthews* to Jacksonville, this route was mostly inland, sometimes the steamer was grounded when the tide was out. $2.00 a piece for the passage. Horseback riding again. A good deal of rainy weather, temperature in the 60s, usually they travelled north in February, left Jacksonville February 27th, 1850 for St. Augustine where they enjoyed the long walks and some horseback riding. Returned home via Richmond".[432]

"In October 1850, Thomas and wife Catherine (Kate) Skirving sailed for the island of Madeira still in search of a healthful climate. They left their two children Jane Emily and John with Tom's sister, Jane Ewart Mowat[433], in Toronto and stayed in Funchal, Madeira, until Tom died on March 22nd, 1851. Kate, six months pregnant with her third child, sailed on April 3rd from Funchal back to Toronto via Southampton and New York. Her daughter, Louise, was born in Toronto on July 2, 1851."[434]

We have no record of the heartbreak of John and Jane Ewart at the passing of yet another child. We cannot project 21st century grief onto those of another era, where early death was more common. They had already lived through the infant deaths of Jenniot, Agnes, James, and the first John Jr. between 1814 to 1816 in England. In 1835, when most of Ewart's architectural work was completed, his second son named James, died of drowning, aged 10. His oldest son William would be killed in unknown circumstances, in 1843 at the age of 21. Two years before his own death, Ewart's son-in-law James Maxwell Strange (married to Margaret) would die. Subsequent to Ewart's own death, Jane would go through the loss of two more children: daughter Margaret Ewart Strange in 1860 and the suicide of her second son John Jr. in 1861.

John Ewart Jr. (1822-1861) was a bachelor. He shared some property with his father along Jarvis Street and may have been part of running the family building yard beside Ewart's Wharf.[435] He also owned a wholesale dry-goods shop at 23 Front Street in partnership with Messrs. Bowes and Hall. His home was at 148 Yonge Street, also listed in John Ewart's name.[436] On 2 July 1861, John Ewart Jr. committed suicide, without recorded explanation. "He had been executor with Oliver Mowat of Margaret's estate (Jane's sister) and joint guardian of her four children. Exactly three months later, the youngest Mowat child, fourteen-month-old John, died."[437] The devastation such an event would create for his mother, sisters and Margaret's children is not recorded anywhere.

17. John Ewart, Jr. [TPL T-35169]

George Ewart, (1828-1870) the youngest child of John and Jane Ewart, was a proprietor and merchant who had a shop in the east side of the St. Lawrence Market according to advertisements in the Scotsman of the period and occupied some property leased to him by his father, John Ewart, at the corner of King and Yonge Streets. He married Agnes S. Rogers (1835-1877) and they had three children: John, George and Clara. As we saw earlier, George won six elections as a city alderman.

Howard Joy, a direct descendant, recounts family legend that George was killed in 1870 during a mutiny upon one of the ships that docked at Ewart's Wharf. George was 42 years old at the time. His wife, Agnes, would die seven years later, (also at the age of 42) leaving her three children in the care of Jane Mowat and her husband Oliver, then the Premier of Ontario. The youngest, Clara, lived in the Mowat home on Simcoe Street while the boys boarded at Upper Canada College. Clara could see the school from her home and the boys visited on the weekends.

John Ewart's Death (1856)

Ewart died on September 18, 1856 at the age of 68 of gangrene, a common ailment among builders whose arteries hardened from their labour.[438] *The Globe* obituary appeared two days later on Saturday, September 20, 1856 in this way: "Death notice: on the 18th last, John Ewart, Esq., of the city, aged 68. The funeral will take place to-morrow (Sunday) at 8 o'clock p.m. from the residence of the deceased on Front Street. Friends and acquaintances are hereby invited to attend without further notice."[439] Ewart was buried in his Necropolis Cemetery in Section M, Lot 98 with a tomb stone approximately 10 feet high topped by a Celtic cross. He also owned Lot 94 for other family members.

18. The Ewart Monument in the Necropolis Cemetery, Toronto. [JEF]

Only nine months before, he would have celebrated his son-in-law's appointment (Oliver Mowat) as a Queen's Counsel on the recommendation of his former law master, John A. Macdonald, then the attorney general for Canada West. "The dinner to celebrate Oliver's QC was the last given by the Mowats in the Church Street cottage. Their new house, 'Northfield', in the fashionable residential area on the west side of Jarvis Street north of Carlton, was almost ready. In this luxurious Georgian-style home there was plenty of space for their four children: Jane Helen, now almost nine; Frederick, five; the two-year old Laura, born 23 May 1853; and the baby Arthur, born 29 October 1855. The grounds were large enough to keep horses for riding, which was still a popular form of relaxation for Oliver and Jane."[440] The house was admired throughout the city for its stately drawing rooms, well-stocked library and several large fireplaces.[441]

At the time of his death, Ewart owned a substantial piece of the Coffin Block[442] (his office would be located in present-day Berczy Park) and a substantial piece of property around Jarvis and Carlton Streets which he had purchased from Samuel Jarvis in 1843.[443] He also owned a larger estate, a lot east of Woodbine Avenue. "The Ewart Estate was undivided on the 1884 Goad's Atlas of the City of Toronto just east one lot size from Woodbine Avenue. Ewart's estate includes part of the area called "Norway" after the Norway Steam Saw Mill at the intersection of Woodbine and Kingston Roads 'which started in 1835 and supplied white pine, hemlock, oak and particularly valuable and scarce article, the Norway Pine.'"[444] In an 1892 map, it shows the Ewart estate near Woodbine as being subdivided below Kingston Road and undivided north of it. The northern part is owned by Justice Maclennan. Kenilworth and Waverley are new streets running north and south on the old Ewart Estate.[445] He owned 148 Yonge Street in addition to his 30 Front Street address.[446]

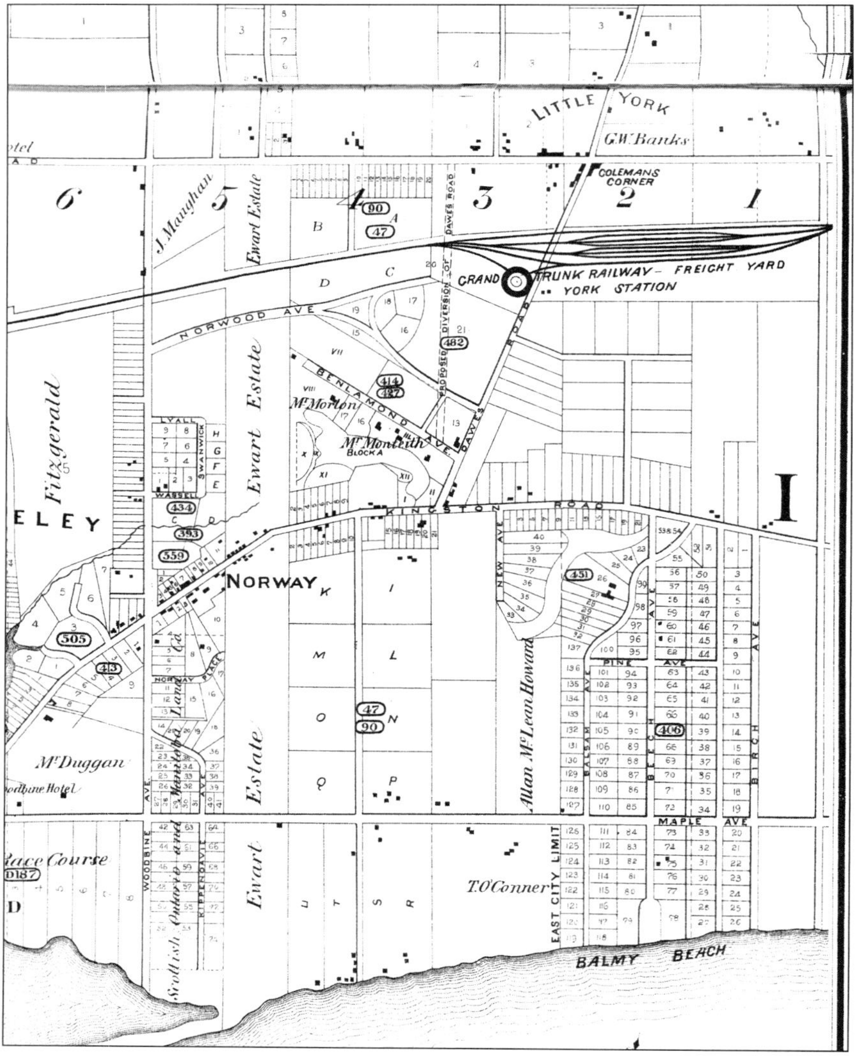

19. The Ewart Estate's property starting at the beach up to Danforth Road. Present-day Woodbine Ave. is just to the west of the Ewart property while Kingston Road bisects it at the community of Norway. [TPL cropped Goad Map of 1884, p. 38]

Ewart's Last Will and Testament[447] (dated 1854, after his daughter, Margaret's husband died) was witnessed by Joshua E. Cooper of Toronto and Andrew Patterson, a merchant in Belleville. Below are the extracts of its most important points:

Fourth point: "I give to my Wife Jane an annuity of two hundred and fifty pounds a year for her life such Annuity to commence from my decease—and to be paid quarterly the first of these payments to be made in three Calendar months after my decease. This Annuity is to be accepted by my said Wife in lieu of her Dower in all and every part of the real Estate which I may have at the time of my death."

Fifth point: "I likewise bequeath to my said wife all her own wearing apparel, trinkets and other personal ornaments and all the Household Goods furniture pictures books plates linen and provisions which may be in my house at the time of my death."

Sixth point: £1,000 to granddaughter Elizabeth Strange when she becomes 21 or is married.

Seventh point: "I forgive to my son George one thousand pounds of the amount which he may owe me at the time of my death if he should happen to owe me less than one thousands pounds then I forgive him the amount of his indebtedness to me whatever the same may be at the time of my decease."

Eighth point: "I direct the residue of my real and personal Estate to be divided as follows:" [summarized below]

1/5 of estate each to sons John and George, daughters Margaret and Jane and late son Thomas' family.

Ninth point: Re: estate portion for Thomas's widow and children (pages long)

Tenth point: If any of his children die before him, their 1/5 share be divided among the spouse and children.

Eleventh: appoints sons John and George and daughter Margaret Strange and son-in-law Oliver Mowat as executors. If Mowat dies before Ewart, Jane will become executrix as well.

Ewart's estate was estimated at £100,000[448] making him one of the wealthier men in Toronto. Put into context, his estate was larger than the total assessed property values of Toronto in 1841 (£81,610 for a population of 14,249).[449] Five years before his death in 1856, the total assessment for the city was only £186,983, with a population of 30,775.[450] In different terms, his estate was worth ten times the cost of constructing the largest building in York in 1832, the Third Parliament buildings.[451]

By the time of Ewart's death, Toronto had grown to over 30,000 people and was now second only to Montreal as a major colonial trading hub, as well as the military and government centre of what would soon be Ontario.[452] Toronto was still far away from being a metropolis, however. Even at Confederation, a decade after Ewart's death, log dwellings still accounted for almost half of all housing in Ontario.[453] Eric Arthur describes it as a "nice Georgian town with an esplanade, and its water front as yet undefiled by railways and industry."[454]

20. Two years before Ewart's death W. Whitfield did a lithograph of the waterfront and city from atop the jail giving an eastern viewpoint. We have divided the print into two close-ups of the built-up city to show the bustling harbour, the steeples of the St. James Cathedral and the wide esplanade. This half shows the bustling harbour. [TPL T-32081]

21. The second half of W. Whitfield's drawing shows the steeples of the St. James Cathedral and the wide esplanade. Three and four storey buildings are now quite typical compared to what Ewart saw a scant 36 years before upon his arrival in York. [TPL T-32081]

Remnants of the early city of Toronto can be seen on walking tours throughout the 'old town' and 'new town' of what is now the downtown core of the city. Little of Ewart's architecture remains except for Osgoode Hall and the Bank of Upper Canada buildings in Toronto and the Middlesex Courthouse in London, Ontario. What he started, however, would be built upon by the second and third generation of architects and builders, such as John George Howard.

The measure of a person's worth cannot be described by the value of their estate, nor their accumulated awards or honours. Ewart's legacy can only be measured by the journey he took, his responses to the triumphs and tragedies of life, and how he fulfilled his dreams and met his obligations. Mostly, his legacy can be measured by whether his life made a positive difference to those around him. By that measure, John Ewart, Upper Canada's first architect in York and London, left an impression that lasts to the present day. His buildings were the landmarks of his day. His community services led to Toronto's public library system and the Mount Pleasant Group of Cemeteries. His corporate and political work influenced the leadership of the time. Historical societies and building sites in Toronto and London all exemplify some of the fruits of his labour over 150 years ago. His efforts were part of the first building blocks that were to help Toronto eventually become one of the world's great cities.

---

340 Eric Arthur. (1964). *Toronto: No Mean City*, p. 54.

341 *Ibid*, pp. 54 & 55: from "The Story of Toronto" in Ontario Historical Society, *Papers and Records*, 1934. Vol. XXX, pp. 205 & 206.

342 Eric Arthur. (1964). *Toronto: No Mean City*, pp. 54 & 55: from "The Story of Toronto" in Ontario Historical Society, *Papers and Records*, 1934. Vol. XXX, p. 206. Accurate statistics for this period are difficult to establish, but in 1832 probably out of a population of 5,502, there were 535 cases of cholera and 205 deaths, Arthur endnote, p. 241.

343 J.M.S. Careless. (1984). *Toronto to1918*, p. 203.

344 Patricia McHugh. (1989). *Toronto Architecture: A City Guide*, p. 8.

345 Ewart's signed copy of Loudon's book, (1833). *An Encyclopedia of Cottage, Farm and Villa Architecture*, p. 1 of the Preface.

346 *Dictionary of Canadian Biography.* Vol. VIII, pp. 281-282, "John Ewart", by Marion MacRae.

347 *Dictionary of Canadian Biography.* Vol. VIII, pp. 281-282, "John Ewart", by Marion MacRae.

348 J. Ross Robertson. (1896). *Landmarks of Toronto.* Vol. 1: pp. 367-376 the assessment roll for York 1833 based on the assessments recorded in Walton.

349 Marion MacRae and Anthony Adamson. (1983). *Cornerstones of Order*, p. 47. Christopher Moore's footnote in (1997). *The Law Society of Upper Canada and Ontario's Lawyers 1779-1997*, p. 82.

350 J. Ross Robertson. (1896). *Landmarks of Toronto,* Vol. 1: p. 406.

351 (Council Journal, 13 February 1835; *Patriot* 20 February 1835).

352 J.M.S. Careless. (1984). *Toronto to 1918*, p. 126.

353 According to the statute incorporating the City of Toronto (4 William IV c. 23) article 18, voting was restricted to "male Inhabitant Householders". Householder meant owning or renting a "Town Lot or Dwelling-house...Provided always that a portion of a House in which any Inhabitant shall reside as a Householder, and not as a Boarder or Lodger, and having a distinct communication with the street by an outer door, shall be considered a Dwelling-house within the meaning of this Clause". Voters had to have lived in the city for 12 months, and in the ward for three months, before the election.

354 Land just beyond the city limits at Queen Street to the north.

355 Act of Incorporation for the City of Toronto, 4th William IV., Cap. 23, Section 16.

356 F.H. Armstrong. (1965). *Toronto in Transition: The Emergence of a City*, p. 11.

357 Jesse Edgar Middleton's 1923 *The Municipality of Toronto: A History, Vols. 1-3*, check index for numerous listings.

358 A quick comparison of the names of the men involved in these projects with their names on Allison Ewart and Julia Jarvis's article (1926): "The Personnel of the Family Compact, 1791-1841" in *Canadian Historical Review*, Vol. VII, No. 3 (Sept., 1926): pp. 209-221, with verify both Tory and Reformer affiliations.

359 Jesse Edgar Middleton. (1923). *The Municipality of Toronto: A History, Vols. 1-3,* pp. 168 & 169.

360 She is quoted earlier in this book about her visit with Colonel Talbot and his influences in the London area of Upper Canada.

361 Eric Arthur. (1964). *Toronto: No Mean City*, p. 54 from Anna Jameson's (reprinted 1923), *Winter Studies and Summer Ramblings.* pp. 17, 67, 89, 64. Arthur concludes that "Mrs. Jameson was a highly educated, talented woman, but her views may have been prejudiced by her unhappy marriage to the Attorney-General of Upper Canada."

362 Eric Arthur. (1964). p. 54.

363 J.M.S. Careless. (1984). *Toronto to 1918*, pp. 201 and 202.

364 *Toronto Mirror*, April 3, 1840.

[365] Edwin C. Guillet. (1933). *Pioneer Days in Upper Canada,* p. 144: letter of William Hutton in the *British Farmer's Magazine*, April 1835, p. 114.

[366] *Ibid,* p. 144: M.A. Garland and J.J. Talman. *Pioneer Drinking Habits, and the Rise of the Temperance Agitation in Upper Canada.* Ontario Historical Society, Papers and Records, Vol. XXVII, p. 345.

[367] Eric Arthur. (1964) *Toronto: No Mean City*, p. 54 from Charles Dickens, *American Notes* (Everyman ed., pp. 202-3) Quoted in John Forster's *Life of Charles Dickens* (Household ed., London, n. d.), p. 123.

[368] William Kilbourn. (ed). (1976). *The Toronto Book: An Anthology of Writings Past and Present*, p. 36.

[369] Eric Arthur. (1964) *Toronto: No Mean City*, p. 54 from Charles Dickens, *American Notes* (Everyman ed., pp. 202-3) Quoted in John Forster's *Life of Charles Dickens* (Household ed., London, n. d.) p. 123.

[370] *Dictionary of Canadian Biography.* Vol. VIII, p. 282 "John Ewart", by Marion MacRae.

[371] St. Andrew's Society's web site: www.standrews-society.ca/index.cfm

[372] F.H. Armstrong. (1988). *A City in the Making*, pp. 59 & 60.

[373] Toronto Public Library digital directories circa 1830-1860:
http://mtrl.toronto.on.ca:80….ge.html:sessionid=01-6233-41995397

[374] *Dictionary of Canadian Biography.* Vol. VIII, p. 282 "John Ewart", by Marion MacRae; Jesse Edgar Middleton. (1923). *The Municipality of Toronto: A History*, p. 226.

[375] F.H. Armstrong. (1988). *A City in the Making*, p. 67.

[376] Mike Filey. (1994). *Toronto Sketches 3*, pp. 34 & 35.

[377] F.H. Armstrong. (1988). *A City in the Making*, p. 67.

[378] Lucy Booth Martyn. (1983). *A View of Original Toronto*, p. 66.

[379] Marion MacRae and Anthony Adamson. (1975). *Hallowed Walls,* pp. 82 & 83. William Cooke makes no mention of Ewart's work on St. James, pp. 190 & 193.

[380] Nelson J. Gordon. (2001). *Old Town Toronto: A Heritage Landscape Guide*, p. 15.

[381] Marion MacRae and Anthony Adamson. (1975). *Hallowed Walls,* p. 87 upon Dr. Strachan's specific instructions.

[382] *Ibid*, p. 87.

[383] William Cooke. (1998). *The Parish and Cathedral of St. James', Toronto 1797-1997* makes no mention of Ewart in its architectural history of the era, pp. 190-193.

[384] William Dendy. (1993). *Lost Toronto*, p. 22.

[385] *Dictionary of Canadian Biography Online.* "Talbot, Thomas" by Alan G. Brunger.

[386] Randall White. (1985). *Ontario 1610-1985: A Political and Economic History.* p. 108.

[387] Marion MacRae. (1971). *MacNab of Dundurn*, pp. 107-108. For more on MacNab see Dictionary of Canadian Biography Online:
www.biographi.ca/EN/ShowBio.asp?Biold=38687.

388 Marion MacRae. (1971). *MacNab of Dundurn*, p. 107.

389 *Ibid*, pp. 107 & 108.

390 *Ibid*, pp. 129 & 130.

391 *Ibid*, p. 121.

392 William Dendy. (1993). *Lost Toronto: Images of the City's Past*, p. 22.

393 George Walton (Compiler). (1833-34). *The York Commercial Directory*. York, p. 82.

394 *Dictionary of Canadian Biography*. Vol. VIII, p. 282 "John Ewart", by Marion MacRae.

395 Toronto Public Library digital directories circa 1830-1860: http://mtrl.toronto.on.ca:80….ge.html:sessionid=01-6233-41995397

396 *Ibid.*

397 *Ibid.*

398 Jesse Edgar Middleton. (1923). *The Municipality of Toronto: A History*, p. 747; and *Dictionary of Canadian Biography*. Vol. VIII, p. 282 "John Ewart", by Marion MacRae.

399 Toronto Public Library digital directories circa 1830-1860: http://mtrl.toronto.on.ca:80….ge.html:sessionid=01-6233-41995397

400 Bea McCowan's Toronto Bay web site: www.beamccowan.com/toronto.htm.

401 Toronto Public Library digital directories circa 1830-1860: http://mtrl.toronto.on.ca:80….ge.html:sessionid=01-6233-41995397

402 When the new jail was built in 1840 the old jail built by Ewart became the first insane asylum. Lucy Booth Martyn. (1982). *The Face of Early Toronto: An Archival Record 1797-1936*, p. 14.

403 From 1849 until 1851. Mike Filey. (1994). *Toronto Sketches 3*, pp. 6 & 7.

404 *Dictionary of Canadian Biography*. Vol. VIII, p. 282 "John Ewart", by Marion MacRae.

405 John George Howard. *The Journals of John George Howard* 1833-1849. Editor Shirley G. Morriss, Vol. 6.

406 August 3, 1844, Howard's submission to be named architect is in the Public Archives of Canada [RG5 C1 Vol. 133]. Howard, John George. *The Journals of John George Howard* 1833-1849. editor Shirley G. Morriss, Vol. 4, p. 179.

407 John George Howard. *The Journals of John George Howard* 1833-1849. Editor Shirley G. Morriss, Vol. 6, p. 147. Footnote 1: Ewart was a commissioner in charge of building the Provincial Lunatic Asylum. He had suggested a reservoir and waterworks for supplying the asylum and city with fresh lake water.

408 Lucy Booth Martyn. (1982). *The Face of Early Toronto: An Archival Record 1797-1936*, p. 89.

409 John George Howard. *The Journals of John George Howard 1833-1849*. Vol. 6, p. 147, Footnote 1 January 3, 1848.

410 John George Howard. *The Journals of John George Howard 1833-1849*. Vol. 5, April 18, 1845

411 *Ibid*, Vol. 2. Footnote 9 "Ewart moved to York establishing himself as an architect and builder. He provided the city with many of its important early buildings, among them St.

Paul's Church for the Roman Catholics, and St. Andrew's for the Presbyterians, Upper Canada College, and the west wing [sic] of Osgoode Hall"

412 Howard, John George. *The Journals of John George Howard* 1833-1849. Editor Shirley G. Morriss, Vol. 3, p. 163. Reference to one of at least several commissions that Ewart gave his personal recommendation to Howard acquiring the work.

413 John George Howard. *The Journals of John George Howard* 1833-1849. editor Shirley G. Morriss, Vol. 4, p. 37. *Dictionary of Canadian Biography*. Vol. VIII, p. 282 "John Ewart", by Marion MacRae.

414 *Ibid*, Vol. 4, p. 133

415 *Ibid*, Vol. 4, p. 179.

416 *Ibid*, Vol. 4, p. 197.

417 *Ibid*, Vol. 5.

418 *Ibid*, Vol. 5, June 4, 1846.

419 *Ibid*, Vol. 6, p. 135.

420 *Ibid*, Vol. 4, Vol. 6 p. 65. On page 66 a footnote explains that a large number of Irish immigrants were arriving with diseases or were enfeebled. A shed was built onto the hospital site to receive them. The hospital was turned into an immigrant fever hospital. The regular patients were cared for in the Temple Building on King Street.

421 *Ibid*, Vol. 6, p. 165

422 See footnote 61, to understand how Oliver Mowat and writer Farley Mowat are related.

423 C.R.W. Biggar. (1905). *Sir Oliver Mowat: A Biographical Sketch: Two Volumes*, p. 39.

424 Margaret Evans. (1992). *Sir Oliver Mowat*, p. 13: She writes about: "whose good sense and studiousness [Mowat] had admired while both were law clerks under Burns."

425 Margaret Evans. (1992). *Sir Oliver Mowat,* p. 14.

426 C.R.W. Biggar. (1905). *Sir Oliver Mowat: A Biographical Sketch: Two Volumes*, p. 39.

427 Mike Filey. (1996). *Toronto Sketches 5*. This land was part of the parcel that Ewart bought from Samuel Jarvis in May 1843. Today that parcel comprises the block between Carlton and Maitland streets on the west side of Jarvis Street. Austin Seton Thompson. (1980). *Jarvis Street: A Story of Triumph and Tragedy*, p. 108.

428 Austin Seton Thompson. (1980). *Jarvis Street: A Story of Triumph and Tragedy*, p. 184. *Northfield*'s name changed to *Coverley House* after it was sold to Havergal Ladies' College in 1913. It later became the CBC Ontario Regional office buildings in 1978.

429 John Mowat, according to James King's book *The Life of Farley Mowat*, was the father of Sir Oliver Mowat. John immigrated to Upper Canada to fight in the War of 1812 and settled in Kingston in 1919 where he married Helen Levak. Their eldest of five was Sir Oliver and their third born was John Bower (one of the first three students admitted to Queen's University. John's only child, Robert McGill (Gill) was the father of Angus Mowat. Angus married Helen and they were the proud parents of one of Canada's best-loved authors, Farley Mowat, born on May 12, 1921. p. 8.

430 Margaret Evans. (1992). *Sir Oliver Mowat,* p. 14.

[431] C.R.W. Biggar. (1905). *Sir Oliver Mowat: A Biographical Sketch: Two Volumes*, p. 19.

[432] Handwritten page of notes about Thomas Ewart by his great granddaughter Mabel Ewart (Steele) Grubbe in the private papers of Janet Ewart FitzGerald.

[433] C.R.W. Biggar. (1905). *Sir Oliver Mowat :A Biographical Sketch: Two Volumes*, p. 56.

[434] Handwritten page of notes about Thomas Ewart by his great granddaughter Mabel Ewart Steele Grubbe in the private papers of Janet Ewart FitzGerald.

[435] Archives of Ontario E 17/9. Letter to L-G Maitland requesting extension of wharf and purchase of William Cooper's lot as well to build a wood yard for steamships.

[436] Toronto Public Library digital directories circa 1830-1860:
http://mtrl.toronto.on.ca:80….ge.html:sessionid=01-6233-41995397

[437] Margaret Evans. (1992). *Sir Oliver Mowat,* p. 40.

[438] *Dictionary of Canadian Biography*. Vol. VIII, pp. 281-282, "John Ewart", by Marion MacRae.

[439] P. 2, c. 8.

[440] Margaret Evans. (1992). *Sir Oliver Mowat*, p. 18.

[441] Mike Filey. (1996). *Toronto Sketches 5*.

[442] Agreement between Catherine Ewart and William Thompson regarding the Janus Buildings, Land Registry Office, #4788 SE.

[443] Mike Filey. (1996). *Toronto Sketches 5*. This land was part of the parcel that Ewart bought from Samuel Jarvis in May 1843. Today that parcel comprises the block between Carlton and Maitland streets on the west side of Jarvis Street. Austin Seton Thompson. (1980). *Jarvis Street: A Story of Triumph and Tragedy*, p. 108.

[444] Mary Campbell and Barbara Myrvold. (1988). *The Beaches in Pictures 1793-1932*, p. 6.

[445] *Ibid*, p. 8.

[446] Toronto Public Library digital directories circa 1830-1860:
http://mtrl.toronto.on.ca:80….ge.html:sessionid=01-6233-41995397

[447] Microfiche Roll: 19 128 at Land Registry, Toronto, Section Wills, File MS 638(47)

[448] Marion MacRae. *Dictionary of Canadian Biography*. Vol. VIII, p. 282.

[449] J.M.S. Careless. (1984). *Toronto to 1918*, p. 203.

[450] Ibid, p. 203.

[451] William Dendy. (1993). *Lost Toronto*, p. 52.

[452] Patricia McHugh. (1989). *Toronto Architecture: A City Guide*, p. 9.

[453] Randall White. (1985). *Ontario 1610-1985: A Political and Economic History*, p. 61.

[454] Eric Arthur. (1964). *Toronto: No Mean City*, p. 112.

APPENDIX 1
John Ewart (1788-1856) Family Tree

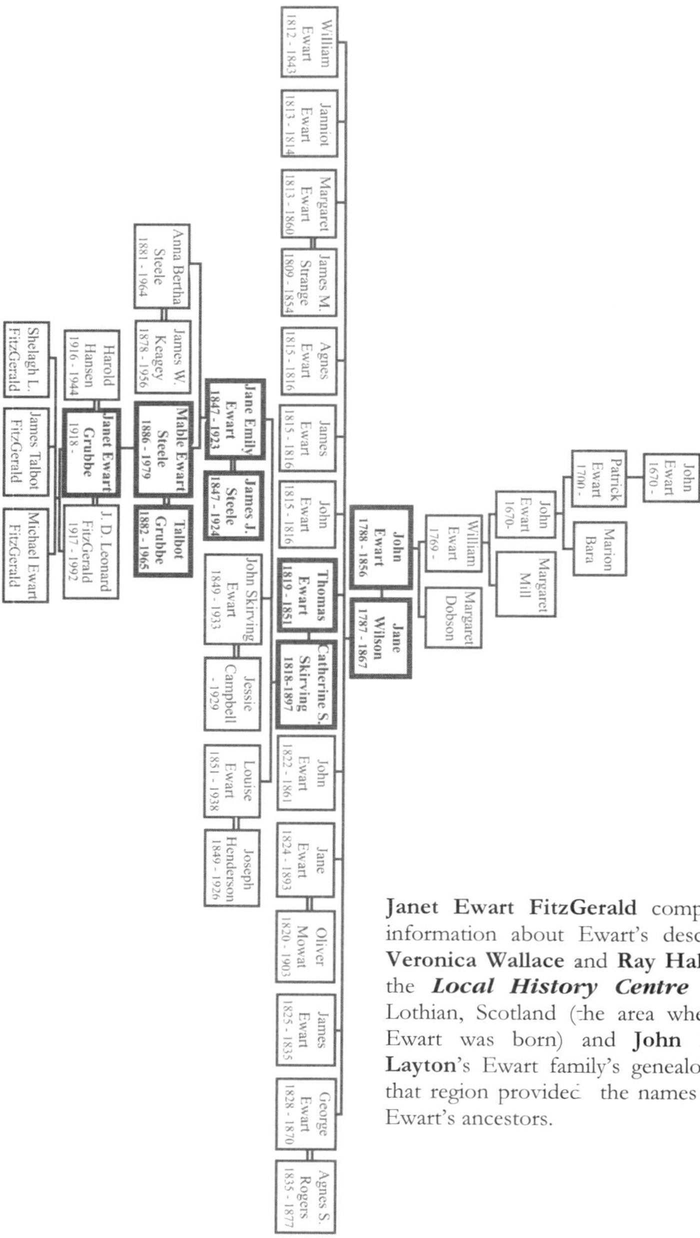

Janet Ewart FitzGerald compiled the information about Ewart's descendants. **Veronica Wallace** and **Ray Halliday** of the ***Local History Centre*** in East Lothian, Scotland (the area where John Ewart was born) and **John Richard Layton**'s Ewart family's genealogy from that region provided the names of John Ewart's ancestors.

APPENDIX 2
Historical Timeline

The following timeline places Ewart's life within the history of early York and Toronto and in the framework of related world historical events—Ewart's age is placed between brackets.

1763 British Crown imposes its own institutions onto Quebec (including what is now Ontario).

1775-83 American Revolution.

1783-84 British Loyalists migrate from US to southeastern Ontario and Niagara; Pennsylvania Germans move into southwestern Ontario.

1788 John Ewart born January 31 in East Lothian, Scotland, Baptized in Scottish Presbyterian Church (that is how birth date known). Lived in Tranent, 16 kilometres from Edinburgh, within 3 kilometres of the Firth of Forth. Town prospered since 13th century from natural resources (coal) and agriculture.

1789 [1] Outbreak of French Revolution.

1791 [3] Britain's Constitution Act divides colony into Upper Canada (capital is Niagara-on-the-Lake) and Lower Canada (capital is Quebec City).

1792-1815 Napoleonic War involving Austria, Britain, Prussia, Russia, Spain and Sweden against France.

1793 [5] Summer, Simcoe lands in Upper Canada to establish "York".

1793 Simcoe passed Act to "to prevent the introduction of slaves" making Upper Canada first British possession to legislate against slavery. (Riendeau, 1984).

1797 [9] Lord Dorchester concluded the "Toronto Purchase" which outlined an area 22 km east of the Humber River, 45 km north of the lakeshore for a total of 250,880 acres. Three Mississauga chiefs signed the agreement in exchange of £1,700, assorted goods including cloth,

	clothes, blankets, fishhooks, farm tools and about 400 litres of rum.
1805	[17] Final sale of lakefront property by The Mississaugas to Britain from Burlington Bay to Etobicoke. Further sales in 1818 and 1819 moved Mississaugas to reservations in Peterborough area.
1807	[19] Britain bans slave trade in the British Empire (750,000 slaves already living in Empire) [Pollard, page 35].
1809-11	[21-23] Tecumseh, a Shawnee chief in the Ohio Valley tries to unite Indian tribes and leaders (including Joseph Brant) to slow or halt the western expansion of the US.
Abt 1810	[22] Ewart earned his qualifications as a craftsman in Edinburgh before learning further in London and New York. May have visited Glasgow and its St. George Church by William Stark as it is quite similar to Ewart's St. Andrew's Church.
1810	Married *Jane Wilson* [23] of Cranston before moving to London.
1811	[23] Moved to London for five years. Broadened his architectural and building skills. Probably encountered works by John Soane, Nicolas Hawksmoor and Sir John Nash.
1812	[24] Birth of first child, *William* (April 5).
1812	America declares war on Britain and invades Canada from Detroit; Upper Canadians victorious at the Battle of Queenston Heights; France invades Russia and loses at Moscow.
1813	[25] Americans attack and occupy York. Tecumseh, brigadier general for the British is killed fighting for Canadian independence.
1813	[25] Birth of twins, *Margaret* and *Jenniot* (Nov 23).
1813-1815	Fort York built.

1814	[26] *Jenniot* died within two months (January 13).
1814	Dec 24, Treaty of Ghent ends War of 1812 and restores Canada-US borders.
1815	[27] Birth of triplets: *Agnes, James, John* (February 24th).
1816	[28] Deaths of the triplets (unknown why or if they died at about the same time. All died in England before family moved to New York).
1816	Moved to New York City for two years with Jane and children William (4) and Margaret (3).
1817-18	*The Grange* built in York.
1818	[30] Moved north to York, Upper Canada.
1819	[31] First steamship crosses Atlantic (*Savannah*) to America.
1819	Petitioned Lieutenant-Governor Peregrine Maitland for 200 acres of Crown "waste" land and wharf rights.
1819	*Thomas* born in York (August 12).
1820	York General Hospital (Georgian style) built.
1820s	Underground Railway would become very active with up to 3,000 helping to bring slaves into Canada until slavery abolished in 1863 by Abraham Lincoln.
1822	[34] *John Ewart Jr.* born February 25 (day after triplets born in 1815).
1822	*Hazelburn* built.
1822	*Campbell House* built.
1822	Camera invented by Niepce in France.
1823	[35] St. Paul's Roman Catholic Church (Regency style).
1823-24	Second Jail in York.
	Second Courthouse in York.
1824	[36] *Jane* born (March 5).

1824-29 Welland Canal is completed partly in response to American initiatives in building Erie Canal.

1825 [37] *James* born (May 8).

1825 Census shows Upper Canada has 157,923 people and Lower Canada 479,288.

1825 Founding trustee of Stranger's Burial Ground (aka "Potters' Field"). First burial in 1826.

1825 Started work on Bank of Upper Canada with W.W. Baldwin.

1826 [38] Workers' Residence, London (Otto Letter).

1827-29 [39] *Moss Park*.

1827-30 [39-42] London Courthouse and Jail.

1828 [40] *George* born (April 16).

1829 [41] Third Parliament Buildings.

1829 The Welland Canal opens.

1829 York General Hospital opened, after being used as the legislative building between 1824-1829.

1829-31 Ewart Wharf at foot of Church Street.

1829-31 [41-43] Upper Canada College.

1829-32 [41-44] Osgoode Hall (East wing) designed by Ewart.

1830 [42] Upper Canada College opened in January.

1830 Bank of Upper Canada opened with William Allan as 1st President (1822) and owner of *Moss Park*.

1830 Emigrants' Asylum built.

1830-31 Market Building built at King and Jarvis (2nd floor used by town council).

1830 Sir John Beverley Robinson becomes Chief Justice (until 1862).

1830s	193,000 people immigrate from Ireland to Upper Canada (including York). Europe's population was about 230 million, almost twice the number since 1730s. There was insufficient food to feed the growing population.
1831	[43] *Margaret Ewart* marries James Maxwell Strange (September 1).
1831	The original St. Andrew's Church built (later replaced by new church in 1876).
1831	Ewart First President of Mechanics Institute (to become Toronto Public Library).
1831	Ewart is one of the petitioners to allow more boys to enter UCC without certain subjects (e.g. Latin) taught.
1831	First Market Town Hall (burned down in 1849).
1832	[44] Osgoode Hall completed.
1832	*Thomas* becomes second Head Boy of UCC.
1832	Cholera epidemic begins and most dangerous during summer months. In Britain, one in 130 people died. Further outbreaks in 1848 and 1854.
1832	York's first windmill built (lasted till 1859) by James Worts at east end of harbour near Don River and started partnership of Gooderham and Worts. Mill was main supplier for York's flour and alcohol.
1833	[45] Feb 8 a bill passed providing £10,000 to macadamize (make gravel roads) of Yonge, Dundas and Kingston Road to improve traffic into and out of the city (Kingston Road had tolls to pay back their £2,000).
1833	Wholesale Grocers Store.
1833	William Warren Baldwin extends Osgoode Hall with a three-storey addition later replaced by Cumberland and Storm's central section.
1833	Britain frees slaves across the empire.

1834 [46] City of Toronto incorporated, population 9,254 (Rosen, 1999). William Lyon Mackenzie is first mayor.

1834 Emancipation Act abolished slavery in the British Empire.

1834 *John Jr.* becomes fourth Head Boy of UCC.

1835 [47] *James* dies (December 23, aged 10) from drowning.

1836 [48] 9,652 population of Toronto.

1836-37 *Colborne Lodge* built by owner John G. Howard (now part of High Park).

1837 [49] An economic depression in Toronto and worldwide.

1837 Queen Victoria's coronation.

1837 Rebellion led by William Lyon Mackenzie was defeated by loyal troops, and he escapes to America.

1837 Osgoode Hall taken over by government as a military barracks for 6 years.

1837 Telegraph invented by Morse in America.

1838 [50] Britain frees slaves in the colonies.

1838 Lord Durham's Report, after investigating the Rebellion, recommends government reforms and the union of Upper and Lower Canada to speed the assimilation of French-speaking Canadians.

1839 [51] St. James' Church of England (renovation after fire).

1840 [52] John Jr. and Thomas participate in Curling match against Scarborough Club and lost with the Governor General in attendance.

1841 [53] Act of Union--Upper and Lower Canada are joined to create Province of Canada with Canada West and Canada East as divisions. A single Assembly met under the plan laid out by Lord Durham in 1838.

1842 [54] Toronto had 10,000 people. Most men worked in manufacturing, or as shoemakers, tailors, blacksmiths and construction craftsmen. Toronto also had several breweries by families like the Gooderhams, Joseph Bloor, the Severn family and John Farr brewery. (MacNab, 1955). Good yearly salary was $500. Home rental about $100-125 a year. Beef and pork cost 5-7 cents a pound. Two chickens cost 25 cents. Working men earned: bricklayer ($1.50/day), carpenter ($1/day), labourers (75 cents per day plus any extra pay they could acquire). Glazenbrook, G.P. DeT. (1971) page 89. Twenty percent of people were Catholic (Wise and Gould, p. 168).

1842 Charles Dickens visits and writes about Toronto.

1842 St. James Cemetery laid out by John G. Howard.

1843 [55] *William* dies (May 27, aged 31) records at Potters' Field list cause as "killed".

1843 Military leaves Osgoode Hall.

1844 [56] New City Hall opened.

1844-46 Osgoode Hall remodelled and west wing added by Henry Bowyer Lane.

1845-47 [57-59] The Great Famine in Ireland with resulting large immigration to Canada. Almost 1,000,000 starved to death. Germany also hard hit.

1845-46 The Church of the Holy Trinity (Henry Bowyer Lane) built at Trinity Square (beside present day Eaton Centre).

1846 [58] *Thomas* marries Catherine Seaton Skirving.

1846 *Hazelburn* torn down, land sold in parcels including one to John Ewart (Jarvis, Carlton, Mutual and Maitland Streets).

1846 [58] *Jane* marries Oliver Mowat (May 19).

1846 Gives part of Jarvis property to daughter Jane and Oliver Mowat as a wedding present.

1846 City of Toronto and Lake Huron Railroad Co. founded with Ewart as a director.

1846-47 *Thomas* opens up law firm with Price at 42 Yonge Street.

1846	Ewart becomes a commissioner for the development of the Provincial Lunatic Asylum.
1847	21,050 population of Toronto.
1847	[59] *Jane Emily* born to Thomas and Catherine, first grandchild.
1847	17,000 immigrants to Canada died of typhus ('ship's fever') either during or after the journey (Pollard, p. 31) Bishop Power (aged 42) dies in Toronto of disease tending to sick (Wise and Gould, p. 169).
1847-48	Karl Marx (1818-1883) and Friedrich Engels (1820-1895) write the *Communist Manifesto,* rebellions occur throughout Europe.
1848	[60] Provinces of Canada and Nova Scotia get responsible government.
1848	Further outbreak of cholera.
1849	49th parallel is extended to the Pacific Ocean as border.
1849	[61] *John Skirving* born to Thomas and Catherine (grandchild).
1849	The GREAT FIRE destroys much of downtown area of city including Market Town Hall and 3rd St. James Cathedral that Ewart renovated after 1839 fire. Covered blocks around King, Adelaide, Church, Jarvis and George Streets. Only 3 pre-1834 buildings survived: 1827 Upper Canada Bank (Adelaide and George), 1834 Residence of Postmaster J.S. Howard, 1822 *Campbell House* (Frederick and Adelaide before move).
1849	An Act of Amnesty allows William Lyon Mackenzie to return from exile in America.
1850	[62] St. Lawrence Market (William Thomas) built on old Market Town Hall site.
1850	Provincial Lunatic Asylum, designed by John G. Howard, opens under supervision of 3 Commissioners, including

	John Ewart who had become quite close to Howard professionally.
1850-53	Present day St. James Cathedral built.
1850-55	The Necropolis cemetery laid out with chapel designed by Henry Langley in 1872.
1850s	Population reached about 50,000 with 1,000 Blacks (Riendeau, 1984).
1850-51	*John Sr.* has a home and office on Front Street, another house at 148 Yonge Street, *John Jr.* at 23 Front Street (Wholesale Dry Goods); *Thomas* has law firm with Mowat and Helliwell on Church Street across from Roman Catholic Church.
1851	[63] April 23, Canada's first postal stamp issued (3-cent beaver stamp).
1851	The Great Exposition is held in London, England.
1851	*Thomas* dies in Madeira from tuberculosis (March 21, aged 32).
1851	*Louise* born to Thomas (after his death from consumption) and Catherine (grandchild for John Ewart).
1851	34% of population born in Canada (Goheen, pp. 55, 76).
1852	[64] Harriet Beecher Stowe publishes *Uncle Tom's Cabin,* a melodramatic novel that depicted slavery as a passion play with a cast of saintly blacks and sadistic whites (she was the daughter and sister of clergymen). Book outsold every other book of 19th century America except the Bible.
1853-56	[65-68] Crimean War with Britain, France, Sardinia and Turkey against Russia.
1853	[65] George and John Jr. play against Scarborough in important curling match and lose (Feb. 22) although George's team won their match.
1854	[66] Further outbreak of cholera.

1854 Toronto General Hospital's new building opened on Gerrard Street and designed on a Scottish hospital model. (G. Mercer Adam, 1972, pp. 113-114).

1854 Son-in-law James Maxwell Strange dies (married to Margaret Ewart).

1854 Reciprocity Treaty signed with USA.

1855 [67] Last burial in Potters' Field, January 21. Burials moved to Necropolis.

1855 Bytown is incorporated as Ottawa.

1856 [68] *John Ewart* dies (September 18). Buried in Necropolis under ten-foot Celtic Cross.

1856 Oliver Mowat and Jane build *Northfield* on land given to them by Ewart in 1846. House later becomes Havergal College and then part of CBC.

1856 The Grand Trunk Railway opens its Toronto to Montreal line.

1856-60 Osgoode Hall's centre block rebuilt by Messrs. Cumberland and Storm.

1857 *George* marries Agnes S. Rogers; owns a shop on east side of St. Lawrence Market. Also leased land from father at King and Yonge Streets.

1857 Canada adopts the decimal system for currency (i.e., dollars instead of pounds). (FH Armstrong, 1988); $4 to 1£ (John Honsberger, p. 290).

1857 December 31, Queen Victoria names Ottawa as new capital of Canada.

1857-59 Depression in Canada with banks failing (deT Glazebrook, p. 188).

1858 A storm cuts the peninsula free from the mainland at Ashbridges Bay forming the Eastern Gap to the east of the harbour. (Firth, p. 239).

1859 Charles Darwin publishes *The Origin of the Species.*

1859 100th anniversary of Battle of the Plains of Abraham.

1860 *Margaret* dies (September 8).

1860 Population of Toronto is 42,000.

1860 Edward Albert, Prince of Wales (future King Edward VII) is the first royal visitor to Ontario, lays cornerstone for Parliament Buildings in Ottawa.

1861 *John Jr.* dies by suicide (July 2), never married.

1861-65 American Civil War between Union States against southern Confederacy States.

1863 *Clara* born to George Ewart and Agnes.

1864 Charlottetown Conference for Maritime union; talks take first steps toward Confederation.

1866 Osgoode Hall's iron fence by W.G. Storm and made at St. Lawrence Foundry.

1866 Defeat of Fenians (Irish Republican Brotherhood founded in New York in 1858 to end British Rule) during Irish-American Civil War who invaded the Niagara Peninsula in 1866 and January 1867. Invaded Canada in hopes of drawing English troops away from Ireland.

1866 Bank of Upper Canada failed.

1867 *Jane Wilson Ewart* dies (April 26), just over 2 months before the birth of Confederation, she outlives her husband and 9 of her 11 children.

1867 July 1st, confederation of Ontario, Quebec, Nova Scotia and New Brunswick.

1870 *George* dies (January 2, aged 42).

1870 First Canadian coins struck. Over the following year or two, foreign coins no longer legal tender in Canada.

Early 1870 Toronto population was 56,092 with 51% born in Canada. Anglicans, then Catholics then 17% Methodists. (Goheen pp. 55, 76) Economy grew from 1867 to 1890s without any real negative growth periods. (Bliss, 1974, p.

11). Toronto (33%) and Montreal (27%) were central areas of manufacturing in Canada. Secondary industries expanded rapidly for local and regional consumption. (Chambers 1964) Wages were relatively constant with unskilled labour at $1/day; tradesmen $2-3.50/day, businessmen and professionals had a good salary at $2,000 per annum (Bliss, 1978, p. 3) Taxation was always low (federal income and corporate taxes did not appear until World War I). Administrative and sales staff earned between $200 to $700 per annum. In 1890 that would grow to $320 for junior staff and $1,500 for senior staff (Assessment Rolls).

1872 Oliver Mowat becomes Premier of Ontario until July 1896.

1876 Telephone invented by Alexander Graham Bell with long-distance call between Brantford and nearby Paris.

1876 Intercolonial Railway links central Canada and the Maritimes to Halifax-Truro line.

1881 96,198 population.

1885 Last spike in Eagle Pass, BC concludes CPR line across Canada.

1893 *Jane Ewart Mowat* dies (March 12).

APPENDIX 3
John Ewart's Buildings

The following are a sampling of supporting citations attesting to Ewart's design and/or building of these projects—the dates reflect the period of construction. We have tried to secure at least three different sources to attest to Ewart's involvement with a specific building project but for several projects that was not possible because construction records for the early years in York are incomplete.

York General Hospital 1820-1824

W.G. Crosbie. (1975). *The Toronto General Hospital 1819-1965*, p. 10.

Edith Firth. (1962). *The Town of York 1815-1834*, p. 41.

Harold Kalman (2000). *A Concise History of Canadian Architecture*, credit to both Ewart and Baldwin p. 128.

Marion MacRae. *Dictionary of Canadian Biography*. Vol. VIII, pp. 280-282. (Georgian style).

Lucy Booth Martyn (1982), *The Face of Early Toronto: An Archival Record 1797-1936*, p. 88.

Hazelburn 1822

Liz Lundell. (1997). *The Estates of Old Toronto*, p. 54.

Lucy Booth Martyn. (1983). *A View of Original Toronto*, p. 44. "…is believed to have been designed and built by John Ewart."

J. Ross Robertson. (1896). *Landmarks of Toronto*, Vol. 2 p. 1023. "In this house, which was built by the late Mr. John Ewart, as contractor for the masonry work…"

Austin Seton Thompson. (1980). *Jarvis Street: A Story of Triumph and Tragedy*, p. 86.

Leonard Wise and Allan Gould. (2000). *Toronto Street Names*, p. 122.

St. Paul's Roman Catholic Church 1823

Marion MacRae. *Dictionary of Canadian Biography*. Vol. VIII, pp. 280-282.

MacRae and Adamson. (1975). *Hallowed Walls*, p. 84. (calls it a Regency style).

Lucy Booth Martyn. (1983). *A View of Original Toronto*, p. 41. "John Ewart was engaged to draw plans for the church…"

Jesse Edgar Middleton. (1923). *The Municipality of Toronto*, p. 719.

Shirley G. Morriss (ed.) *The Journals of John George Howard 1833-1849*, editor, Vol. 2, Footnote 9 "Ewart moved to York establishing himself as an architect and builder. He provided the city with many of its important early buildings, among them St. Paul's Church for the Roman Catholics, and St. Andrew's for the Presbyterians, Upper Canada College, and the west wing [sic] of Osgoode Hall."

Henry Scadding. (1873). *Toronto of Old*, p. 141.

Second Courthouse and Jail in York 1823-1824

Eric Arthur. (1964). *Toronto: No Mean City*, p. 83.

Dendy and Kilbourn. (1986). *Toronto Observed*, pp. 60, 71-72.

Harold Kalman. (2000). *A Concise History of Canadian Architecture*, p. 128. "both by W.W. Baldwin[455] and John Ewart".

Marion MacRae and Anthony Adamson. (1983). *Cornerstones of Order*, p. 41.

Lucy Booth Martyn. (1982). *The Face of Early Toronto*, p. 14: "Architect John Ewart assisted by Dr. W.W. Baldwin."

Lucy Booth Martyn. (1983). *A View of Original Toronto*, p. 48. "…designed by John Ewart and Dr. W.W. Baldwin."

Ontario Archives, Minutes of the Magistrates of the Home District Quarter Sessions, 17 May 1823; and 27 August 1823.

Stephen Otto. (1983). *Toronto: No Mean City*, p. 47: built to John Ewart's plans by contractors Ford and Hayden.

Jennifer Parsons and Kevin Lillian. (1995). *Toronto 1837: A Model City*, p 13.

J.R. Robertson. (1894). *Landmarks of Toronto*, p. 83, Ewart's name misspelled.

Leonard Wise and Allan Gould. (2000). *Toronto Street Names*, p. 161.

Bank of Upper Canada 1825-1827

City of Toronto's Inventory of Buildings of Architectural and Historical Importance (2nd edition). (April 1981), p. 9: "Bank of Upper Canada attributed to W.W. Baldwin".

Marion MacRae. *Dictionary of Canadian Biography*, VIII, p. 281: "Ewart's smooth, spare trim still curves around the original entrance [of Osgoode Hall]. Trim of the same plasticity, so characteristic of his work, also informs the doorway of the Bank of Upper Canada begun at the corner of Duke (Adelaide) and George streets in 1825. This is probably another result of the successful collaboration between Ewart, who understood the design of buildings, and Baldwin, who recognized the architectural needs of York."

Stephen Otto. (1983). *Toronto: No Mean City*, pp. 75 & 80. "either the obliging Dr. Baldwin or John Ewart."

Stephen Otto. (22 March 1983). "Architects of the Bank of Upper Canada: Francis Hall" monograph. *Toronto: The Town of York Historical Society*. "Another candidate for the honour of designing the Bank is John Ewart, based on stylistic similarities common to the Bank, his York County Court house of 1825-6, and the original Osgoode Hall, now incorporated in the east wing, which he designed in 1829."

Workers' Residence, London 1826

Courier of Upper Canada, 28 April 1832, c 2 reprinted from a lost issue of the London (UC) Sun.

Pat Morden's chapter on the courthouse in Edward Phelps. (1989). *Middlesex: Two Centuries*, p. 26.

London Court House and Jail 1827-1830

William E. Corfield. (1974). *Towers of Justice*, pp. 1, 2, 3, 4.

A traveller's letter in the *Gore Gassette* of July 31, 1827 published by George Gurnett of Ancaster notes: "Mr. Ewart, an architect of first rate ability."

Harold Kalman. (1994). *A History of Canadian Architecture*, Vol. 1 (of 2), p. 275. Refers to the building as first example in Upper Canada of Early Gothic Revival.

London and Middlesex Historical Society (1908).

Marion MacRae and Anthony Adamson. (1983). *Cornerstones of Order*, p. 95. She refers to the castlegated building as Regency Gothic (p. 37).

Pat Morden`s chapter on the courthouse in Edward Phelps. (1989). *Middlesex: Two Centuries*, p. 27.

Moss Park 1827-1829

Stephen Otto in a letter to Janet FitzGerald, June 23, 2001.

Stephen Otto in a telephone interview April 16, 2004.

Mary Allodi and Stephen Otto. (Spring, 2001). "Landmark Sketches: Two Drawings Preserve the Likeness of the 1830s Home of One of Toronto's Wealthiest and Most Influential Citizens" in *Rotunda: The Magazine of the Royal Ontario Museum, pp 18-23*: "It was probably Ewart, a Scot like Allan, who was responsible for designing and constructing Allan's last and most luxurious home, Moss Park."

Coffin Block 1826- 1830

C.R.W. Biggar. (1905). *Sir Oliver Mowat*, p. 39. Goads 1894 Map.

Lucy Booth Martyn. (1982). *The Face of Early Toronto*, p. 37.

Parsons, Jennifer and Lillian, Kevin. (1995) *Toronto 1837: A Model City*, p. 10, Footnote 11.

Upper Canada College 1829-1831

William Dendy. (1993). *Lost Toronto: Images of the City's Past*, p. 59.

William Dendy and William Kilbourn. (1986). *Toronto Observed*, pp. 71-72..

Lucy Booth Martyn. (1982). *The Face of Early Toronto*, p. 99.

Shirley G. Moriss (ed.). *Howard, John George. The Journals of John George Howard 1833-1849*, Vol. 1, p. 19.

Stephen Otto. (1983). *Toronto: No Mean City*, p. 64.

Third Parliament Buildings 1829-1832

Eric Arthur. (1964). *Toronto: No Mean City*, p. 45 (re: design competition); p. 45 (superintend the job).

C.R.W. Biggar. (1905). *Sir Oliver Mowat*, p. 39.

William Dendy. (1993). *Lost Toronto: Images of the City's Past*, p. 52 (re: design competition).

William Dendy and William Kilbourn. (1986). *Toronto Observed*, pp. 71-72.

Jesse Edgar Middleton. (1923). *The Municipality of Toronto*, Vol. 1 of 3, p. 167 (re: contracting work).

Lucy Booth Martyn. (1983). *A View of Original Toronto*, p. 51. "Designed by James Grant Chewett (1793-1862) and built by John Ewart (1788-1856).

Mount Pleasant Cemetery Mausoleum plaque re: contract work on buildings.

Stephen Otto, letter to Janet FitzGerald, June 23, 2001 (re contracting west wing, also competed for design).

Osgoode Hall 1829-1832

Angela K. Carr. "Hopkins, Lawford & Nelson at Osgoode Hall: The Debacle of 1855" in *17 SSAC BULLETIN* 4:88, pp. 17-25, p. 17 "The east wing was constructed in 1829-32 by John Ewart."

City of Toronto's Inventory of Buildings of Architectural and Historical Importance (2nd edition). (April 1981), p. 77: "Osgoode Hall 1829-1932 East Wing, John Ewart" architect.

William Dendy and William Kilbourn. (1986). *Toronto Observed*, pp. 71-72.

John Honsberger (2004). *Osgoode Hall: An Illustrated History*, p. 116.

Dana Johnson and Leslie Maitland. (December 1985). "Osgoode Hall and the development of public architecture in Canada," in *14 SSAC BULLETIN* 4:85, pp. 14-15.

Marion MacRae and Anthony Adamson. (1983). *Cornerstones of Order*, p. 45, 47. (MacRae: Regency)

Lucy Booth Martyn. (1982). *The Face of Early Toronto*, p. 80. "Architect John Ewart under supervision of Dr. W.W. Baldwin."

Lucy Booth Martyn. (1983). *A View of Original Toronto*, p. 59. "The original building, now the East Wing, was designed by the master builder, John Ewart…"

Shirley G. Morriss (ed.) *The Journals of John George Howard 1833-1849*, editor, Vol. 2, Footnote 9 "Ewart moved to York establishing himself as an architect and builder. He provided the city with many of its important early buildings, among them St. Paul's Church for the Roman Catholics, and St. Andrew's for the Presbyterians, Upper Canada College, and the west wing [sic] of Osgoode Hall."

Christopher Moore. (1997). *The Law Society of Upper Canada and Ontario's Lawyers 1779-1997*, p, 82.

Larry Richards. (1992). *Toronto Places*, p. 69. "Osgoode Hall east wing by John Ewart 1831-32."

Ewart Wharf 1829-1831

Edwin C. Guillet. (1939). *Toronto: Trading Post to Great City*, p. 68.

Edith Firth. (1962). *The Town of York 1815-1834*, p. 124, footnote 17: William Lyon Mackenzie "claimed that before the 1828 election, town waterlots which were valuable because of the building of wharves and storehouses, were given to Thomas Helliwell, Henry Hamilton and John Ewart, to win their support for Robinson."

Jesse Edgar Middleton. (1923). *The Municipality of Toronto*, p. 440: "Between 1818-1834 there were only 3 new wharfs: Ewart's at the bottom of Church street east of Cooper's. He received the patent to the waterlot on August 15, 1828 and probably built the wharf that year."

J. R. Robertson. (1896). *Landmarks of Toronto*, Vol. 1, p. 343: "Waterlot patents—Lot D John Ewart All—1 of it September 11, 1828. Lot D John Ewart S. Pt., 3-10 June 1 1832."

Emigrants' Asylum 1830

Kingston Chronicle, 29 August 1830, p. 2, c. 4. Ewart the contractor.

Stephen Otto in a letter June 2001 to Janet FitzGerald.

St. Andrew's Church 1831

F.H. Armstrong. (1983). *Toronto: The Meeting Place*, p. 65 "St. Andrew's Presbyterian Church, built between 1830 and 1833 by John Ewart."

Eric Arthur. (1964). *Toronto: No Mean City*, p. 47 "John Ewart, the architect and builder."

Harold Kalman. (2000). *A Concise History of Canadian Architecture*, p. 149. "designed and built in 1830-34 by John Ewart."

Marion MacRae and Anthony Adamson. (1975). *Hallowed Walls*, p. 86. (Regency).

Ibid, p. 82-83: "The three churches were all the work of John Ewart, *the first architectural designer of demonstrable merit to appear in York*." [emphasis added]

Lucy Booth Martyn. (1982). *The Face of Early Toronto*, p. 66.

Shirley G. Morriss (ed.) *The Journals of John George Howard 1833-1849*, editor, Vol. 2, Footnote 9 "Ewart moved to York establishing himself as an architect and builder. He provided the city with many of its important early buildings, among them St. Paul's Church for the Roman Catholics, and St. Andrew's for the Presbyterians, Upper Canada College, and the west wing [sic] of Osgoode Hall."

Stephen Otto. (1983). *Toronto: No Mean City*, p. 46-47.

Wholesale Grocers Store 1833

Brockville Recorder. Friday 11 October 1833, Vol. XIII, No. 41, p. 2, c. 5 & 6 and a reprint of same article from Colonial Advocate, October 3, 1833 "Growth and Trade in the Town of York".

St. James' Anglican Church (renovation) 1839

Marion MacRae and Anthony Adamson. (1975). *Hallowed Walls*, p. 82, 83, 87: J.S. Buckingham, in his work Canada, Nova Scotia, New Brunswick published in 1843, writes about Toronto's churches: "The three churches (which had been named in reverse order of construction dates) were all the work of John Ewart, the first architectural designer of demonstrable merit to appear in York…He rebuilt the 1839 version of St. James' Church of England on King Street." "Ewart's unenviable task at St. James' had been to rebuild that edifice following its destruction by fire in 1839. He had been instructed to reproduce the preceding building but to give it a higher ceiling, greater length in the nave, and a different pulpit...It was very much a church designed by the building committee, and the grateful sigh with which its builders turned over completion of the bell tower to John G. Howard carries down the years. Howard does not appear to have fared much better at the hands of the building committee; the abridgement of a spire, which incurred James Buckingham's censure, was his contribution."

Provincial Lunatic Asylum 1846-1850

Dictionary of Canadian Biography. Vol. VIII, p. 282 "John Ewart", by Marion MacRae.

John G. Howard. *The Journals of John George Howard 1833-1849*, editor Shirley G. Morriss, Vol. 6 p. 147, Footnote 1, January 3, 1848: "shewed him the Plan for the Reservoir". Ewart was a commissioner in charge of building the Provincial Lunatic Asylum. He had suggested a reservoir and waterworks for supplying the asylum and city with fresh lake water.

General Comment

Nancy Zwart Tausky and Lynne Delehanty DiStefano. (1986). *Victorian Architecture in London and Southwestern Ontario*, Symbols of Aspiration, p. 12 they write about Ewart: "one of the most talented architects then in Upper Canada."

---

[455] Dr. W.W. Baldwin is often listed first when combined with John Ewart's name (Courthouse and Jail, Osgoode Hall, Bank of Upper Canada). This is more likely because he was one of York's most prominent citizens, rather than because he did most of the collaborate work. As Dr. Baldwin was a physician, lawyer, part-time 'amateur' architect, and a legislator it is more likely that John Ewart did the lion's share of the architectural designing with input from Dr. Baldwin—after all, John Ewart was a full time architect and builder.

APPENDIX 4
Toronto/York Street Names

Many early books about the history of Toronto give the old and new names of streets within the text of the book. For example, Lot Street was later changed to Queen Street in honour of Queen Victoria (1844). Reading these books can be cumbersome as one has to remember which street was Adelaide (Duke) and which was Richmond (Duchess). Therefore, we use only the current names for streets in old York and the new Toronto. Below is a reference list of street names to help you in your further readings of this frontier town and early city.[456]

Current Name	Original Name
Adelaide Street	Duke Street east of Jarvis New Gate Street west of Jarvis
Berkeley Street	Parliament Street, changed when new Parliament Street built
Power Street	Chapel Street
Front Street	Palace Street east of Jarvis Front Street west of Jarvis
Jarvis Street	New Street
Lombard Street	March Street
Mill Street	Front Street (extension of earlier Front Street west of Jarvis)
Queen Street	Lot Street (changed in 1844)
Richmond	Duchess Street
Sherbourne Street	Caroline Street
Trinity Street	Mill Street
Victoria Street	Upper George Street
Wellington Street	Market Street

456 Most of this information comes from Eric Arthur. (1964). *Toronto: No Mean City*. Toronto: University of Toronto Press; Jennifer Parsons and Kevin Lillian. (1995) *Toronto 1837: A Model City;* Leonard Wise and Allan Gould. (2000). *Toronto Street Names: An Illustrated Guide to Their Origins*. Toronto: Firefly Books.

APPENDIX 5
Members of the Family Compact[457]

Throughout this book, and most books about that era, the 'Family Compact' is mentioned as the group of powerful men who made the most important political, administrative, commercial and religious decisions of the day. Allison Ewart (no known relation to John Ewart) and Julia Jarvis discovered in 1926 that no list existed of the members of this most influential network of families. They used membership lists of the Upper Canada Executive and Legislative Councils to compile the first roster of members of 'the family compact' and published their findings in the *Canadian Historical Review.*

Some members were more influential as 'family compact' members through marriage and commerce while others were, or became, Reformers opposed to the compact, such as Robert Baldwin. Some members were on both the Executive Council and the Legislative Council.

We could refer you to their article but it is not readily available. Therefore, we have summarized the 13-page article for your convenience. Below are just their names without the descriptions researched by Ewart and Jarvis. You will notice many of the same people with whom Ewart worked during his years as York's first architect.

Members (36) of the Executive Council of Upper Canada (the most powerful body):

William **Allan**, Henry **Allcock**, Jacques Duperron (James) **Baby**, Augustus **Baldwin**, Robert **Baldwin** [briefly before mass resignation one month later in March 1836 after dispute with Lieutenant Governor], Sir Isaac **Brock**, Sir William **Campbell**, William **Claus**, William Henry **Draper**, Sir Gordon **Drummond**, John Henry **Dunn**, John **Elmsley**, John **Elmsley Jr.**, Alexander **Grant**, Sir James Buchanan **Macaulay**, John **McGill**, George Herchmer or Herkimer **Markland**, Jacob **Mountain**, William **Osgoode**, William Dummer **Powell**, William **Robertson**, Sir John Beverley **Robinson**, Baronet; Peter **Robinson**, John **Rolph**, Baron Francis **de Rottenburg**, Peter

Russell, Thomas **Scott**, Prideaux **Selby**, Æneas **Shaw**, Sir Roger Hale **Sheaffe**, Sir David William **Smith**, Baronet; Samuel **Smith**, John **Strachan**, Robert Baldwin **Sullivan**, Richard Alexander **Tucker**, Joseph **Wells**.

Members (69) of the Legislative Council of Upper Canada were: [* = also on Executive Council above]

Peter **Adamson**, *William **Allan**, *Henry **Allcock**, * Jacques Duperron (James) **Baby**, *Augustus **Baldwin**, Walter **Boswell**, Zacceus **Burnham**, Duncan **Cameron**, *Sir William **Campbell**, Richard **Cartwright, Jr**., Thomas **Clark**, *William **Claus**, James **Crooks**, George **Crookshank**, Hon Peter Boyle **de Blaquière**, William **Dickson**, Richard **Duncan**, *John Henry **Dunn**, *John **Elmsley**, *John **Elmsley Jr**., Adam **Fergusson**, Alexander **Fraser**, Isaac **Fraser**, Thomas **Fraser**, Henry **Graham**, *Alexander **Grant**, Alexander **Grant Jr**., James **Gordon**, George **Hamilton**, John **Hamilton**, Robert **Hamilton**, Charles **Jones**, Jonas **Jones**, James **Kerby**, John **Kirby**, Arthur **Lloyd**, John **Macaulay**, John Simcoe **Macaulay**, John **McDonald**, Alexander **Macdonnel**, Alexander **Macdonnel**, *John **McGill**, John **McGillivray**, Angus **McIntosh**, Archibald **McLean**, Neil **McLean**, *George Herchmer or Herkimer **Markland**, William **Morris**, *Jacob **Mountain**, John **Munro**, Abraham **Nelles**, *William **Osgoode**, *William Dummer **Powell**, Thomas **Radcliffe**, Thomas **Ridout**, *William **Robertson**, *Sir John Beverley **Robinson**, Baronet., *Peter **Robinson**, *Peter **Russell**, *Thomas **Scott**, *Æneas **Shaw**, Thomas Alexander **Stewart**, *John **Strachan**, *Robert Baldwin **Sullivan**, Thomas **Talbot**, Philip **Vankoughnet**, *Joseph **Wells**, Robert Charles **Wilkins**, John **Willison**.

---

[457] Allison Ewart and Julia Jarvis provide 13 pages of biographical sketches of the membership. of the Family Compact. (1926) "The Personnel of the Family Compact, 1791-1841" in *Canadian Historical Review*, Vol. VII, No 3 (Sept., 1926): pp. 209-221.

Glossary

Adamesque after Robert Adam (1728-1792), English architect and designer known for his refined, elegant classicism.

arcade a row of arches, carried on piers or columns, sometimes having a covered walkway above them.

cupola is a small dome on a roof.

entablature is the upper horizontal parts of a Classical order of architecture resting on the capital of a column; it includes the architrave, frieze and cornice.

order In classical architecture there are five orders that use columns and entablature, each with their own established proportions and ornament: Doric, Ionic, Corinthian, Tuscan and Composite.

Palladian 18th century English architectural tradition is based on the Renaissance style of the northern Italian architect, Andrea Palladio (1508-80). A Palladian door or window is divided into three parts: the centre is round-arched, the sides are flat.

parapet is a low wall at the edge of a roof, balcony or terrace.

pediment is a low-pitched triangular gable on the front of a building, especially above a portico.

portico is a roofed porch, often with columns and a pediment, and usually the centre-piece of an architectural composition (Osgoode Hall, Bank of Upper Canada).

tessellated a wall or floor made from small flat pieces of stone in various colours arranged in a pattern.

Bibliography

Architectural References

Alberti, Leon Battista. (1986). *The Ten Books of Architecture.* New York Dover Publications. Reprint of 15th century work.

Allodi, Mary and Otto, Stephen A. (Spring, 2001). "Landmark Sketches: Two Drawings Preserve the Likeness of the 1830s Home of One of Toronto's Wealthiest and Most Influential Citizens [William Allan]. His Estate Occupied a Sizeable Portion of What is Now Downtown Toronto." In *Rotunda: The Magazine of the Royal Ontario Museum.* Toronto: ROM, pp. 18-23.

Arthur, Eric. (1952). "The History and Architecture of Fabric" in C.H.A. Armstrong. (1952). *The Honourable Society of Osgoode Hall.* Toronto: Clark, Irwin & Company.

Arthur, Eric. (1964). *Toronto: No Mean City.* Toronto: University of Toronto Press.

Asher, Benjamin. (1994). *Practice of Architecture The Five Orders of Architecture) and The Builder's Guide.* New York: Da Capo Press. Introduction by Thomas Gordon Smith, Notre Dame, Indiana.

Blumenson, John. (1990). *Ontario Architecture: A Guide to Styles and Building Terms 1784 to the Present.* Toronto: Fitzhenry & Whiteside.

Britton, John. (1817 & 1820). *The History and Antiquities of the See and Cathedral Church of Lichfield and Wincester.* London: Longman, Hurst, Rees, Orme and Brown.

Carr, Angela K. "Hopkins, Lawford & Nelson at Osgoode Hall: The Debacle of 1855" in *17 SSAC BULLETIN* 4:88, pp. 17-25.

Carr, Angela. (1995). *Toronto Architect Edmond Burke: Redefining Canadian Architecture.* Montreal: McGill-Queen's University Press.

City of Toronto's Inventory of Buildings of Architectural and Historical Importance. (2nd ed.). (April 1981). Toronto: Toronto Historical Board.

Collett-Sandars, W. (1889). *A Handbook of Architectural Styles.* Translated from the German edition of A. Rosengarten and Jean-Claude Corbeil. (1992). PONS: Bildwörterbuch. Stuttgart, Germany:

Ernst Klett. Four-language visual dictionary with excellent architectural drawings.

Corfield, William E. (1974). *Towers of Justice*. London: London and St. Thomas Real Estate Board.

Crawford, Pleasance and Otto, Stephen. (Fall, 1997). "André Parmentier's 'Two or Three Places in Upper Canada'" in *Journal of the New England Garden History Society*, 5: pp. 1-8.

Gowans, Alan. (1992). *Styles and Types of North American Architecture*. New York: Harper Collins.

Jones, Owen. (1856). *Grammar of Ornament*. London: Day and Son.

Klein, Marilyn W. and Fogle, David P. (1985). *Clues to North American Architecture*. Toronto: Fitzhenry & Whiteside.

Kalman, Harold. (1994). *A History of Canadian Architecture*, Vol. 1 (of 2). Toronto: Oxford University Press.

Kalman, Harold. (2000). *A Concise History of Canadian Architecture*. Toronto: Oxford University Press.

Loudon, J.C. (1833). *Encyclopaedia of Cottage, Farm and Villa Architecture and Furniture*. London: Longman, Rees, Orme, Brown, Green & Longman.

MacRae, Marion and Adamson, Anthony. (1983) *Cornerstones of Order: Courthouses and Town Halls of Ontario, 1784-1914*. Toronto: for The Osgoode Society by Clarke Irwin.

MacRae, Marion and Adamson, Anthony. (1975). *Hallowed Walls: Church Architecture of Upper Canada*. Toronto: Clarke Irwin.

McAlester, Virginia and Lee (2003). *A Field Guide to American Houses*. New York: Alfred A. Knopf.

McHugh, Patricia. (1989). *Toronto Architecture: A City Guide*. (2nd ed.). Toronto: McClelland and Stewart.

McKelvey, Margaret and McKelvey, Merilyn. (1984). Toronto: Carved in Stone. Toronto: Fitzhenry & Whiteside.

McKendry, Jennifer. (1991). *William Coverdale and the Architecture of Kingston from 1835 to 1865*. Ph.D. Thesis for University of Toronto published by the National Library of Canada in Ottawa.

Nicholson, Peter. (no publication date, however he lived from 1765-1844). *Architectural Directory: The Student's Instructor in Drawing and Working with the Five Orders of Architecture*. London: M. Taylor. Two large volumes.

Oresko, Robert. (ed.). (1975). *The Works in Architecture of Robert and James Adam*. London: Academy Editions.

Otto, Stephen. (1983). *Architects of the Bank of Upper Canada: Francis Hall* monograph. Toronto: The Town of York Historical Society.

Otto, Stephen A. (1986). Revised edition of Eric Arthur's (1964). *Toronto: No Mean City*. Toronto: University of Toronto Press.

Rickman, Thomas. (1881). *An Attempt to Discriminate the Styles of Architecture in England from the Conquest to the Reformation with a Sketch of the Grecian and Roman Orders*. (7th ed.). London: Parker and Company.

Serlio, Sebastiano. (1982) *The Five Books of Architecture*. New York: Dover Publications. Unabridged reprint of English edition of 1611.

Stitt, Fred A. (1990). *Architect's Detail Library*. New York: Van Nostrand Reinhold.

Tausky, Nancy Zwart and DiStefano, Lynne Delehanty. (1986). *Victorian Architecture in London and Southwestern Ontario, Symbols of Aspiration*. Toronto: University of Toronto Press.

Historical References

Account Books of the General Board of Education. Vol. 114, p. 136 in University of Toronto Archives.

Act of Incorporation for the City of Toronto, 4th William IV, Cap. 23.

Adam, G. Mercer. (1972). *Toronto, Old and New: A Memorial Volume*. Toronto: The Mail Printing Company, 1891 by the Mail Printing Company and reprinted by Coles Publishing Company.

Armstrong, C.H.A.. (1952). *The Honourable Society of Osgoode Hall.* Toronto: Clark, Irwin & Company.

Armstrong, Frederick Henry. (1988). *A City in the Making: Progress, People & Perils in Victorian Toronto.* Toronto: Dundurn Press.

Armstrong, F.H.; Stevenson, H.A. and Wilson, J.D. (eds). (1974). *Aspects of Nineteenth-Century Ontario.* Toronto: University of Toronto Press.

Armstrong, Frederick Henry (1985). *Handbook of Upper Canadian Chronology* (revised edition). Toronto: Dundurn Press.

Armstrong, Frederick Henry (1983). *Toronto: The Place of Meeting.* Burlington, ON: Windsor Publications (Canada).

Armstrong, Frederick Henry. (1965). *Toronto in Transition: The Emergence of a City.* Toronto: University of Toronto Thesis.

Arthur, Eric. (1979). *From Front Street to Queen's Park: The Story of Ontario's Parliament Buildings.* Toronto: McClelland & Stewart.

Baine, Richard P. and McMurray, A. Lynne. (1977). *Toronto: An Urban Study.* Toronto: Clarke, Irwin and Company.

Ball, Edward. (1998, 1999). *Slaves in the Family.* New York: Ballantine Books.

Bartlett, W.H. (1830-1845) *Canadian Scenery.* See N.P. Willis.

Baskerville, Peter. (ed.) (1987). *The Bank of Upper Canada: A Collection of Documents.* Toronto: The Champlain Society in cooperation with the Ontario Heritage Foundation.

Biggar, C.R.W. (1905). *Sir Oliver Mowat: A Biographical Sketch: Two Volumes.* Toronto: Warwick Brothers and Rutter.

Boa, Ann Jarvis. (2002). *My Eventful Life: Stephen Jarvis, U.E. 1756-1840.* Montreal: Price-Patterson.

Bothwell, Robert. (1986). *A Short History of Ontario.* Edmonton: Hurtig Publishers.

Bradbury, Bettina. (1992). *Canadian Family History: Selected Readings.* Toronto: Copp Clark Pitman.

Campbell, Mary and Myrvold, Barbara. (1988). *The Beaches in Pictures 1793-1932.* Toronto: Toronto Public Library.

Careless, J.M.S. (1984). *Toronto to 1918.* Toronto: James Lorimer and Company.

Clarke, C.K. (1913). *A History of the Toronto General Hospital.* Toronto: W. Briggs.

Cooke, William. (1998). *The Parish and Cathedral of St. James', Toronto 1797-1997: A Collaborative History.* Toronto: University of Toronto Press.

Cosbie, W.G. (1975). *The Toronto General Hospital 1819-1965: A Chronicle.* Toronto: Macmillan of Canada.

Craig, Gerald M. (1963). *Upper Canada: The Formative Years 1784-1841.* Toronto: McClelland & Stewart.

Crowder, Norman K. (1988). *Inhabitants of Toronto, Ontario 1848.* Toronto: Ontario Genealogical Society, Toronto Branch.

Davies, Gill. (1993). *The Chronicle of World History.* London: Studio Editions.

de Volpi, Charles P. (1965). *Toronto: A Pictorial Record 1813-1882.* Montreal: Dev-Sco Publications.

Dier, Elspeth; Dier, Paul, and Hubbard, Keith. (1982). *Canada: Years of Change from 1814.* Toronto: Holt, Rinehart and Winston.

Dendy, William. (1993). *Lost Toronto: Images of the City's Past.* McClelland and Stewart.

Dendy, William and Kilbourn, William. (1986). *Toronto Observed: Its Architecture, Patrons, and History.* Toronto: Oxford University Press.

Dictionary of Canadian Biography. Vol. VIII, pp. 280-282 "John Ewart", by Marion MacRae.

Dictionary of Canadian Biography Online. "Catherine Seaton Skirving" by Ruth Compton Brouwer.

Dictionary of Canadian Biography Online. "Talbot, Thomas" by Alan G. Brunger.

Duff, J. Clarence. (1967, 1972). *Pen Sketches of Historic Toronto,* Vols. 1 & 2. Toronto: J. Clarence Duff.

Duff, J. Clarence with Sarah Yates. (1984). *Toronto: Then and Now.* Toronto: Fitzhenry & Whiteside.

Evans, A. Margaret. (1992). *Sir Oliver Mowat.* Toronto: University of Toronto Press.

Ewart, John. (1819). Land Petition to Lieutenant Governor Peregrine Maitland. Ontario Archives Roll C –1889 document #E–17-9.

Ewart, John. (1854). The Last Will and Testament. Toronto: City of Toronto Registrar's Office, File MS638(47).

Ewart, Allison and Jarvis, Julia. (September, 1926) "The Personnel of the Family Compact, 1791-1841" in *Canadian Historical Review*, Vol. VII, No 3: 209-221.

Executive Council papers. National Archives of Canada. RG1, Vol. 23, pp. 47-50 re: Emigrant's Asylum.

Filey, Mike. (1999). *Mount Pleasant Cemetery: An Illustrated Guide*, (2nd revised ed.). Toronto: Dundurn Press.

Filey, Mike. (1970). *A Toronto Album: Glimpses of the City that Was.* Toronto: University of Toronto Press.

Filey, Mike. (1994 to 2003). Toronto sketches 3-7: "The Way We Were." Columns from the Toronto Sunday Sun. Toronto: Dundurn Press.

Fink, Dean. (1971). *Life in Upper Canada 1781-1841: An Inquiry Approach.* Toronto: McClelland & Stewart.

Firth, Edith. (1983). *Toronto in Art: 150 Years Through the Artists' Eyes.* Toronto: Fitzhenry and Whiteside.

Firth, Edith.(ed.) (1962). *The Town of York 1793-1815: A Collection of Documents of Early Toronto.* Toronto: University of Toronto Press, and the Champlain Society for Government of Ontario.

Firth, Edith. (1962). *The Town of York 1815-1834: A Further Collection of Documents of Early Toronto.* Toronto: University of Toronto Press.

FitzGerald, James. (1994). *Old Boys.* Toronto: Macfarlane Walter and Ross.

FitzGerald, Janet Ewart. (2001). *The Grubb Pioneers of Etobicoke.* Toronto: Pro Familia Publishing.

Fouts, C.R., Freeman, E.B., Kemp, K.M., Marmont, C., and Minnes, D.G. (1991). *Building Stone and Historic Structures in Downtown Toronto.* Toronto: Geological Association of Canada, Toronto '91 Committee.

Gad, Gunter and Holdsworth, Deryck W. "Streetscape and Society: The Changing Built Environment of King Street, Toronto" in Hall, Roger; Westfall, William; and MacDowell, Laurel Sefton. (eds.) (1988). *Patterns of the Past: Interpreting Ontario's History: A Collection of Historical Articles Published on the Occasion of the Centenary of the Ontario Historical Society.* Toronto: Dundurn Press. pp. 174-205.

Glazenbrook, G.P. DeT. (1971). *The Story of Toronto.* Toronto: University of Toronto Press.

Godfrey, Sheldon and Godfrey, Judy. (1984). *Stones, Bricks and History: The Corner of Duke and George.*" 1798-1884 (3rd ed.). Toronto: Lester & Orphan Dennys

Gourlay, Robert. (1822). *Statistical Account of Upper Canada,* Volume 1. London: Marshall Stationers Court. Reprinted (1966) New York: Johnson Reprint Corporation.

Guillet, Edwin C. (1933). *Pioneer Days in Upper Canada.* Toronto: University of Toronto Press. Reprinted six times up to 1979.

Guillet, Edwin C. (1939). *Toronto Illustrated: From Trading Post to Great City, with a Short History.* Toronto: Ontario Publishing Co.

Hacker, Carlotta. (2002). *The Kids Book of Canadian History.* Toronto: Kids Can Press.

Hall, Roger and Dodds, Gordon. (1991). *Ontario: 200 Years in Pictures.* Toronto: Dundurn Press.

Harney, Robert F. (ed.). (1985). *Gathering Places: Peoples and Neighbourhoods of Toronto, 1834-1945.* Toronto: Multicultural History Society of Ontario.

Harris, R. Cole and Warkentin, John. (1974). *Canada Before Confederation.* Toronto: Oxford University Press.

Hartt, Shirley E. (2003). *Old Town Toronto: Images of Past and Present.* Toronto: Enoch Turner Schoolhouse.

Historic Atlas of York Country 1878. (1972). Belleville: Mike Silk Screening Company.

History of Toronto and County York, Ontario, illustrated. (1885). Vols. 1 & 2. Toronto: C. Blackett Robinson, Publishers.

Home District Quarter Sessions. Minutes of the Magistrates. 17 May 1823, 27 August, 1823. Ontario Archives.

Honsberger, John. (2004). *Osgoode Hall: An Illustrated History.* Toronto: The Osgoode Society for Canadian Legal History.

Hounsom, Eric Wilfred. (1970). *Toronto in 1810.* Toronto: Ryerson Press

Howard, John George. *The Journals of John George Howard 1833-1849.* Vols. 1-7 transcribed by editor Shirley G. Morriss for the Ontario Heritage Foundation and bound by the Toronto Public Library (Reference, special collections). Covering his day-to-day notes of a very active career. Ewart cited in all volumes. Vol. 1=1833-34; Vol. 2=1836, 1837, 1839; Vol. 3=1840-42; Vol. 4=1843-44; Vol. 5=1845-46, Vol. 6=1847-48, Vol. 7=1849.

Hudson, Edna. (2000). *The Provincial Asylum in Toronto: Reflections on Social and Architectural History.* Toronto: Toronto Regional Architectural Conservancy.

Jeffreys, C.W. (1945). *The Picture Gallery of Canadian History, Vol. 2 1763-1830.* Toronto: The Ryerson Press. A three-volume set of "illustrations drawn & collected" by Jeffrey's and assisted by T.W. McLean. Vol. 1 covers the beginning of Canadian History to 1763; Vol. 2 from 1763-1830, and Vol. 3 from 1830-1890.

Jones, Donald. (1992). *Fifty Tales of Toronto.* Toronto: University of Toronto Press.

Johnson, Dana and Maitland, Leslie. "Osgoode Hall and the Development of Public Architecture in Canada" in *14 SSAC BULLETIN* 4:85 Dec 1985, pp. 14-18.

Journal of the House of Assembly. Upper Canada, Appendix 1832-32, pp. 179-83 re: Upper Canada College, York; Appendix, 1829, p. 39 re: Second Parliament House in York

Keane, David and Read, Colin. (eds.). (1990). *Old Ontario: Essays in Honour of J.M.S. Careless.* Toronto: Dundurn Press.

Kilbourn, William. (1956). *The Firebrand: William Lyon Mackenzie and the Rebellion in Upper Canada.* Toronto: Clarke, Irwin.

Kilbourn, William. (Ed.) (1976). *The Toronto Book: An Anthology of Writings Past and Present.* Toronto: The Macmillan Company of Canada.

Kilbourn, William. (1984). *Toronto Remembered: A Celebration of the City of Toronto.* Toronto: Stoddart.

King, James. (2002). *Farley: The Life of Farley Mowat.* Toronto: HarperFlamingo Canada.

Law Society of Upper Canada. Minutes. February 5, 1832.

Law Society of Upper Canada Archives. Minutes of Convocation, 1829-32. Passim. Re: Osgoode Law building.

Layton, John Richard. (1993). *The Ewarts of Tranent, East Lothian.* Devon, England: Self-published.

London and Middlesex Historical Society (ON). (1908). Programs of the London and Middlesex Historical Society: transactions 1902-1907. London, Ontario: The Society.

Lundell, Liz. (1997). *The Estates of Old Toronto.* Toronto: Boston Mills Press.

MacNab, John E. "Toronto Industrial Growth to 1891" in *Ontario History*, Vol. 47, pp. 59-80.

MacNab, John E. (1955). "Toronto's Industrial Growth to 1891" in *Ontario History*, Vol. 47, pp. 64-66.

MacRae, Marion. (1971). *MacNab of Dundurn*. Toronto: Clarke, Irwin and Company.

Marsh, James H. (Editor in Chief). (1985). *The Canadian Encyclopedia*. Edmonton, Alberta: Hurtig Publishers.

Martyn, Lucy Booth. (1980). *Aristocratic Toronto: 19th Century Grandeur*. Toronto: Gage Publishing.

Martyn, Lucy Booth. (1978). *100 Years of Grandeur: The Inside Story of Toronto's Great Homes and the People Who Lived There*. Toronto: Pagurian Press.

Martyn, Lucy Booth. (1983). *A View of Original Toronto: The Fabric of York/Toronto Circa 1834*. Sutton West, Ontario: The Paget Press.

Martyn, Lucy Booth. (1982). *The Face of Early Toronto: An Archival Record 1797-1936*. Toronto: The Pagent Press.

Mays, John Bentley. (2002). *Arrivals: Stories from the History of Ontario*. Toronto: Penguin Books.

Mays, John Bentley. (1994). *Emerald City: Toronto Visited*. Toronto: Viking Press.

McInnes, Edgar. (1963). *The North American Nations*. Toronto: J.M. Dent & Sons.

"*The Middlesex Court House*", 21 loose pages, typewritten in early 1970s? and "*Middlesex Court House and Jail: A Study of Proposed Future Uses*" by law students in 1973. Cerlox bound, typewritten. In private collection of Colter, William E. C., Toronto, Ontario.

Middleton, Jesse Edgar. (1923). *The Municipality of Toronto: A History*, Vols. 1-3. Toronto: Dominion Publishers.

Minhinnick, Jeanne. (1970). *At Home in Upper Canada*. Toronto: Clarke, Irwin and Company.

Moore, Christopher. (1997). *The Law Society of Upper Canada and Ontario's Lawyers 1779-1997*. Toronto, University of Toronto Press.

Morden, Pat. (See Phelps, Edward).

Morley, John. (1903). *The Life of William Ewart Gladstone*. 3 vols. London: Macmillan and Company.

Mosser, Christine. (ed.) (1984). *York, Upper Canada Minutes of Town Meetings and List of Inhabitants 1797-1823*. Toronto: Metro Toronto Library Board.

Mulvany, C. Pelham. (1884, reprinted by Toronto's Ontario Reprint Press in 1970). *Toronto: Past and Present: A Handbook of the City*. Toronto: W.E. Caiger.

Myrvold, Barbara. (1997). *The People of Scarborough: A History*. Toronto: Grenville Printing for The City of Scarborough Public Library Board.

Nelles, H.V. (1974). *The Politics of Development: Forest, Mines & Hydro-Electric Power in Ontario, 1849-1941*. Toronto: Macmillan of Canada.

Nelson, J. Gordon. (2001). *Old Town Toronto: A Heritage Landscape Guide*. Waterloo, Ontario: The Heritage Resource Centre, University of Waterloo.

Noel, S.J.R. (1990). *Patrons, Clients, Brokers: Ontario Society and Politics 1791-1896*. Toronto: University of Toronto Press.

Oliver, Peter. (1975). "On Being an Ontarian" in *Public and Private Persons*. Toronto: Clark, Irwin and Company; pp. 1-14.

Ontario Heritage Foundation. York Mechanics' Institute (1830-1382) plaque on Adelaide Street. Agency of the Government of Ontario.

Ontario Statistics. (1978). Toronto: Ministry of the Treasury and Economics.

Parker, Reverend Stuart C. (1930). *The Book of St. Andrew: A Short History of St. Andrew's Presbyterian Church in Toronto*. Toronto: The Centenary Committee of the Congregation.

Parsons, Jennifer and Lillian, Kevin. (1995) *Toronto 1837: A Model City*. Toronto: The Town of York Historical Society.

Phelps, Edward. (ed.). (1989). *Middlesex: Two Centuries*. London: Frontline Publications.

Pollard, Michael. (1993). *The Nineteenth Century*. New York: Simon and Schuster Young Books.

Radcliff, Thomas. (Ed.). (1953). *Authentic Letters from Upper Canada.* Toronto: The Macmillan Company of Canada.

Richards, Larry. (1992). *Toronto Places: A Context for Urban Design.* Toronto: University of Toronto Press.

Richmond, Jon and West, Bruce. (1969) *Around Toronto.* Toronto: Doubleday Canada.

Riendeau, Roger and staff of the Ontario Ministry of Citizenship and Culture. (1984). *An Enduring Heritage: Black Contributions to Early Ontario.*

Robertson, J. Ross. (1896). *Landmarks of Toronto: A Collection of Historical Sketches of the Old Town of York from 1792-1833 and of Toronto from 1834 to 1895.* Based on his columns in the *Toronto Evening Telegram.* (Republished by the Mika Publishing Company, Belleville, ON in 1976 for Vol. 1 and 1987 for Vol. 2). Six vols. (1894, 1896, 1898, 1904, 1908, 1914).

Romney, Paul. "A Struggle for Authority: Toronto Society and Politics in 1834" in Russell, Victor L.(ed.) (1984). *Forging a Consensus: Historical Essays on Toronto.* Toronto: University of Toronto Press.

Rose, George Maclean (Ed.). (1886). *A Cyclopedia of Canadian Biography.* Toronto: Rose Publishing Company.

Rosen, Eric S. (1991, 1998). *The Don: The History of the Don Valley.* Toronto: The Metropolitan Toronto and Region Conservation Authority.

Rowsell, H.W. (1850-51). *Toronto City Directory.*

John Ruskin. (1907). *Sesame and Lilies: The Two Paths.* New York: J.M. Dent & Co.

Scadding, Henry. (1873). *Toronto of Old.* Abridged and edited by F.H. Armstrong (1966). Toronto: Oxford University Press.

Scadding, Henry. (1886). *Supplement to Toronto of Old.* Toronto: W.C. Chewett & Company.

Sewell, John. (2002). *Doors Open Toronto: Illuminating the City's Great Spaces.* Toronto: Alfred A. Knopf.

Slaight, Annabel (Ed). (1972). *Exploring Toronto.* Toronto: Toronto Chapter of Architects.

Smith, Mary Larratt. (1980). *Young Mr. Smith in Upper Canada.* Toronto: University of Toronto Press.

Splane, Richard B. (1965). *Social Welfare in Ontario 1791-1893: A Study of Public Welfare Administration.* Toronto: University of Toronto Press.

Swainson, Donald. (1972). *Oliver Mowat's Ontario.* Toronto: Macmillan of Canada.

Thompson, Austin Seton (1980). *Jarvis Street: A Story of Triumph and Tragedy.* Toronto: Personal Library Publishers.

Thompson, Austin Seton. (1975). *Spadina: A Story of Old Toronto.* Toronto: Pagurian Press Limited.

The Toronto City Directories. (1850 to 1940). Toronto: R.C. Polk and Company.

Toronto Illustrated 1893. (1992). Toronto: Ontario Genealogical Society, Toronto Branch reprint of 1893 original book.

Toronto Public Library. (1954) *The Guide to the Manuscript Collection.* Toronto: Toronto Public Library.

Upper Canada Sundries, RG 5, A 1, pp. 43443-45, 12 December 1826 in National Archives of Canada. Re: Third Parliament Buildings.

van Bommel, Harry. (2000). *Canada 150: Recording Your Life Story or Family History.* Scarborough: Resources Supporting Family and Community Legacies Inc.

van Bommel, Harry. (2005). *John Macdonald: Merchant Prince.* Scarborough: Resources Supporting Family and Community Legacies Inc.

Wallace, W. Stewart. (1963). *The MacMillan Directory of Canadian Biography.* Toronto: Macmillan Company of Canada.

Walton, George (Compiler). (1833-34). *The York Commercial Directory.* York: Thomas Dalton printer.

West, Bruce. (1967). *Toronto.* Toronto: Doubleday Canada.

White, Randall. (1985). *Ontario 1610-1985: A Political and Economic History*. Toronto: Dundurn Press.

Willis, Nathaniel Parker. (1967). *Canadian Scenery Illustrated from drawings of W.H. Bartlett.* Toronto: Peter Martin Associates. Originally published by J.S. Virtue in London between 1838-1842.

Wills, Gabriele. (2003). *A Place to Call Home: A Novel.* Lindsay, Ontario: Mind Shadows.

Wise, Leonard and Gould, Allan. (2000). *Toronto Street Names: An Illustrated Guide to Their Origins.* Toronto: Firefly Books.

Yeigh, Frank. (1893). *Ontario's Parliament Buildings or a Century of Legislation 1792-1992.* Toronto: Williamson Book Company.

Interviews

Stephen Langmead, May 10, 2004 outside Osgoode Hall. Mr. Langmead is a recently retired Professor of Architecture (Part-time) at Ryerson University in Toronto.

Stephen Otto, telephone interview April 16, 2004. Mr. Otto is a consulting historian who updated the 3rd edition of Eric Arthur's *Toronto: No Mean City* in the mid 1980s. In doing that book, he did extensive research including newspapers of the era from which he was able to extract references to John Ewart.

Jenny Rieger of *The Grange* and Melissa Wright of *Campbell House*, May 14, 2004 by telephone.

Correspondence

Stephen Otto, letter dated June 23, 2001. Mr. Otto is a consulting historian who updated the 3rd edition of Eric Arthur's *Toronto: No Mean City* in the mid 1980s. In doing that book, he did extensive research and read a lot of newspapers from the era from which he was able to extract references on John Ewart and pass them along to the author, Janet FitzGerald.

May 31, 2004 E-mail from Louise Winton, Public Relations and Communications Co-ordinator, Mount Pleasant Group of Cemeteries, Toronto. mpginfo@MountPleasantGroup.com.

Toronto Public Library "Ask a Librarian" e-mails asking specific questions of fact and receiving answers throughout the research.

Judy Craig, Guelph Historical Society, Fall 2004.

Paul Gains, personal correspondence regarding the value of pounds, shillings and pence, Fall 2004.

Maps

The following maps are from the map collection at the Toronto Public Library (Reference branch) on Yonge Street just north of Bloor Street.

- June 3, 1818 Plan of the Town of York in the Toronto Reference Library.
- J.G. Chewett. Township of York map.
- 1834 City of Toronto map by Bonnycastle for Sir John Colborne (including Ewart's Wharf)
- Toronto Map, March 30, 1839 by Rordans and Carter, Lan.
- Bryce's New Index Map of Toronto. (1888). Toronto: Office of the Minister of Agriculture.
- Charles E. Goad. (1884). Atlas of the City of Toronto and Suburbs.

Newspapers

- *Brockville Recorder*. Friday 11 October 1833, Vol. XIII, No. 41 p. 2, c. 5 and a reprint of same article from *Colonial Advocate*, October 3, 1833 "Growth and Trade in the Town of York".
- *Colonial Advocate*. Thursday 7 April, 1825, No. 40 & 41, Appendix c. 37 "Increase of Private and Public Buildings" re: Bank of Upper Canada.
- *Colonial Advocate*. 22 March 1827 (re: Canada House in Guelph).
- *Courier of Upper Canada* [York]. 26 February 1832, p. 2 c. 5. Re: Infant School; 28 April 1832, p 2, c. 2 re: Workmens' Residence. Reprinted from a lost issue of the London (US) Sun.
- *The Globe and Mail.* Saturday, September 20, 1856. "Death Notice" p. 2, c. 8.
- *The Globe and Mail.* (Monday, April 30, 1984). "150 years of Toronto: Hogtown becomes Boomtown", pp. T1-T26.

Commemorative special section celebrating the sesquicentennial of Toronto.

- *Gore Gazette* (Ancaster), 24 November 1827, p. 153 re: London Courthouse and Jail.
- *Illustrated London News,* 30 January 1847, Vol. 10, p. 68.
- *Kingston Chronicle.* 29 August 1830, p. 2 c. 3-4 copied from lost issue of York Courier re: Emigrant's Asylum.

Web Sites

- City of Toronto Arts and Culture site including history of the city: www.city.toronto.on.ca/culture/museums
- Bea McCowan's Toronto Bay web site: www.beamccowan.com/toronto
- The First Parliament Buildings, York web site: www.firstparliament.ca
- Public Accounts of the Inspector General, 7 January 1831. www.canadiana.org/ECO/PageView/9_00942_7/001?id=04f58050bf5990e7
- St. Andrew's Society's web site: www.standrews-society.ca/index.cfm
- Toronto Public Library digital directoriescirca1830-1860: http://mtrl.toronto.on.ca:80….ge.html:sessionid=01-6233-41995397
- Upper Canada Schedule of Accounts sent to the House of Assembly, the 2d February 1831. www.canadiana.org/ECO/PageView/9_00942_7/0018?id=04f58050bf5990e7

Index

Note: This index does not include listings for the appendices.

Aberdeen, 38

Aberdeenshire, 36, 91

Adams, Robert, 27, 48

Adams, James, 48

Adelaide Street, 32, 38, 75, 77, 79, 110, 137, 164

Aitkin, Thomas, 165

Allan Gardens, 93

Allan, William, 35, 36, 53, 76, 91, 92, 95, 111, 127, 138, 149, 155, 156, 164

Allan, George William, 92

Anderson, R, 165

Anglican, (Church of England) 38, 39, 60, 108, 115

Architects, 15, 18, 24, 39, 48

Amateur, 18, 19, 20, 48, 99 (note 141)

Architecture, 18, 19, 21, 24, 26, 28, 48, 118, 119, 148

Armstrong, J.A., 166

Arthur, George, 166

Assessment Rolls, 149

Atkinson, William, 156

Aurora, 157

Baby, Jacques Duperron (James), 59, 61, 105

Badenach, Alex, 165

Baldwin, J.S., 134, 164

Baldwin, Robert, 35, 36, 116, 117, 120, 134, 164

Baldwin, William Warren, 35, 49, 63, 66, 69, 74, 76, 77, 78, 80, 111, 115, 118, 119, 120, 123, 130, 132, 164

Bank of Upper Canada, 16, 19, 24, 32, 36, 70, 74, 75, 76, 77, 78, 79, 80, 91, 92, 149, 156, 164, 184

Bates, Joseph, 132

Bartlett, W.H., 128

Bathurst, Lord, 63

Beikie, John, 41

Berkeley Street, 40, 110

Bible, 26

Bible Society, 164

Billings, F.T., 134

Bloor, Joseph, 156

Bloor Street, 32, 73, 74, 92, 122,

Bond, Thomas, 61

Boulton, D'Arcey, 35, 37, 76, 128, 137, 164

Boulton, Henry, 60, 76

Boulton, Matthew, 162

Boulton, William, 156, 164

Bradley's Hotel, 138

British America Fire & Life Assurance Co., 164

British American Assurance Company, 36

British Hotel and Tavern, 108

Brooke, Daniel, 134

Buckingham, James, 160

Buffalo, NY, 161

Building and Loan Society, 164

Building Supply, 30

Burley, Cornelius, 89

Burns, Robert, 25

Burnside, Alexander, 164, 165

Burwell, Mahlon, 83

Cambridge, 108

Cameron, Duncan, 138

Campbell House, 19, 38

Campbell, Mrs. & Miss, 162

Campbell, William, 35, 37, 38, 74, 76, 122

Canada Company, 36, 156

Canadian Broadcasting Corporation Building, 112

Canadian National Railway System, 157, 163

Carfrae, Hugh, 138

Carfrae, Robert, 86

Carfrae, Thomas, 72, 73, 74, 137, 138, 149

Carlton Street, 57

Carlton Place, 118

Carthew, Arthur, 57

Cathcart, Lord, 162

Cawthra House, 67

Champion, Thomas, 165

Charleston, 174

Chewett, J.G., 108, 114, 168

Cholera Epidemics, 20, 130, 147, 151

Church Street, 32, 40, 43, 51, 62, 96, 103, 134, 137, 179

Churchill, Winston, 15

City of Toronto & Lake Huron Railroad Company, 155, 156

Clarence Square, 119

The *Cobourg*, 129

Colborne, John, 108, 109, 119, 133, 134, 137, 140

Coffin Block, 51, 94, 95, 96, 97, 179

Collingwood, 157, 158, 160

Cooper, Joshua, 180

Cooper, Mrs. E., 166

Cooper, William, 129

Confederation (1867), 20

Court of Requests, 165

Court House and Jail (London), 16, 19, 24, 70, 71, 80, 81, 82, 83, 87, 88, 89, 114, 119, 184

Courthouse and Jail (Second in York), 16, 19, 23, 24, 30, 32, 35, 38, 48, 62-65, 66, 78, 87, 116, 118, 137, 153

Cow Proofing Gates, 113, 125

Crowther, 111

Cumberland, F.W., 80

Currency, 46 (note 33), 76, 99 (note 137), 105

D'Almaine, George, 168

Daly, 162

Danforth Road, 180

De La Salle Institute, 75, 79

Deer Park, 57, 107

Deihl, Dr., 164

Denholm, George, 165

Denison, George Taylor, 156

Detroit, 59, 157, 160

Dickens, Charles, 153

Dixon, Alex, 166

Don River, 32, 40, 71, 73, 74

Draper, William Henry, 156

Dublin, 82, 103

Duggan, George Jr., 164, 165

Duke of Kent, 52

Duncan Street, 110

Dundas, Henry, 81

Dundurn Castle, 161, 162

Dunlop, Dr., 132, 137, 138

Dunn, John Henry, 132, 164

Dundas Street (London), 84

East Lothian, 25, 26, 119

Edinburgh, 15, 25, 27, 103, 131

Elgin, Lord and Lady, 156

Elisabeth College, 108

Ellah, John, 164

Ellice, Edward, 37

Elmsley, John, 156

Elmsley, Mrs., 73

Emigrants' Asylum, 98, 104, 130

Executive Counsellor, 36

Ewart, Agnes (daughter of John Ewart), 175

Ewart, Catherine Skirving (daughter-in-law of John Ewart), 173, 175

Ewart, James (son of John Ewart), 175

Ewart, James (second son of

same name of John Ewart), 175

Ewart, John (uncle of John Ewart), 25, 26

Ewart, John (1788-1856), 15, 16, 153, 162, 173, 174, 175

Architect, 18, 19, 22, 23, 27, 30, 38, 39, 48, 53, 59, 63, 64, 65, 77, 78, 80, 82, 83, 84, 87, 90, 92, 93, 100 (note 167), 105, 108, 111, 114, 115, 116, 118, 119, 137, 139, 148

Arrival in York, 17, 18, 24, 28, 30, 39, 40, 48, 70

Birth, 25

Builder, 18, 19, 27, 30, 48, 53, 55, 56, 61, 62, 84, 86, 104, 105, 108, 111, 116, 117, 118, 123, 136, 137, 141, 158, 159, 164

On Budget, 20, 61

Contribution to Civic Life, 29, 73, 74, 131, 132, 133, 134, 137, 138, 140, 150, 151, 155, 156, 164, 165, 166, 167

Death, 177

Income and Assets, 85, 100 (note 173), 105, 116, 117, 120, 144 (note 267), 149, 181, 182

Last Will and Testament, 180

Legacies, 20, 21, 29, 30, 184

New York, 28

Properties, 29, 44, 57, 95, 149, 179, 180

Water Lots, 34, 42, 43, 125, 126, 127

Training, 24, 26, 27, 28

Work (other), 129, 148, 170, 171, 172

Ewart, George (son of John Ewart), 151, 155, 173, 174, 176, 177

Ewart, Jane (daughter of John Ewart), 24, 57, 140, 171, 172, 173, 175, 176, 177, 179

Children, 177, 179

Ewart, Jane Wilson (wife of John Ewart), 16, 17, 20, 27, 28, 175, 181

Ewart, Jenniot (daughter of John Ewart), 175

Ewart, John Jr. (son of John Ewart, died in infancy), 175

Ewart, John Jr. (second son named after John Ewart), 48, 109, 165, 175, 176

Ewart, Margaret (mother of John Ewart), 25, 26

Ewart, Margaret (daughter of John Ewart), 175, 176, 180

Ewart, Thomas (son of John Ewart), 48, 109, 165, 171, 173, 174, 175

Children, 173, 175

Ewart, William (father of John Ewart) 25, 26

Ewart, William (son of John Ewart), 17, 164, 175

Ewart Wharf (*see also Wharves*), 30, 32, 33, 51, 96, 98, 125, 126, 127, 128, 163, 176, 177

Fairbanks, L., 134

Family Compact, 34, 36, 38, 44, 47 (note46), 76, 91, 150, 151

Firemen's Hall, 62

Fish Market, 40, 95, 96

FitzGibbs, James, 111

Ford, John, 111

Fort Erie, 161

Fort York, 52, 97

Four Nations Corner, 107

Fraser, Archibald, 24

Frederick Street, 38

Front Street, 40, 51, 94, 95, 96, 97, 103, 110, 115, 162, 176, 177, 179

Gamble, Clarke, 156, 166

Garrison Soldiers, 41

George Street, 32, 57, 74, 75, 76, 79

Georgian Architectural Style, 19, 28, 53, 139, 179, 182

Georgian Bay, 157, 160

Gerrard Street, 166

Gibraltar Lighthouse, 40

Gibraltar Point, 129

Glasgow, 60, 103, 118

Glasgow Colonial Society, 138

Goderham Building, 94, 96

Goderich, 161

Gore, Francis, 34

Gothic Architectural Style, 20, 28, 83, 87, 88, 90, 114

Government House, 53, 105, 106, 107, 108

Grand Truck Railway, 157, 161, 163

The Grange 19, 37

Grassett, J.J., 165, 166

Great Western Railway Company, 160, 161, 162, 163

Station, 163

Greek Revival Architectural Style, 91, 92

Grubbe Family, 15

Grubbe, Talbot Page, 11, 15

Gurnett, George, 86, 165

Gwynne, William Charles, 167

Haddington, Scotland, 25

Hagerman, Christopher, 116, 117

Hale, William, 86

Halfway Tavern, 41

Hall, Francis, 77, 78, 80

Hamilton, 97, 160, 161

Hamilton, Alex, 164

Harper, John, 119, 150

Harris, Dr., 165

Harris, James, 140, 165

Harris, Thomas D., 166

Hawksmoor, Nicolas, 59

Hazelburn, 16, 48, 55, 56, 57

Helliwell, John, 165

Helliwell, Joseph, 73

Helliwell, Thomas, 73, 164

Higgins, William, 165

Holloway, C.B., 168

Hopkins, Lawson & Nelson, 114

Horne, R.C., 134

Howard, John George, 16, 56, 57, 62, 65, 77, 80, 136, 159, 167, 168, 169, 170, 184

Hunter, Peter, 56

1st Hussars Regiment, 91

Industrial Revolution, 131

Immigration, 29, 41, 42

Insane Asylum, 112

Institute of British Architects, 24

Ireland, 35, 87

Jacksonville, Florida, 174, 175

Jail Cells, 65, 89, 90

Jamieson, Anna, 83, 100 (note 164), 152

Jamieson, Robert, 100 (note 164), 152

Jamieson, Robert Sympson, 167

Janus Building, 95

Jarvis, Samuel Peter, 55, 56, 57, 92, 172

Jarvis, William (Sheriff), 56, 132, 156, 164, 167

Jarvis Street, 40, 55, 56, 57, 172

Jennings, Rev Dr., 171

John Street, 41, 52

Johnstone, 167

Joy, Howard, 177

Kennedy, Duncan, 104, 112

Kenney, Kidd & Co., 78

Kennilworth Street, 179

Ketchum, Jesse, 132, 140, 149, 164

King George VI, 107

King Street, 23, 31, 32, 40, 52, 62, 64, 104, 107, 108, 115, 122, 137, 140, 147, 154, 177

King's Bench, 37

King's College, 112, 114, 115, 154, 167

Kingston, 38, 59, 60, 73, 138

Kingston Road, 40, 179

Knox, John, 26

Knox Presbyterian Church, 140

Lake Erie, 82, 157

Lake Huron, 161

Lake Ontario, 29, 40, 157

Lane, Henry Bowyer, 123, 164

Langley, Henry, 80

Latham, Jacob, 134, 138

Law Society of Upper Canada, 39, 63, 80, 105, 114, 115, 116, 117, 118, 122

Leache, W.T., 165

Leake, William, 108

Legislative Counsellor, 36

Lesslie, James, 121, 122, 132, 133, 134

Library, Toronto Public (*see also Mechanics Institute*), 135, 145 (note 311)

Literacy, 26

Liverpool, 29, 106

London, England, 18, 20, 25, 27, 42, 103, 119, 131, 138

London, Ontario, 15, 17, 18, 21, 81, 82, 160

London Workers' Residence, 80, 81, 86

Lots

Town and Farm, 32, 33, 34

Water, 34, 42, 43

Louden, 27, 148

Macaulay, John Simcoe, 165

Macdonald, Alexander, 137

Macdonald, John (wholesaler), 20

Macdonald, John A., 178

Macdonnel, Alexander, 60, 111

Mackenzie, William Lyon, 72, 132, 137, 139, 140, 149

Maclennan, Justice, 179

MacNab, Allan, 160, 161, 162

MacNab, Sophia, 162

Madeira, 175

Maitland, Peregrine, 52, 56, 63, 119, 128-129

Maitland Street, 57

Malahide Castle, 82, 87

Masonic Lodge, 134

McCaul, Dr., 165

McGill, Andrew, 39

McGill, Ann, 39

McLean, Neil, 138

McMahon, E., 134

McNab, David, 112

The Mechanics Institute, 24, 30, 131, 132, 133, 134, 135, 137, 173

Holdings, 135

Metcalf, Thomas, 165

Metcalfe, Charles T., 164, 167

Metro Hall, 112

Mitchell, Robert, 165

Montreal, 36, 91, 97, 138, 160, 161, 162, 168, 182

Montreal Telegraph Company, 95

Moore, Thomas, 134

Morris, William, 137, 138

Morrison, Angus, 165

Morrison, Thomas D., 73, 150

Moss Park, 16, 36, 70, 80, 91, 92, 93

Mowat, Farley, 188 (note 429)

Mowat, John, 173, 174

Mowat, Oliver, 24, 30, 57, 112, 140, 151, 171, 172, 176, 177, 178, 179

"Muddy York", 18, 20, 30, 71, 122

Munroe, George, 165

Murchison, John, 134

Murray, Alexander, 138

Museum, first, 91

Mutual Street, 57

Napoleonic War, 28

Nash, John, 28

Necropolis Cemetery, 74, 177, 178

New York City, 18, 20, 28, 29, 42, 106, 174, 175

Newbigging, 164

Niagara, 160

Niagara-on-the-Lake (Newark), 33, 63, 114

Niagara River, 161

Nicholson, Peter, 25, 27, 28, 118

Nixon, Joseph, 111

Nixon, Walter, 86

Northern Railway, 157, 160

Northfield, 57, 172, 173, 179

Norway, Ontario, 179, 180

Notman, William, 169

O'Reilly, 87

"Old Log Court House", (London), 85

Ontario Heritage Conservation Movement, 24

OS&H Railway, 157

Osgoode, William, 115

Osgoode Hall, 19, 24, 30, 35, 38, 39, 55, 74, 78, 79, 80, 98, 105, 113, 114, 115, 118, 119, 122, 123, 124, 125, 137, 184

  Costs, 117, 120, 149

  Cumberland and Storm Renovation, 113, 123

Ossington Street, 49, 169

Oswego, 29

Otto, Stephen, 12, 24, 30, 62, 77, 78, 80, 92, 114

The Palace, 19, 38, 110

Palais de Justice, Brussels, 117

Paley, 27

Palladin Architectural Style, 88, 123

Parks (or Parke, or Sparks), 104, 105, 112, 130

Parke, Thomas, 86

Parliament Buildings

  First, 31, 48, 62, 110

  Second, 110

  Third, 16, 19, 24, 30, 35, 98, 104, 107, 110, 112, 113, 114, 115, 118, 137, 156, 167, 168

    Costs, 111, 182

  Fourth (Queen's Park), 110, 112, 115

  Temporary, 18, 52, 54

Parliament Street, 40, 48, 62, 166

Paterson, David, 132

Patterson, Andrew, 180

Patterson, Peter, 73, 164, 165

Patrick, 73

Pattern Books, 19, 27, 28

Peter Street, 41

Phillpotts, Col., 165

Phillpotts, R.E., 31

Playter, George, 97

Potters' Field, 70, 72, 74

Powell, Grant, 111, 137

Powell, William Dummer, 56

Power, Michael, 59

Power Street, 58

Primrose, F.S., 165

Prisoner's Box, 66

Proudfoot, William, 156, 164

Provincial Lunatic Asylum, 16, 49, 56, 141, 167, 168

Public Executions, 66, 89

Queen Street, 32, 38, 40, 49, 55, 56, 58, 114, 116, 118, 119, 121, 147, 149, 169

Queen Victoria, 52, 153

Queen's College, 108

Rebellion of 1837, 20, 26, 66, 87, 89, 90, 140

Reform Movement, 35, 36, 73, 115, 150, 151, 156

Regency Architectural Style, 20, 28, 59, 77, 119, 139

Rennie, John, 25, 27, 28

Richardson, H., 134

Richardson, James, 165

Richmond, 175

Richmond Street, 40, 92

Ridout, George P., 156, 164, 166

Ridout, John, 56

Ridout, Thomas, 78, 80, 92, 140

Ridout Street (London), 84

Rintoul, William, 165

Ritchie, John, 114

Robinson, John Beverley, 114, 138, 149

Robinson Hall, 86

Rogers, Agnes, 177

Rogers, Joseph, 156

Rogers, Thomas, 24, 63, 111, 119

Rolph, John, 122, 132

Romanesque Architectural Style, 113

Rose, Walter, 138

Ross, John, 156, 165

Ross, William, 166

Royal Grammar School, 108

Royal Military Academy, 28, 87

Russell, Peter, 35

Russell Square, 109, 114

Rychman, 27

Ryerson, William, 165

St. Augustine, 175

St. Andrew's Presbyterian Church, 16, 19, 24, 59, 98, 108, 136, 138, 139, 140, 159, 171, 173

St. Andrew's Society, 155

St. Clair Avenue, 107

St. Clair River, 157

St. George, Laurent Quetton, 31

St. George's Parish Church in Glasgow, 59, 60

St. James' Anglican Church, 16, 19, 23, 24, 40, 59, 62, 64, 73, 129, 148, 151, 153, 154, 158, 159, 160, 183

St. Lawrence River, 29, 63, 160

St. Marylebone Estate, 28

The *St. Matthews*, 175

St. Paul's Roman Catholic Church, 16, 19, 24, 48, 58, 59, 60, 61, 105, 137, 159

Sarnia, 161

Savannah, 174, 175

Scadding, Henry, 30, 61

Scarborough, 165

Schooling, 26

Scott, James, 97

Scott, Thomas, 95

Scott, Walter, 25

Scott Street, 94

Scottish Immigrants, 15, 24, 28, 29, 42

Scottish Presbyterian Church, 25

71st and 79th Highlanders, 138

Sherbourne Street, 91, 92

Sherwood, Henry, 156

Sherwood, L.P., 165

Shuter Street, 55, 56

Sidewalk, York's First, 122

Simcoe, John Graves, 35, 81, 82, 94, 110

Simcoe Street, 107, 156, 177

Small, Charles, 165

Small, James E., 134, 164

Smith, James F., 103, 138, 166

Soane, John, 138

The *Southerner*, 174

Southampton, 175

Spadina, 35

Spadina Avenue, 37, 119

Sports, 41, 71

Stagecoach Travel, 95, 97

Stanton, Robert, 150

Stark, William, 59

Steele, Mabel Ewart, 11, 174

Stennett, William, 156, 165

Stephenson, George, 162

Storm, Thomas, 164

Storm, William, 27, 66

Stotebury, Charles, 164

Strachan, John, 19, 34, 35, 38, 56, 76, 95, 110, 115, 138, 149, 151, 158, 159, 167

Strange, James Maxwell, 175

Sudd, John, 53

Talbot, Freeman, 86

Talbot Settlement, 81, 83

Talbot, Thomas, 81, 82, 83, 87, 101 (note 182), 160

Tantallon, 87

Tasmania, 89

Telford, 27

Theller, E.A., 89

Thomas, William, 164

Thompson, William, 111

Thomson, W.J., 75

Toronto, 15, 32, 147, 157, 161, 175

Toronto Board of Trade, 135

Toronto Bowling Club, 165

Toronto Cricket Club, 165

Toronto Curling Club, 165

Toronto General Hospital, 52, 166

Toronto Islands, 31, 129

The *Toronto* locomotive, 156-157

Toronto School of Practical Science, 27

Toronto Street, 23, 32, 62, 137

Tory (Conservatives), 36, 73, 115, 150, 151, 154, 155, 161

Tradesmen, skilled, 20, 32, 53

Tranent, Scotland, 25, 26

Massacre of, 26

Trinity College, 38

Turton, 111, 112

Union Station, 162

Upper Canada College, 16, 19, 24, 55, 98, 104, 107, 108, 109, 114, 118, 137, 177

Tuition, 109, 133, 134, 153, 173

University Avenue, 115, 119, 122, 154

University of Toronto, 115

Van Dieman's Land, Tasmania, 89

Van Every, Peter, 84

Voting Rules, 185 (note 353)

Walton, George, 163, 165

War of 1812, 31, 34, 37, 52, 62, 71, 110

Wards (political boundaries in Toronto), 150-151

Ware, 141

Washburn, Simon, 164

Waterfront, 34, 40, 41

Waterloo, battle of, 108, 162

Watt, James, 27

Waverley Avenue, 179

Welland Canal, 157

Weller, William, 97

Wellington Hotel, 96, 97

Wellington Street, 51, 94, 95, 96, 97, 119

Weston, Ontario, 15

Wharves, 127

Commissariat, 127

Coppers', 127, 129

Ewart's (*see Ewart's Wharf*)

King's (also called Navy), 127

Merchants', 127, 128

White, 104

Whitfield, W., 183

Wholesale Grocers Store, 140

Widder, Frederick, 156

Widmer, Christopher, 166, 167

Willcocks, Phoebe, 35

Willcocks, William, 35

William the Conqueror, 87

Winchester Street, 74

Windsor, 160

Wolsencroft, John, 73

Wood, Alexander, 156

Woodbine Avenue, 179

Workers' Residence, London (*see London Workers' Residence*)

Workmens' Compensation Building, 112

Wyatt, James, 28, 87

Wyman, F.E., 124

Yonge Street, 32, 40, 62, 73, 74, 140, 147, 177, 179

York, 15, 17, 21, 24, 30, 32, 33, 40, 42, 97

Building, 32, 39, 60, 71, 104

Daily Life (includes wages, costs), 21, 41, 70, 103, 105, 109, 152, 153

Economics, 31, 32, 71, 104, 149

Environment, 17, 19, 21, 30, 31, 82

Population, 17, 18, 31, 34, 42, 48, 58, 70, 74, 103, 147, 153, 182

Swamp Land, 40

York General Hospital (*see also Toronto General Hospital*), 16, 18, 19, 24, 48, 49, 52, 62, 110, 130

York Harbour, 39, 41, 92, 129, 168, 183

York Street, 118, 119, 121, 122, 162

York's First Post Office, 79

Yorkville, 74

Young, Thomas, 23, 62, 65, 77, 107, 110

About the Authors

Janet Ewart FitzGerald (nee Grubbe) first wrote about her ancestors in *The Grubb Pioneers of Etobicoke* (1987, revised 2001). Her interest in early local history came naturally through her father's (Talbot Grubbe) early writing and research about his family in Scotland and Etobicoke. On her mother's side (Mabel Ewart Steele of Dundas), the family could be traced back to John Ewart (1788-1856), another Scottish immigrant who was Upper Canada's first architect in York and London, Ontario.

Janet's methodical research into Ewart's life and times built upon the skills she developed early in her career as a young U of T graduate in the employ of William Stephenson (later Sir) in New York. Mainly Canadians staffed this wartime secret service, established by Winston Churchill, headed by Stephenson and approved by Roosevelt (who also used the communications). Janet also worked in a similar manner in the British embassy in Guatemala for a year.

As well as raising three children, Janet returned to University of Toronto's University College in 1970 and worked in various capacities, including the running of the Alumni Office. She is a founder of the UC Book Sale and a member of the UC Art Centre. In 2003 she received the U of T's Arbour Award for Volunteerism.

Harry van Bommel is the author of 27 books. He is Co-Executive Director of *Resources Supporting Family and Community Legacies Inc.*, a Canadian not-for-profit organization (www.legacies.ca) with a mission to provide free or low-cost written resources in the areas of home and hospice care, community development and family history. His 20-year project ***Canada 150*** encourages Canadians to record their life stories or family histories and deposit them, in perpetuity, with ***Library and Archives Canada*** in celebration of Canada's 150th birthday in 2017.